Miracles and the Kingdom of God

Miracles and the Kingdom of God

*Christology and Social Identity in
Mark and Q*

Myrick C. Shinall Jr.

LEXINGTON BOOKS/FORTRESS ACADEMIC
Lanham • Boulder • New York • London

Published by Lexington Books
An imprint of The Rowman & Littlefield Publishing Group, Inc.
4501 Forbes Boulevard, Suite 200, Lanham, Maryland 20706
www.rowman.com

Unit A, Whitacre Mews, 26-34 Stannary Street, London SE11 4AB

British Library Cataloguing in Publication Information Available

Library of Congress Cataloging-in-Publication Data

Names: Shinall, Myrick C., author.
Title: Miracles and the kingdom of God : Christology and social identity in Mark and Q / Myrick C.
    Shinall Jr.
Description: Lanham : Lexington Books-Fortress Academic, 2018. | Includes bibliographical refer-
    ences and index.
Identifiers: LCCN 2018005347 (print) | LCCN 2018000258 (ebook) | ISBN 9781978701120 (Elec-
    tronic) | ISBN 9781978701113 (cloth : alk. paper)
Subjects: LCSH: Bible. Mark--Criticism, interpretation, etc. | Q hypothesis (Synoptics criticism) |
    Miracles. | Kingdom of God.
Classification: LCC BS2585.52 (print) | LCC BS2585.52 .S44 2018 (ebook) | DDC 226/.066--dc23
LC record available at https://lccn.loc.gov/2018005347

Printed in the United States of America

To Jennifer, for everything

Table of Contents

Acknowledgments

As with any first-time author, I owe much to my teachers and mentors for bringing me to the point where I could write this book. Thanks must first go to my *Doktormutter* Amy-Jill Levine. Keith Meador has been an invaluable resource to me as he has helped me think about how I can integrate expertise in the New Testament with my career in medicine. I wish to thank both of them, along with Robin Jensen, Joe Rife, and Todd Klutz for their help in bringing this book to fruition. I also wish to acknowledge and thank the leadership of the Vanderbilt General Surgery Residency and the Department of Surgery for their openness to my work and their support for it. Thanks especially to Drs. John Tarpley, Naji Abumrad, Seth Karp, and Kyla Terhune.

My family, of course, supported me in all the education that got me to the point of writing this book, and I owe them more than I can say. My wife, Jennifer Shinall, has displayed the patience of both Job and Penelope in living with me as I completed a surgical residency, a clinical fellowship, and a PhD. This book is dedicated to her for all that she has done to support me even as she has built her own independent career as a scholar.

Introduction

One of literature's most famous stories within a story, the Grand Inquisitor from Dostoyevsky's *The Brothers Karamazov,* causes an impassioned dispute between two of the titular brothers:

> Ivan paused. He had grown flushed from talking, and talking with passion; now that he had stopped, however, he suddenly smiled.
> Alyosha, who had listened to him all this time without saying anything, though towards the end, in a state of extreme agitation, he had several times attempted to interrupt the flow of his brother's speech, but had evidently held himself in check, suddenly began to speak as though he had leapt into motion.
> "But . . . that is preposterous!" he exclaimed, turning red.[1]

Like many passionate disagreements, the conflict between Ivan and Alyosha Karamazov arises from biblical exegesis. Ivan, the world-weary intellectual, tells his story of the Grand Inquisitor to Alyosha, the pious novice in an Orthodox monastery. Ivan upsets Alyosha because his Grand Inquisitor, while glossing Jesus' Temptation (Matt 4:1–11//Luke 4:1–13), claims that Jesus rejects miracles as a means of demonstrating his divine power, while the Church has adopted such a use of miracles. This present book argues for a modified version of the Grand Inquisitor's claim: Mark uses miracles to demonstrate the divine power resident in Jesus, while Q, the hypothetical source for Matthew and Luke, instead uses miracles to demonstrate the triumph of the kingdom of God over the kingdom of Satan. To see why the Grand Inquisitor's distinction between Jesus and the Church should be transposed to a distinction between Mark and Q, it is necessary to examine Ivan Karamazov's story in detail. In Ivan's tale, Jesus appears in sixteenth-century Seville and performs several miracles for an astonished public. Investigating the ado, the Cardinal Grand Inquisitor finds Jesus and arrests him. That night the Inquisitor comes to Jesus' cell alone to talk. Jesus says nothing, and the Grand Inquisitor delivers a monologue interpreting Christian history in light of Jesus' three-fold Temptation by the devil.

The Inquisitor views Jesus' responses to the Temptation as a triple refusal to assume coercive power over humanity. After Jesus spent forty days and nights fasting in the desert, Satan approached the famished Jesus and tempted him to turn stones into bread. The Inquisitor rephrases this temptation, "Look, see those stones in that naked, burning hot wilderness? Turn them into loaves and mankind will go trotting after you like a flock, grateful and obedient, though ever fearful that you may take away your hand and that your loaves may cease to come their way."[2] Jesus refused. Next, the devil took him to the pinnacle of the temple in Jerusalem.[3] There, Satan tempted Jesus to test God by leaping to certain death so that God would send angels to save him. Jesus again refused, which the Inquisitor takes as evidence for a faith in God that is "able to reject the miracle, and to make do . . . with only a free decision of the heart."[4] Finally, the devil led Jesus up a mountain over-looking all the kingdoms of the world and offered to give Jesus all their power if Jesus would bow down to him. According to the Inquisitor, accept-ing this offer to become a universal king would have given humanity "some-one to bow down before, someone to entrust ones conscience to, and a way of at last uniting everyone into an undisputed, general and consensual ant-heap."[5] For a third time Jesus refused. In the Inquisitor's telling, Jesus re-jected these temptations because he "did not want to enslave man with a miracle and . . . thirsted for a faith that was free, not miraculous . . . thirsted for a love that was free, not for the servile ecstasies of the slave before the might that has inspired him with dread once and for all."[6] Jesus, according to the Inquisitor, offered humanity freedom.

The Inquisitor goes on to say that humanity cannot bear the burden of such freedom. Servile by nature, humans seek a power that awes them into obedience. Jesus' great deed in rejecting Satan's temptations encapsulates his general program of giving humanity the terrible gift of freedom, a program which the Inquisitor disavows. Speaking for and about the Church, the Inqui-sitor tells Jesus, "We corrected your great deed and founded it upon *miracle, mystery,* and *authority.* And people were glad that they had once been brought together into a flock and that at last from their hearts had been removed such a terrible gift."[7] While Jesus avoided coercion, the Church adopts coercion in his name. While Jesus promoted the decision of the indi-vidual, the Church rejects independent thought in favor of its own authority. Since the Church nullifies Jesus' gift of freedom, the Inquisitor cannot allow Jesus to wander the streets of Seville. When the Inquisitor announces that he will execute Jesus, Ivan pauses, and so gives Alyosha the chance to object.

Alyosha objects, but he cannot refute the Inquisitor's argument. His agita-tion shows how the Inquisitor's monologue strikes at the foundation of Alyosha's life of devotion—maybe the Church has betrayed the true message of Jesus so that it could rule in his name, maybe the Inquisitor is right. Examinations of whether the Inquisitor was right about the church's infidelity to Jesus could fill a library—the argument about whether the Christ of faith is true to the historical Jesus goes on. This current book has a more modest aim: to investigate in what sense the Inquisitor is right about the significance of Jesus' rejecting miracles in the Temptation story.

The Grand Inquisitor does not say what he means by miracle, but John Meier has given a very useful definition of miracle as an action that satisfies three criteria: "(1) an unusual, startling, or extraordinary event that is in principle perceivable by any interested and fair-minded observer, (2) an event that finds no reasonable explanation in human abilities or in other known forces that operate in our world of time and space, and (3) an event that is the result of a special act of God, doing what no human power can do."[8] Under this definition, Jesus did not repudiate miracles wholesale. Whatever rejection comes in the Temptation narrative does not carry on to the rest of Matthew and Luke. Even in Ivan's story, Jesus performs miracles. Before the Inquisitor arrests him, Jesus has healed a blind man and raised a little girl from the dead. The palpable healing power emanating from Jesus attracted the crowd, which attracted the Inquisitor's attention. Ivan clearly models these miracles on the similar stories that Matthew, Mark, and Luke share. Although all three Synoptic Gospels share these miracle stories, only Matthew and Luke share the Temptation narrative, so the Temptation forms part of the hypothetical source Q. The Inquisitor's claim that Jesus rejects miracles in the Temptation suggests we examine Q for other indications of such rejection.

Mark also tells a story of Jesus encountering the devil after his baptism, but a much shorter one: "He was in the wilderness forty days, tested by Satan; and he was with the wild beasts; and the angels waited on him" (Mark 1:13). Mark lacks Jesus' repudiation of miracles, and elsewhere in the gospel Mark uses miracles as just the sort of proofs of Jesus' divine identity that the Inquisitor imputes to the Church. What the Inquisitor thought was a distinction between Jesus and the Church is a distinction between Q and Mark: the former rejects the use of miracles to claim a divine identity for Jesus, and the latter embraces miracles for just this purpose.

Such a distinction between Mark and Q echoes the sentiments of Rudolf Bultmann, who noted the difference between Mark and Q in that "miracle stories are almost entirely absent from Q," and went on to explain, "The deeper reason for their absence is the different light in which Jesus appears. In Q he is above everything else the eschatological preacher of repentance and salvation, the teacher of wisdom and the law. In Mark he is . . . the very Son of God walking the earth."[9] This distinction between Mark and Q might tempt one to view Jesus' encounter with Satan in the Temptation as Q's straightforward rejection of miracles and the identity of Jesus they imply. However, as Bultmann notes, miracles are *almost* entirely absent from Q—that is, Q does contain miracles. Besides the Temptation, Q has six pericopae where Jesus performs miracles or talks about performing miracles:

1. The Healing of the Centurion's Child/Servant (Matt 8:5–13//Luke 7:1–10)
2. The Commissioning of Disciples (Matt 10:7–8//Luke 10:9)
3. The Response to John the Baptist (Matt 11:2–6//Luke 7:18–23)
4. The Woes on Chorazin and Bethsaida (Matt 11:21–22//Luke 10:12–14)
5. The Beelzebul Controversy (Matt 12:22–31//Luke 11:14–26)
6. The Refusal to Give a Sign (Matt 12:38–42//Luke11:16, 29–33)

The Inquisitor's distinction between a miracle-rejecting Jesus and a miracle-embracing Church cannot be mapped onto Q and Mark. Rather, to determine the truth in the Inquisitor's interpretation of the Temptation Narrative requires investigating why and to what effect both Mark and Q tell stories about miracles. In Q's Temptation, Jesus rejects Satan's inducement to perform miracles and Satan's offer of kingdoms. Similar connections between miracles and kingdoms—either the kingdom of God or the kingdom of Satan—occur also in Q's version of the Commissioning of the Disciples and the Beelzebul Controversy. In the Q version of these stories, miracles indicate the victory of God's kingdom over Satan's. Mark also has versions of the Commissioning and the Beelzebul Controversy, but in Mark these stories lack the connection between miracle and kingdom, just as Mark's Testing narrative lacks these elements. For the sake of convenience, I will refer to these three stories shared by Mark and Q—the Temptation, the Commissioning, and the Beelzebul Controversy—as the miracle overlaps. Closely examining these miracle overlaps allows us to test a modified version of the Inquisitor's claim, that Mark uses miracles to demonstrate the divine power resident in Jesus while Q instead uses miracles to demonstrate the triumph of the kingdom of God over the kingdom of Satan.

Mark and Q use the same basic stories about miracles to depict Jesus' relation to God differently—the former to blur the distinction between Jesus and God and the latter to reject such blurring. In the past few decades, many biblical scholars have grappled with the question of how the earliest followers of Jesus conceived of Jesus vis-à-vis God. Typically, scholars couch the debate in terms of Christology, with a prominent group offering the view that high Christology (usually defined as attributing divinity to Jesus) developed very early and was ubiquitous among Jesus followers. Other scholars argue that high Christology developed more slowly in the first hundred years (or more) following Jesus' death.[10] Students of early Christology have frequently availed themselves of Mark and Q's miracle stories as sources of data.[11]

Although comparing the miracle overlaps contributes to debates about New Testament Christology, this comparison also contributes to the study of Christian origins beyond the subfield of New Testament theology. This book assumes that Christological claims do not occur in a vacuum, but rather they arise in response to the social situation in which followers of Jesus find themselves.[12] Making claims about who Jesus is and the significance of his actions is also a way of defining the identity of his followers. Therefore, investigating the Christology of Mark and Q gives access to the process of identity formation at work among some of Jesus' earliest followers. Examining how certain ways of depicting Jesus could generate a positive sense of identity among his followers allows us to understand why his followers would depict Jesus in these ways.

Comparing the miracle overlaps in Mark and Q illustrates one aspect of the diverse ways that early Jesus followers constructed both their memory of him and their identity as his followers. Telling the stories of the miracle overlaps was a means to remember two aspects of Jesus' ministry: his miracle working and his proclamation of the coming kingdom of God.[13] Mark and Q demonstrate distinct ways of conceptualizing the relationship between Jesus and these two aspects of his ministry:

Mark:

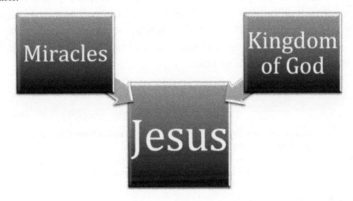

Figure 0.1.

Q:

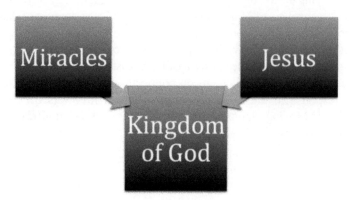

Figure 0.2.

In Mark, the miracles and the kingdom of God point to Jesus, whereas in the Double Tradition, Jesus and the miracles point to the kingdom of God. These two alternate configurations reflect different ways that early Jesus followers conceptualized their identity as a group: as the community participating in the in-breaking kingdom of God that Jesus announced and that will ultimately overcome the kingdom of Satan (Q) or as the group whose fidelity to Jesus will allow them to live in the state of eschatological blessedness, which Jesus calls the kingdom of God, when Jesus ultimately returns with his divine identity made manifest to all as he overcomes Satan and judges the world (Mark). Demonstrating how the miracle overlaps illustrate these two distinct ways of constructing memory and identity among Jesus' early followers will be the task for this book.

NOTES

1. Fyodor Dostoyevsky, *The Brothers Karamazov: A Novel in Four Parts and an Epilogue*, trans. David McDuff (London: Penguin, 1993), 299.

2. Ibid., 290.

3. This order of temptations follows that in Matthew, which the Inquisitor follows as well. Luke inverts the order of the second and third temptations.

4. Dostoyevsky, *Brothers*, 294.

5. Ibid., 296.

6. Ibid., 294.

7. Ibid., 295.

8. John P. Meier, *A Marginal Jew: Rethinking the Historical Jesus*, vol. 2, *Mentor, Message, and Miracles* (New York: Doubleday, 1994), 512. Such a definition coheres with that used recently by other authors: "an astonishing event, exciting wonder in the observers, which carries the signature of God, who, for those with the eye of faith, can be seen to be expressing his powerful eschatological presence," Graham H. Twelftree, *Jesus the Miracle Worker: A Historical and Theological Study* (Downers Grove, IL: InterVarsity, 1999), 350; "a wonderful rescue or salvation of someone [that] takes place by the overturning of the 'canons of the ordinary' through the intervention of a deity or hero," Wendy J. Cotter, *Miracles in Greco-*

Roman Antiquity: A Sourcebook for the Study of New Testament Miracle Stories (London: Rutledge, 1999), 2.

9. Rudolf Bultmann, *History of the Synoptic Tradition*, trans. John Marsh (New York: Harper & Row, 1968), 240–41.

10. For a review of the *status quaestionis* see Andrew Chester, "High Christology: Whence, When, and Why?" *Early Christianity* 2, no. 1 (2011): 22–50.

11. For miracles and Christology in Q, see Siegfried Schulz, *Q: Die Spruchquelle der Evangelisten* (Zurich: Theologischer Verlag Zurich, 1972), 177–269; Michael Hüneburg, *Jesus als Wundertäter in der Logienquelle: Ein Beitrag zur Christologie von Q* (Leipzig: Evangelische Verlagsanstalt, 2001); Larry W. Hurtado, *Lord Jesus Christ: Devotion to Jesus in Earliest Christianity* (Grand Rapids, MI: Eerdmans, 2003), 247–54. For miracles and Christology in Mark, see Theodore J. Weeden, *Mark—Traditions in Conflict* (Philadelphia: Fortress, 1971), 52–69; Edwin Keith Broadhead, *Teaching With Authority: Miracles and Christology in the Gospel of Mark* (Sheffield: JSOT Press, 1992); J. R. Daniel Kirk and Stephen L. Young, "'I Will Set His Hand to the Sea:' Psalm 88:26 LXX and Christology in Mark," *JBL* 133.2 (2014): 333–40.

12. For a similar approach looking at the sociological implications of Christological claims in Matthew, see Bruce J. Malina, *Calling Jesus Names: The Social Value of Labels in Matthew* (Sonoma, CA: Polebridge Press, 1988).

13. For arguments in favor of the historicity of Jesus' proclamation of the kingdom of God, see Dale C. Allison, Jr., *Constructing Jesus: Memory, Imagination, and History* (Grand Rapids, MI: Baker Academic, 2010), 164–204; Marinus De Jonge, *God's Final Envoy: Early Christology and Jesus' Own View of His Mission* (Grand Rapids, MI: Eerdmans, 1998), 34–43; Meier, *Marginal Jew*, 2:237–508; for arguments in favor of the historicity of Jesus' miracles see Allison, *Constructing* 17–19; Meier, *Marginal Jew*, 2:509–970; Twelftree, *Jesus the Miracle Worker*; Eric Eve, *The Healer from Nazareth: Jesus' Miracles in Historical Context* (London: SPCK, 2009).

Chapter One

Preliminary Objections

No character effectively refutes the Grand Inquisitor's interpretation of the Temptation. Ivan Karamazov's Jesus sits silently as the Grand Inquisitor talks about the Church abandoning Jesus' true message. On hearing the story, Alyosha calls it absurd, but he offers no substantive objection to gainsay the claims of Ivan's protagonist. Within the novel, Dostoyevsky allows the Grand Inquisitor's claims to stand essentially unchallenged.

In contrast, the first step in testing this book's thesis, that Mark tells miracle stories to affirm a divine identity for Jesus while Q tells the same stories to illustrate the kingdom of God rather than Jesus' exalted nature, will be to examine potential objections. One objection is that Q is a hypothetical document, and so there is little value in examining what it has to say since it might not exist. This book compares Mark and Q to investigate attitudes about Jesus' identity, what is usually termed "Christology." Thus, another possible objection is that speaking about Christology in the New Testament is anachronistic, that this sort of sustained theological reflection was a later development. To demonstrate how this book will meet these objections, this chapter uses an example from the study of folklore to illustrate this book's methods. Using folkloristic methodology opens this study to another objection: the Bible is not folklore. To address these objections, this chapter starts with the example, the folkloristic analysis of a famous urban legend.

THE KENTUCKY FRIED RAT

In the 1970s a story began circulating in North America about a person who inadvertently ate a rat from a fast-food restaurant.[1] Many versions of the story exist, but one representative example goes as follows:

2					*Chapter 1*

The story begins with a local woman on her way home from work one evening. She decided to stop at Kentucky Fried Chicken and pick up some dinner, rather than cooking. Upon arriving at her home, she disposed of the packaging and attempted to pass off the meal as home-cooked. When her family returned home for dinner, they all agreed it was the best fried chicken that Mom had ever made. The mother basked in their compliments while enjoying the meal herself. When she bit into her piece of chicken, however, she noticed an unpleasant taste and texture. She spat the mouthful into her napkin and discovered that she had been chewing on a ball of hair and a rat's tail. Her family was horrified and she, of course, fainted on the spot. When she came to, she was at the hospital where she had just had her stomach pumped. She had to tell the doctors where she had purchased the "chicken," and thus her secret was revealed to the family.[2]

While the setting of this story is decidedly contemporary, stories of contaminated foodstuffs have a long pedigree. In medieval Europe, stories circulated that the plague resulted from Jews poisoning the water supply.[3] In the 1930s as Sino-Japanese tensions rose, rumors circulated in China that Japanese manufacturers were adding ground glass to canned goods destined for China.[4] In early twentieth-century America, stories about restaurants serving a noxious meat (rat, mouse, cat, dog) circulated, but in these cases the offending restaurants were Chinese or Italian. In the 1970s, similar stories were told of ethnic minority restaurants in Europe.[5] By the 1980s and 1990s the Kentucky Fried Rat made its way to the United Kingdom and other European countries, as well.[6]

In the vast majority of accounts from contemporary North America, Kentucky Fried Chicken is the offending restaurant. In almost all other cases it is an outlet of another national fast-food chain. The ubiquity of the food contamination stories across cultures speaks to a widespread human anxiety about the safety of our food supply, an essential ingredient in our survival. Those viewed as somehow foreign but who nevertheless have access to societies, like Jews in medieval Europe or Japanese manufacturers in 1930s China, pose an especial threat and recur as the perpetrators of food contamination. As people's fears vary over time and regionally, the perpetrators of the contamination change. When ethnic minorities are the feared threat to national cohesion, ethnic restaurants serve the fried rat, as in the European stories and the American stories from the early twentieth century. The corporate villain in the Kentucky Fried Rat story speaks to a different set of anxieties present in late twentieth-century America.

The rise of fast-food restaurants conspicuously manifested how American society changed in the twentieth century. Certain basic societal needs remained constant, such as preparing food, acquiring clothing, consuming entertainment, and supporting the needy. The source of meeting these needs had traditionally been local institutions, such as the home, the small business, and the Church. Over the course of the twentieth century these responsibilities increasingly shifted from local to supra-local institutions, especially governments and national corporations. The Kentucky Fried Rat story expresses anxiety about the transfer of food preparation from the home to the corporation, a manifestation of the more general anxiety about the shift from the local to the supra-local.[7] The fast food corporation becomes the insidious foreigner contaminating the local food supply.

The rise of fast-food reflected not only the greater role of the corporation in American culture, but also the changing pace of American life. In the version above, the purchaser of the tainted food dishonestly presents it as a home-cooked meal, a detail shared by many other variants.[8] This recurring theme indicates anxiety about how fast-food displaced home-cooked meals. However, a number of other variants present the setting not as a faked family meal, but as some dark place where the eater is distracted—in a car while driving, or in a movie theater, or in front of the television. On one level the darkness and distraction add plausibility to the eater's failure to notice the battered rodent until it was too late. Yet these settings also highlight the decline of eating as a communal, leisure activity.[9] Eating happens while doing something else, and not as a dedicated activity that the household undertakes together. Consuming the Kentucky Fried Rat occurs either in an ersatz family dinner or in the family dinner's replacement, the distracted meal on the go.

That families could traditionally rely on their food to be prepared at home and have the leisure to eat it together depended on women accepting food preparation as their primary roles and staying at home to prepare it so the family could eat together after the men had returned from work and the children from school. Given the anxieties the Kentucky Fried Rat story expresses, it should come as no surprise that when a storyteller includes the gender of the victim, it is a woman over 80 percent of the time.[10] After all, one of the most significant changes in the twentieth century was the shift in gender expectations and gender roles. Indeed, the 1970s, when these stories first arose and proliferated, was a period of especially vocal protest against the constraints of traditional gender roles. Many variants of the story that specify a woman as victim also note that she was on her way home from work, as the one quoted above does. The specification of a woman as a victim provides an implicit reactionary moral to the story: women should cook and not work outside the home.[11]

The foregoing analysis of the Kentucky Fried Rat story assumes that the folk tale contains clues about the tellers of the tale and the society in which they live. Such analysis recognizes four interconnected objects of study for the folklorist: 1) the narrative content of the story itself; 2) the internal state of the narrator, including memory, mood, and personality; 3) the immediate setting in which the story is told, including audience expectations; and 4) the larger social and cultural structures in which the narrator and audience find themselves. The societal and cultural structures partially condition both the internal state of the narrator and the immediate setting in which the narration takes place; the internal state of the narrator and the immediate setting, in turn, condition whether and how the story is told.[12] This model conceptualizes how folktales indirectly reflect the psychological state of the tellers, the immediate setting of their telling, and the larger social structures active in the time and place the story is told. The analysis of the Kentucky Fried Rat story has focused on how the narrative content of the story reflects the social forces of change in the twentieth century and the psychological results of these changes, chiefly anxiety, which condition the telling of the story. This model allows one to use folktales to study the setting in which they arise by assuming that the content of a folktale is conditioned by who does the telling, to whom, and in what setting.

OBJECTION 1: THE BIBLE IS NOT FOLKLORE

Adapting the methodology of folklorists in studying multiple variants of similar stories calls to mind the work of classical form critics, like Bultmann and Dibelius, who drew upon the academic study of folklore of their time.[13] Folkloristics seemed an apposite method because the form critics viewed the gospels as somewhat haphazard written collections of originally discrete oral elements.[14] Most today would argue that the gospel writers did not merely collect oral tradition, but rather shaped narratives to suit their own purposes.[15] It might seem inappropriate to study written texts, like Mark and Q, the way folklorists study short units of oral lore that are repeated and modified by innumerable tellers.[16] However, authors composing a written text do so on the basis of their psychological response to the conditions in which they write, just as a teller of a tale does. Every use of language is influenced by the setting in which it occurs, and literature does not constitute a unique set of linguistic phenomena uninfluenced by their social milieu.[17] Gospel texts bear traces of their tellers' and hearers' social situations just as the Kentucky Fried Rat story does. One key aspect of a folktale that gives access to the situation of its telling is the existence of variants of the story that reflect concerns common to multiple tellers; the miracle overlaps represent variants of the same stories that allow a similar analysis. The existence of multiple variants is arguably the defining factor of folklore, and, since on so many occasions the Bible contains multiple versions of the same story, it can be studied as folklore.[18]

However, there remain important differences between studying variants of gospel stories and studying variants of a folktale. Folklorists interested in the Kentucky Fried Rat story have as many variants to examine as they can collect, whereas our study of the miracle overlaps provides only two variants of each story. The folklorist is usually not as interested in what any one individual variant says as in the collective weight of the elements that are repeated in multiple versions of the story. Having only two variants of each story to examine, this book is much more focused on what these two individual versions say.

Although studying the gospels limits the number of variants available to examine, Mark and Q provide another resource for studying these variants: the surrounding text of Mark and Q themselves. The rest of Mark and Q provide context for the miracle overlaps; I will refer to the remainder of Mark and Q as the co-texts for the miracle overlaps.[19] This book will use the most relevant aspects of these co-texts to illuminate what Mark and Q accomplish in their respective variants of the miracle overlaps.[20]

OBJECTION 2: THERE IS NO Q

Scholars posit the existence of Q as one way to solve the so-called Synoptic Problem: Matthew, Mark, and Luke (the Synoptic Gospels) share so many parallels and verbatim repetitions that they must share written sources.[21] The Two-Source Hypothesis, that Matthew and Luke used Mark as a source along with another no longer extent source "Q," has achieved a dominant position within New Testament studies. From time to time, those who accept the Two-Source Hypothesis have turned to examine the stories that Mark and Q share, the Mark-Q overlaps. To the extent that scholars have attended to these overlaps, they have done so most often to establish a literary relationship between Mark and Q or to study the evolution of various elements in the Jesus tradition to recover their earliest forms and/or their origins in the life of the historical Jesus.[22]

Such studies of Mark-Q overlap presume the Two-Source Hypothesis, but other solutions to the Synoptic Problem exist. For instance, the Farrar-Goulder theory posits Mark as the earliest Synoptic, determines that Mark was a source for Matthew, and has Luke coming even later and relying on both Mark and Matthew. The Griesbach theory places Matthew earliest, being a source for Luke, with Mark using Matthew and Luke as sources. The Augustinian theory also has Matthew earliest as a source for Mark, with Luke using Mark and Matthew. None of these theories requires the existence of Q.[23] Thus, one could argue that the entire premise of this current book is flawed—it makes no sense to compare stories in Mark and Q because Q might not exist.

Certainly this objection holds if the purpose of the comparison is to determine the relationship between Mark and Q. If Q does not exist, it is vain to investigate whether Mark used it as a source or vice versa. The diachronic

approaches that trace the development of shared traditions in Mark and Q
rely on the timeline and source relationships presupposed by the Two Source
Hypothesis—change these timelines and the analysis changes with it. Com-
paring the Mark-Q overlaps to discover the earliest version of the story or
Mark and Q's literary relationship rests on accepting the validity of the Two
Source Hypothesis.

Nevertheless, comparing the Mark and Q versions can generate productive insights even when one remains agnostic regarding the existence of Q as
an independent document. The analysis of the Kentucky Fried Rat demonstrates how scholars can study different versions of the same story without
presupposing the relationships among versions. Comparing the different food
contamination tales from different times and different cultures reveals the
ubiquity of human anxiety about the food supply and fear of foreigners, even
as the differences reveal the various foreigners that different communities
fear. The different versions of the Kentucky Fried Rat story reveal the discomfort that the societal changes in twentieth-century America engendered.
The analysis of the Kentucky Fried Rat does not require positing any theory
about the genetic relationship among these various versions. All it requires is
the existence of multiple versions to examine.

Whether or not Q exists, the Double Tradition does exist. Matthew and
Luke manifestly do share material not contained in Mark, and occasionally
Matthew and Luke just do agree substantially against Mark in pericopae that
all three share. Even if there is no independent document behind these agreements, one can still recover this Double Tradition and compare it to Mark.
Therefore, comparing the overlaps in and of itself does not require accepting
the Two Source Hypothesis.

Any comparison is justified by the insight it provides into some phenomena of interest. For folklorists who have examined the Kentucky Fried Rat
story, the phenomena of interest are the societal anxieties that explain why
this urban legend gained such traction. Comparing different versions of the
contemporary American story has revealed the commonly repeated elements—the fast food restaurant, the absence of a home cooked meal, the
gender of the victims. Folklorists can explain these narrative features by the
social transformation of the twentieth century and the discomfort changing
patterns of food preparation engendered. Comparing the Kentucky Fried Rat
story to other stories of food contamination reveals the unease that communities feel about those they view as foreign yet who have access to the
community's resources.

The phenomena of interest in this comparison of Mark and Q are early
Christian attitudes toward miracles. I consider attitudes to miracles an inter-
esting subject in the historical study of Christianity both in itself and as part
of a broader examination of how his first followers thought about Jesus. The
miracle overlaps provide a means of exploring the differences because they

are so similar; the different agendas shine through in the telling of similar stories.[24] Staying neutral with regard to the solution to the Synoptic Problem does not preclude a productive comparison of Mark and the Double Tradition.

Nevertheless, remaining agnostic about Q's existence raises some nomenclature issues that potentially bedevil the discussion. Most of the time when people discuss the material shared between Matthew and Luke but not with Mark, they call it "Q" because the Two Source Hypothesis has become the default position in New Testament Studies. Calling this material "Q" is highly prejudicial against other solutions to the Synoptic Problem. "Double Tradition" is a more neutral term, but has not become standard, and sometimes people who accept the Two Source Hypothesis refer to material shared by Mark and Q as "Double Tradition." In a rigorous attempt to remain agnostic about the Synoptic Problem, one might avoid "Q" altogether and stick to "Double Tradition," as cumbersome as this phrase can be. However, "Q" has become such a ubiquitous and conveniently brief term for this material that I have chosen to use it interchangeably with "Double Tradition" and will alternate between the two of them. Partisans of the Two Source Hypothesis will have no problem with this nomenclature; to doubters or opponents of this hypothesis, I can only offer my apologies for not rigorously sticking with a more neutral nomenclature for the sake of convenience and style.

Maintaining neutrality with respect to Synoptic Problem solutions also complicates the use of co-text in the analysis of the miracle overlaps because using co-texts to understand a pericope assumes that the co-texts and the pericope form a unified text in which one can discover an authorial voice. In the case of the Markan variants of the miracle overlaps, the appropriate co-text is obvious: the Gospel of Mark. For the Q versions, the co-text is somewhat problematic. If Q did exist independently, scholars cannot be sure of its extent or ordering. However, even if Q did not exist as an independent text, the Double Tradition arose from a sequence of authorial choices. Under both the Griesbach and Augustinian hypotheses, the Double Tradition consists of those elements of Matthew that Luke chose to include and Mark chose to excise; for the Farrar-Goulder hypothesis, it consists of those elements Matthew chose to add to Mark that Luke also chose to include. In whatever way the Double Tradition came about, it did so as the result of a sequence of authorial choices, and one would expect these choices to have some coherence. Thus, the other pericopae from the Double Tradition serve as the appropriate co-text for the overlap texts, even if this co-text never existed as an independent text.

The attempt at source hypothetical neutrality raises another methodological question: how to determine the contents of the Double Tradition. When Matthew and Luke agree verbatim and Mark has no parallel, assigning that material to the Double Tradition is uncontroversial. However, when verbatim agreement does not occur, the decision of what belongs to the Double Tradition is influenced by whether or not one posits the Two Source Hypothesis. For instance, in the context of the Beelzebul Controversy, both Matthew and Luke share the following saying that Mark lacks:

> But if by the spirit of God I cast out demons, then the kingdom of God has come upon you. (Matt 12:28)

> But if by the finger of God I cast out demons, then the kingdom of God has come upon you. (Luke 11:20)

This verse belongs to the Double Tradition, but it is not obvious what to do about the one word difference of "finger" vs. "spirit." If Q existed then it must have said that Jesus cast out demons by the finger of God or by the spirit of God or by the something else of God, or there could have been multiple very similar versions of Q that differed in this one word, but this could not just be a blank space—Q must have had something there even if it is not shared by Matthew and Luke. Q and the Double Tradition are not coextensive.

In the effort to remain neutral with regard to the Synoptic source hypotheses, this book will take a strict view of the Double Tradition as that material common to Matthew and Luke but not Mark. This effort means excluding from the comparisons some elements that reconstructions of Q would include. Such a definition of the Double Tradition still involves some judgment when Matthew and Luke's sharing is not verbatim. So, for instance, when this study examines the Beelzebul Controversy, it will say that the Double Tradition includes Jesus claiming that if his exorcisms come by God's power (the sentiment Matthew and Luke express with different words), then the kingdom of God is present. The study can then compare a version of the story that contains this claim (the Double Tradition) with one that does not (Mark).

OBJECTION 3: THERE IS NO NEW TESTAMENT CHRISTOLOGY

It seems ridiculous to question whether Mark and Q have Christologies. New Testament Christology is a major area of contemporary New Testament scholarship, as the subtitles of several monographs, including this one, reveal.[25] Mark and Q certainly talk about Jesus in ways that imply the importance of his identity and his work, so they must each propound some Christology, i.e., a theological articulation of the significance of Jesus' identity and his work within the larger contexts of Christian beliefs. This section argues that the way biblical scholars routinely discuss New Testament Christology is problematic because it supposes theological reflection and articulation as logically prior to the production of texts. This presupposition manifests a larger assumption in the study of religion that beliefs are primary and that expressions of religion, such as texts, flow from these beliefs. The study of ritual has begun to question the assumption that religious actions flow from beliefs, and this section will analogously argue that beliefs and texts are mutually implicating. Thus, this study will not attempt to discover the Christology operative behind Mark and Q, but it will argue that Mark and Q do give evidence of what early Jesus followers thought and felt about Jesus.

Talking about New Testament Christology involves some anachronistic thinking about the New Testament. One of Richard Bauckham's most forceful statements of his perspective reveals the problems:

> The earliest Christology was already the highest Christology. I call it a Christology of divine identity, proposing this as a way beyond the standard distinction between 'functional' and 'ontic' Christology, a distinction which does not correspond to early Jewish thinking about God and has, therefore, seriously distorted our understanding of New Testament Christology. . . . This Christology of divine identity is not a mere stage on the way to the patristic development of ontological Christology in the context of a Trinitarian theology. It is already a fully divine Christology, maintaining that Jesus Christ is intrinsic to the unique and eternal identity of God. The Fathers did not develop it so much as transpose it into a conceptual framework more concerned with the Greek philosophical categories of essence and nature.[26]

Setting aside for a moment the substantive contents of Bauckham's claim, I attend to its presuppositions: there is such a thing as Christology that existed among the earliest Jesus followers and specifically among the authors of the New Testament. Bauckham presumes that the earliest followers of Jesus engaged in ways of thinking that can accurately be described as Christology. He presumes that the theological reflection and disputation of the fourth century has an analogue in the first century such that the earliest followers of Jesus have something (a Christology) that is comparable to the set of statements about Jesus' identity that the later church fathers developed.

Bauckham is not alone in asserting that early Jesus-followers had a Christology (or Christologies). Those investigating early Christologies find evidence for them in the New Testament texts. The relationship between Christology and the New Testament texts is conceptualized in remarkably consistent ways, even if scholars disagree on the nature of the Christologies for which the texts provide evidence. A handful of examples from recent treatments demonstrate this conception (all emphases added):

- "The main thesis of the present chapter offers an explanation for both the great age of this Christology and its prevalence *in our sources.*"[27]
- "New Testament Christology is the Christology *embedded in the text of the New Testament.*"[28]

- "Christology . . . at the same time *formed the core* of the new faith."[29]
- "Christology, which may generally be defined as theological interpretation of the person and work of Jesus of Nazareth, was the focus of early Christian proclamation and is *at the heart of the New Testament witness.*"[30]
- "To *discover Mark's Christology,* therefore, we can only consider the Gospel as it stands today."[31]
- "The New Testament texts *reveal the late first-century Christological developments* that underlie, accompany, or express this evolution."[32]
- "It has been a commonplace of Gospel studies in modernity to set John apart as a late text that *reflects* a more advanced stage of doctrinal development and a 'higher' Christology."[33]
- "Our detailed examination . . . revealed . . . a context where eschatology and Christology are *just below the surface.*"[34]
- ". . . Christology *presupposed in formulas* used by Paul."[35]

When scholars talk about New Testament Christology, they tend to talk about it as something that exists within the texts themselves, embedded there at the heart or core of the message, ready to be discovered just below the surface. The Christology exists in these texts because it existed in the communities that the authors inhabited, so that Christology forms the presuppositions of the texts. The texts reflect and reveal the Christology of the early Christians who created them.

The scholars quoted might rightly object that I am taking their metaphorical language over-literally. Nevertheless, the metaphors with which we—all of us, from the scholar at the lectern to the preacher in the pulpit to the person in the pew—speak about religion constrain the way we think about religion and determine the assumptions we bring to the study of religion.[36] The metaphors with which we talk about New Testament Christology incline us to treat a system of beliefs as the fundamental substance of early Christianity, with the texts that early Christians produced being products of these beliefs.

This idea that religious text flows from religious belief finds a parallel in the assumptions that have historically undergirded the study of ritual. The study of ritual has often operated on the tacit assumption of the dichotomy between thought and action, with thought occupying the position of primacy. Rituals were seen as expressing underlying beliefs, and the investigators who studied rituals treated them as if they were texts to be interpreted to understand the beliefs they expressed.[37] However, a number of ritual theorists have found the idea that rituals express meaning in this way to be untenable.[38] We can no longer presume to study a ritual as a manifestation of a deeper set of beliefs; rituals do not function like texts.

Maybe texts themselves do not function like texts, at least the ways religious texts are frequently conceived, that is, as secondary expressions of beliefs, which are the primary stuff of religion. Rather than seeing texts as the record of a system of thought, we can instead view texts as the record of an activity—storytelling. Indeed, it is likely that the biblical texts were originally read aloud in communities, and this performative aspect of the texts has become a focus of scholarly attention.[39] Performances, such as storytelling or rituals, can develop as a means of communicating and inculcating a preexistent set of beliefs, but they do not necessarily do so. Just as easily can these actions come first and then lead to the development of beliefs, as in the principle of *lex orandi lex credendi*.

Along these lines, Larry Hurtado has argued:

> behind the debates of councils and the framing of creeds, there were the binitarian devotional practices of generations of Christians who reverenced the exalted Christ along with God. . . . The Christological rhetoric of the New Testament and of the later Christological controversies and creeds reflects the attempt to explain and defend intellectually a development that began in human terms in profound religious experiences and in corporate worship.[40]

Hurtado here identifies religious experience and worship as the raw materials out of which Christology was developed, and he views the New Testament texts as part of this reflective activity. I suggest that we adjust Hurtado's schema by viewing worship, texts, and Christological reflection as potentially mutually implicating and stop viewing texts necessarily as secondary results of theological reflection.

Certainly people can tell a story that reflects or illustrates a prior theological stance. *The Pilgrim's Progress*, for instance, clearly illustrates a Puritan view about the nature of Christian life, a view that is the product of theological reflection. If John Bunyan were here, it seems pretty reasonable that he could give a coherent and expansive answer about how a Christian should live, and we can reasonably infer what this answer would look like from reading *The Pilgrim's Progress*. However, religious stories need not reflect pre-existent theological stances. We should not assume that a New Testament writer would have been able to answer the question, "Was Jesus God, and, if so, in what sense?" much less that we can infer how he would answer this question from the text he produced.

Even if the authors of these texts did not have answers to these questions, the texts they produced can still point to such answers. If one asked tellers of the Kentucky Fried Rat story whether national corporations are nefarious intruders into local communities or whether women should not work outside the home, it is possible that some would say yes, but it is also likely that many tellers would not have given these issues much explicit thought. Some might even answer these questions in the negative. Although the story presents an example of the deleterious effects of the changing culture of twentieth-century America, tellers of the story may not have articulated for themselves a stance on the merits and demerits of this cultural change. Indeed, some anxiety about these changes could exist even among people who would overall rate these changes positively. Telling the story could be a way for people to give voice to their own anxieties, or to entertain people who shared these anxieties, or to convince people that they should share these anxieties. However, it would be unwarranted to assume that all who told the story of the Kentucky Fried Rat opposed the cultural shifts of the twentieth century.

Similarly, New Testament authors could have made statements that point toward answers to the question whether Jesus is God without the authors themselves necessarily having formulated explicit answers. For instance, early followers of Jesus might have found the confession, "Jesus is Lord," psychologically appealing in expressing their devotion to Jesus. They might have desired that other members of the group express their devotion in a similar way and encouraged them to do so in their speech and writing. It is likely that part of the psychological appeal of this confession lay in the strong associations of "Lord" with "God of Israel," even if those who made the confession did not make this link explicit for themselves. The use of this confession in New Testament texts can provide evidence for the psychological appeal among some of Jesus' early followers of speaking in ways that assimilated him to the God of Israel, an appeal that could have been operative even in the absence of a conscious attempt to identify Jesus and God. This tendency to blur the distinction between Jesus and God is relevant to people using the New Testament as a document on which to reflect theologically about the identity and work of Jesus, but it does not necessarily provide evidence that the earliest followers of Jesus were engaging in this sort of explicit reflection themselves.

Looking at Mark and the Double Tradition without assuming that there existed a well-articulated Christology to which the texts give voice frees us from the task of trying to discover a systematic theological point of view in their distinct depictions of Jesus.[41] The Christology one could develop based on the texts' depictions of Jesus would be inchoate, perhaps even incoherent or contradictory, but that does not mean that the way the authors depict Jesus is random. We would expect the authors of the texts to talk about Jesus in ways that they thought their audiences would have found appealing or in ways that would convince their audiences to think about Jesus the way the authors wanted. In other words, the authors would depict Jesus in ways that they judged maximally rhetorically effective to reinforce the views of audiences with which they agreed while changing the views of audiences with which they disagreed.[42] Thus, examining depictions of Jesus reveals patterns of what early followers of Jesus found appealing or convincing even if they do not show that these early followers had definite, articulable ideas about precisely how Jesus was related to God.

CONCLUSION

This book aims to examine the depictions of Jesus as miracle worker in Mark and Q to determine what ways of portraying Jesus his early followers found appealing. Comparing Mark and Q versions of the miracle overlaps shows two distinct patterns of portraying Jesus in relation to his miracles and the kingdom of God. That these two patterns coexisted speaks to the diversity of thought among early Jesus followers. However, these two patterns also give insight into the development of the movement of Jesus followers since, as we discussed above, the situation of a story's telling influences the way the story is told. This study therefore goes beyond demonstrating *that* two patterns of relating Jesus, his miracles, and the kingdom of God exist within the Synoptic Tradition to proposing *why* these two patterns would have developed.

Telling stories that use miracles and the kingdom of God to indicate Jesus' god-like status is one way of meeting the pressure that early Jesus followers would have felt to demonstrate why following Jesus was important. Such a story-telling pattern had benefits and drawbacks in generating a positive identity for Jesus' followers. Telling stories that show Jesus and his miracles pointing to coming kingdom of God provides an alternate way of showing why following Jesus was important and had its own distinctive benefits and drawbacks. Comparing Mark and Q allows us to see more clearly the relative advantages and disadvantages of each story-telling pattern and so to understand why some early Jesus followers would have found one pattern appealing while others preferred the other. Choosing one way to depict Jesus is an implicit rejection of others, so comparing different ways of depicting Jesus allows us to see the possible conflict between those who prefer one depiction and those who prefer another. The conflict between the depiction of Jesus in Mark and Q leaves traces in their testing narratives, which we will examine in a later chapter. Comparing Mark and Q thus gives us insight into the dynamics of identity formation and conflict at work among early Jesus followers.

NOTES

1. Gillian Bennett and Paul Smith, *Urban Legends: A Collection of International Tall Tales and Terrors* (Westport, CT: Greenwood Press, 2007), 217; Jan Harold Brunvald, *The Vanishing Hitchhiker: American Urban Legends and Their Meaning* (New York: W.W. Norton, 1981), 81–90. For the development of urban legends, see Richard K. Beardsley and Rosalie Hankey, "A History of the Vanishing Hitchhiker," *California Folklore Quarterly* 2.1 (1943): 13–25. The classic catalogue of urban legends and other American folklore may be found in Ernest W. Baughman, *Type and Motif-Index of the Folktales of England and North America* (The Hague: Mouton & Co., 1966).
2. Cylin Busby, "'This is a True Story': Roles of Women in Contemporary Legend," *Midwestern Folklore* 20, no. 1 (1994): 6.

3. Joseph Byrne, *Encyclopedia of the Black Death* (Santa Barbara: ABC-CLIO, 2012), 194–95.

4. Gary Alan Fine, "The Kentucky Fried Rat: Legends and Modern Society," *Journal of the Folklore Institute* 17.2/3 (1980): 228.

5. Ibid., 231.

6. Bennett and Smith, *Urban Legends,* 217.

7. Fine, "Kentucky Fried," 230–31

8. Busby, "True Story," 26.

9. Fine, "Kentucky Fried," 233–34.

10. Fine, "Kentucky Fried," 232.

11. Busby, "True Story," 42–43.

12. Gary Alan Fine, *Manufacturing Tales: Sex and Money in Contemporary Legends* (Knoxville: University of Tennessee Press, 1992), 5–6.

13. Martin Dibelius, *From Tradition to Gospel*, tr. Bertram Lee Woolf (Cambridge: James Clarke, 1971); Rudolf Bultmann, *History of the Synoptic Tradition*, tr. John Marsh (New York: Harper & Row, 1968). Dibelius and Bultmann were both influenced by the work of Scandanavian folklorist Axel Olrik, especially his essay "Epic Laws of Folk Narrative," reprinted in *The Study of Folklore*, ed. Alan Dundes, 129–41 (Englewood Cliffs, NJ: Prentice-Hall, 1965). For a discussion about the origins of form criticism, see David E. Aune, "Form Criticism," in *The Blackwell Companion to the New Testament*, ed. David E. Aune, 140–55 (Chichester, UK: Wiley-Blackwell 2010).

14. Dibelius, *From Tradition*, 59.

15. Nevertheless, form criticism remains a vital form of Biblical scholarship and has taken into account the fact that the biblical texts are not merely compilations of discrete oral units. See Martin J. Buss, *The Changing Shape of Form Criticism: A Relational Approach* (Sheffield: Sheffield Phoenix, 2010); Werner H. Kelber and Samuel Byrskog, eds., *Jesus in Memory: Traditions in Oral and Scribal Perspectives* (Waco, TX: Baylor University Press, 2009); Roland Boer, ed., *Bakhtin and Genre Theory in Biblical Studies* (Atlanta: Society of Biblical Literature, 2007); Marvin A. Sweeney and Ehud Ben Zvi, eds., *The Changing Face of Form Criticism for the Twenty-First Century* (Grand Rapids, MI: Eerdmans, 2003).

16. In what sense we can consider Q a text will occupy us in the next objection.

17. For justification based on linguistic theory of why gospel texts reflect the psychological state of the authors, the immediate environment of their reception, and the larger environment in which they were composed, see Todd Klutz, *The Exorcism Stories in Luke-Acts: A Sociostylistic Reading* (Cambridge: Cambridge University Press, 2004), 3–28.

18. Alan Dundes, *Holy Writ as Oral Lit: The Bible as Folklore* (Lanham, MD: Rowman & Littlefield, 1999).

19. Borrowing a phrase from Klutz, *Exorcism Stories,* 28.

20. Examining how the unique features of an instance of a repeated story fit an author's purpose has been used in the analysis of Biblical type scenes. The classic description is Robert Alter, *The Art of Biblical Narrative*, rev. ed. (New York: Basic Books, 2010), 55–78. Alter, however, eschews what he terms the excavative function of biblical analysis through which the scholar uses the text to learn about the world in which the texts were produced. Such an excavative function is a major aim of the analysis carried out in this book.

21. For an overview of the Synoptic Problem and the parameters of any acceptable solution, see Mark Goodacre, *The Synoptic Problem: A Way through the Maze* (London: Continuum, 2001), 13–32.

22. Harry T. Fleddermann, *Mark and Q: A Study of the Overlap Texts* (Leuven: Leuven University Press, 1995); Frans Neirynck, "Assessment," in Fleddermann, *Mark and Q,* 263–304; Rudolf Laufen, *Die Doppelüberlieferungen der Logienquelle und des Markusevangeliums* (Bonn: Peter Hanstein, 1980); Joachim Schülling, *Studien zum Verhältnis von Logienquelle und Markusevangelium* (Würzburg: Echter, 1991); Burton L. Mack, "Q and the Gospel of Mark: Revising Christian Origins," *Semeia* 55 (1991): 15–39; David R. Catchpole, "The Beginning of Q: A Proposal," *NTS* 38 2 (1992): 205–21; M. Eugene Boring, "The Syoptic Problem, 'Minor' Agreements and the Beelzebul Pericope," in *The Four Gospels 1992: Fetschrift Frans Neirynck* ed. F. Van Segbroeck, C.M. Tuckett, G. Van Belle, and J. Verheyden

(Leuven: Leuven University Press, 1992): 1:587–619; M. Eugene Boring, "The 'Minor Agreements' and Their Bearing on the Synoptic Problem," in *New Studies in the Synoptic Problem: Oxford Conference, April 2008: Essays in Honor of Christopher M. Tuckett* (Leuven: Peeters, 2011), 227–51; Timothy A. Friedrichsen, "'Minor' and 'Major' Matthew-Luke Agreements Against Mk 4,20–32," in Van Segbroeck et al., *Four Gospels,* 1:541–61; Jan Lambrecht, "Three More Notes in Response to John P. Meier; Mark 1,7–8; 3,27 and 10,1–12," *ETL* 89.4 (2013): 397–409; Jan Lambrecht, "John the Baptist and Jesus in Mark 1:1–15: Markan Redaction of Q?" *NTS* 38.3 (1992): 357–84; David R. Catchpole, "The Mission Charge in Q," *Semeia* 55 (1991): 147–74; Risto Uro, *Sheep Among the Wolves: A Study on the Mission Instructions of Q* (Helsinki: Suomaleinen Tiedeakatemia, 1987), 98–110.

23. Advocates of the Farrar-Goulder theory include Mark S. Goodacre, *The Case Against Q: Studies in Markan Priority and the Synoptic Problem* (Harrisburg, PA: Trinity Press International, 2002) and Francis Watson, *Gospel Writing: A Canonical Perspective* (Grand Rapids, MI: Eerdmans, 2013), 156–216. A modified version of the Griesbach theory finds support from Allan J. McNicol, David L. Dungan, and David B. Peabody, eds., *Beyond the Q Impasse—Luke's Use of Matthew: A Demonstration by the Research Team of the International Institute for Gospel Studies* (Valley Forge, PA: Trinity Press International, 1996) and David B. Peabody, Lamar Cope, and Allan J. McNicol, eds., *One Gospel from Two—Mark's Use of Matthew and Luke* (Valley Forge, PA: Trinity Press International, 2002). The Augustinian theory also has a supporter in J. W. Wenham, *Reading Matthew, Mark, and Luke: A Fresh Assault on the Synoptic Problem,* (London: Hodder & Stoughton, 1991). For a recent assessment of the *status quaestionis* in the Synoptic Problem see C. M. Tuckett, "The Current State of the Synoptic Problem," in Foster et al., *New Studies,* 9–50.

24. A similar comparison of miracle stories used to investigate the different agendas behind them, comes from the analysis of Synoptic and Johannine resuscitations in Philip F. Esler and Ronald Piper, *Lazarus, Mary, and Martha: Social-Scientific Approaches to the Gospel of John* (Minneapolis: Fortress, 2006). Such an approach mirrors that of some contemporary text critics, who have shifted their focus from determining the original form of texts by stripping away corrupted variants to examining the implications of the variants themselves and what they can tell scholars about the development of Christianity, e.g., D.C. Parker, *The Living Text of the Gospels* (Cambridge: Cambridge University Press, 1997).

25. E.g., Marinus De Jonge, *God's Final Envoy: Early Christology and Jesus' Own View of His Mission* (Grand Rapids, MI: Eerdmans, 1998)*;* Richard B. Hays, *Reading Backwards: Figural Christology and the Fourfold Gospel Witness* (Waco, TX: Baylor University Press, 2014); Elizabeth Struthers Malbon, *Mark's Jesus: Characterization as Narrative Christology* (Waco, TX: Baylor University Press, 2009); Michael Tait, *Jesus the Divine Bridegroom in Mark 2:18–22: Mark's Christology Upgraded* (Manchester: University of Manchester Press, 2008); Richard Bauckham, *Jesus and the God of Israel: God Crucified and Other Studies on the New Testament's Christology of Divine Identity* (Grand Rapids, MI: Eerdmans, 2009); Broadhead, *Teaching With Authority.*

26. Bauckham, *Jesus and the God of Israel*, x.

27. Allison, *Constructing,* 303.

28. Frank J. Matera, *New Testament Christology* (Louisville: Westminster John Knox, 1999), 2.

29. "Die Christologie . . . bildete dabei das Herzstück des neuen Glaubens" (Hengel, *Studien,* Vorwort, vii).

30. Richard N. Longenecker, Introduction to *Contours of Christology in the New Testament* (Grand Rapids, MI: Eerdmans, 2005), xii.

31. Morna D. Hooker, "'Who Can This Be?' The Christology of Mark's Gospel," in Longenecker, *Contours,* 80.

32. Paula Fredriksen, *From Jesus to Christ: The Origins of the New Testament Images of Jesus,* 2nd ed. (New Haven: Yale University Press, 2000), 134.

33. Hays, *Reading,* xii.

34. Tait, *Jesus,* 328.

35. de Jonge, *Envoy,* 132.

36. Robert Ford Campany, "On the Very Idea of Religions (In the Modern West and in Early Medieval China)," *HR* 52.2 (2012): 287–319.

37. Catherine Bell, *Ritual Theory, Ritual Practice* (Oxford: Oxford University Press, 2009), 19–54.

38. Ann Baranowski, "A Psychological Comparison of Ritual and Musical Meaning," *MTSR* 10.1 (1998): 3–29; Jenny Blain and Robert J. Wallis, "Ritual Reflections, Practitioners Meanings: Disputing the Terminology of Neo-Shamanic 'Performance,'" *JRitSt* 20.1 (2006): 21–36; Daniel B. Lee, "Ritual and Social Meaning and Meaninglessness of Religion," *Soziale Welt* 56.1 (2005): 5–16; Hans H. Penner, "Language, Ritual and Meaning," *Numen* 32.1 (1985): 1–16; Frits Staal, "The Meaninglessness of Ritual," *Numen* 26.1 (1979): 2–22.

39. David Rhoads, "Performance Criticism: An Emerging Methodology in Second Testament Studies—Part 1," *BTB* 36.3 (2006): 118.

40. Larry W. Hurtado, *One God, One Lord: Early Christian Devotion and Ancient Jewish Monotheism* (Edinburgh: T&T Clark, 1998), 128.

41. Elizabeth Malbon, *Mark's Jesus,* has examined the Gospel of Mark freed from the assumption of a logically prior and uniform Christology.

42. For an analysis of miracles as a rhetorical strategy, see Duane F. Watson, ed., *Miracle Discourse in the New Testament* (Atlanta: SBL, 2012).

Chapter Two

The Purposes of Narrating
Miracle Stories

The Inquisitor suggests that the Church's purpose in telling miracle stories is to arrogate to itself the coercive power that Jesus refused to accept in the Temptation. This chapter examines the purposes of narrating miracle stories to understand why Mark and Q told them. It will look at what positive function miracles serve, but it will also examine how miracle stories function negatively to discredit the doers of such deeds. The analysis of this negative function will be of use in studying two of the miracle overlaps, the Beelzebul Controversy and Q's version of the Temptation, that link miracles with service to Satan.

Investigating these positive and negative functions of miracle stories involves exploring the context of Mark and Q: religious communities in the ancient Mediterranean world striving to create identities for themselves. This investigation will somewhat artificially divide the context into two separate aspects for analysis. The first aspect is that of a religious community creating its own identity, and I will use both social psychology and the study of religion to investigate how telling miracle stories develops positive group identity as well as negative evaluations of other groups. The second aspect of Mark and Q's context of composition is their location in the Roman Empire near the turn of the era. I will investigate this aspect with other literature from the Roman Empire that shows how people at this time used miracles to extol the excellence of some while labeling other people who did such deeds as deviant.

MIRACLES AND IDENTITY FORMATION

While the identity and social locations of the authors of Mark and Q remain obscure, the stories they told exist for us to study because early Jesus followers chose to preserve them. Any time these early Jesus followers read, recited, copied, or distributed these texts, they were making a choice to do so with these texts rather than others. As discussed in the last chapter, the social setting influences the choices people make when telling or retelling a story. The early Jesus followers who continued to tell the stories of Mark and Q found themselves in a nascent religious group, so traces of these group dynamics should exist in what these people transmitted.

At the same time, knowledge of group dynamics helps us understand what occurs in the texts. Insights from social psychology can therefore illuminate the context of these stories' early promulgation. One of the most helpful insights from social psychology in this regard is social identity theory, which emerged within the field of social psychology from Henri Tajfel's experiments. Tajfel demonstrated that merely assigning individuals to a group engendered positive feelings toward fellow members of the group. In the experiment, subjects were randomly assigned to groups that the experimenters falsely told the subjects were based on similar quantitative acuity or aesthetic judgment. When the subjects were allowed to choose rewards for other subjects, they consistently gave larger rewards to the subjects in their own group at the expense of subjects in other groups. Merely informing a subject that he belonged to a group predisposed that subject to reward members of his own group preferentially.[1] This work suggested that human psychology predisposes us to develop groups in which members share positive feelings toward fellow members (termed the in-group) vis-à-vis members of other groups (termed out-groups).

Social-identity theory implies that belonging to a group creates a psychological drive both to develop an identity for the in-group that distinguishes it from out-groups and to make this distinguishing identity as positive as possible. The concept of collective or social memory explains one means by which groups develop such identities. Groups have something analogous to individual memories. Individuals store important past events in their brains and the recollection of these events forms the individual's identity. Likewise, groups have practices, such as storytelling, monument construction, and rituals, that allow current members to connect with the past and help define the group's identity.[2] This analogy does not imply that the group is some organic unity that in and of itself remembers. Only individuals remember, and the social memory results form the group members' individual memories and how they communicate these memories to each other and to new members.

Because social memory results from individual acts of remembering, certain homologies exist between individual and social memory. The life of an individual or group generates experiences too numerous to remember in their totality—there is a limit to the neural capacity of an individual just as there is a limit to the number of stories, rituals, or monuments a society can construct and transmit. Thus, remembering and forgetting are always mutually implicating—most things must be forgotten, and only with effort can certain aspects be preserved in memory.[3] On the individual level, this process of remembering and forgetting involves the subconscious sifting of everyday experience into items to be stored in the long-term memory and thus preserved.[4] Similarly, on the group level, this process involves picking from the ephemera of a group's existence those elements to be commemorated and transmitted widely among the group and to future group members.[5] Within the group there may exist different sub-groups who have selected what to remember differently.[6] For both the individual and the group remembering is always a process of selection.[7]

This selection involves events of the past, but it always occurs in the present. Thus, remembering does not recapitulate the past, but rather it brings present and past into interaction.[8] The memory depends both on the nature of the past events and on the exigencies of the present moment of remembering.[9] Some events forcefully or traumatically impress themselves into individual or social memory even when remembering them provides no present advantage. At other times, the needs of the present determine a memory that diverges radically from the events as they occurred. Away from these two extremes lies what occurs in most processes of remembering—the qualities of both the past event and of the present moment determine the memory.[10]

In the case of miracles, the nature of the events incline them to memorability. The striking violation of expectations evident in these acts of power embed them in the memories of those who witness them and make them captivating subjects for retelling.[11] Even though the miracles might have imprinted themselves on individual and social memories by their striking nature, the needs of the individual or society at the time of remembering influences the memory. Only certain aspects of even the most striking miracle can be remembered and retold, so even in remembering there is also forgetting. In addition to deletion, there is also addition: motivations are supplied, gaps are filled, explanations are added.[12] It is the present state of the individual rememberer that determines how this editing process of the memory unfolds. Telling a story, choosing what words to use and what events to include, provides a way to shape the memory of an event to meet present needs.[13]

Such remembering satisfies the need to create identity. The creation of long-term memories forms a coherent life-story and stable identity for the individual. Similarly, the social memory of a group creates a group identity that is stable over time and that marks the group as distinct from other groups.[14] Social-identity theory predicts that a group develops its collective memory in ways that emphasize the group's positive and distinct identity. Telling stories of a group's founder or early members performing miracles is one way to shape the group's collective memory.[15] Social-identity theory directs attention to those elements of the story that helped Jesus followers form a positive and distinctive identity for themselves since those elements could account for why early Jesus followers found the telling, retelling, and preservation of these stories worthwhile.

Social-identity theory provides one lens through which to view the function of miracles stories in generating positive evaluations of the in-group. However, the negative function of miracles in stigmatizing out-groups does not flow automatically from this tendency to foster positive in-group evaluation. Psychological experiments as well as fieldwork have borne out that in-group positivity and out-group negativity are separate and sometimes not correlated with each other.[16] The tendency toward in-group positivity recognized by social-identity theory does not imply a correlative tendency toward out-group negativity. In-group identification is not sufficient to explain disdain for or conflict with out-groups.[17]

The perception of threat can explain out-group hostility. Such perceived threats can be realistic dangers to the in-group's material well-being. However, groups can also perceive symbolic threats to the in-group's worldview.[18] One way out-groups can pose such symbolic threats is by effacing the boundaries that the in-group sets for itself.[19] In-group positivity relies on the distinctiveness of the in-group from other groups; when the in-group shares similar experiences and beliefs with out-groups, the clarity of intergroup boundaries blurs, which threatens the integrity of the in-group.[20] An out-group can pose a serious symbolic threat to the in-group if its similar worldview causes the in-group to question the validity of its own distinct identity. The in-group then develops out-group negativity as a protective mechanism to defend these threatened ideological boundaries. Here we would expect to encounter what Freud calls the narcissism of minor differences, as the in-group seizes on small differences to distinguish itself from the otherwise similar out-group.[21] Religious groups especially tend to distinguish themselves from other proximate religious groups by magnifying the small differences and attaching immense importance to them.[22]

One effective way that communities create distinctive and positive identities for themselves is by telling stories of miracle workers who operate within their group. The tellers can shape the story to show how the powerful miracle reflects the group's access to the supernatural. Miracle stories also demonstrate how the group's miracle workers have legitimate power, whereas similar deeds done by outsiders constitute illegitimate and dangerous exercises of power. Miracle stories allow religious communities both to articulate their own positive identity and to distinguish themselves from other groups whose proximity and similarity make them symbolically threatening.

A medieval Chinese Buddhist story of an unsuccessful bid to vanquish a demon illustrates how these insights from social psychology and religious studies bear fruit in analyzing miracle stories. The example comes from a fifth-century collection of pro-Buddhist Chinese miracle tales called the *Mingxiang ji* or *Records of Signs from the Unseen Realm*. At this time, Buddhism was a relatively recent entrant in the Chinese religious landscape, and early Chinese Buddhists lived alongside practitioners of many indigenous Chinese religious traditions, including Daoism. Story 67 from the *Minxiang ji* tells of a certain He Danzhi who did not believe in Buddhist teaching and who fell ill. While ill, he saw a demon with a bull's head and a human body standing over him with a pitchfork. He commissioned a Daoist to save him from this demon; the Daoist performed the ritual actions that Daoism prescribed, such as making petitions and talismans, but the demon continued tormenting Danzhi. Danzhi then received a visit from a Buddhist monk. When Danzhi told him about the demon he saw, the monk recognized it as one of the demons from Buddhist purgatory punishing Danzhi in karmic retribution for prior bad acts. The monk encouraged Danzhi to turn toward Buddhist teaching, because if he did so the demon would vanish, but Danzhi would not listen to the monk and died a little later.[23]

This story implicitly contrasts Daoism and Buddhism through the characters of the Daoist and the Buddhist monk. The Daoist, acting as his tradition instructs, fails to save the man from the demon, but the monk, enlightened by the insights of his tradition, correctly recognizes what could have saved Danzhi if only he would have listened. The contrast creates a positive identity for its Buddhist tellers by implying that the teachings of Buddhism overcome supernatural threats; at the same time it creates a negative identity for the out-group as it shows that Danzhi's reliance on Daoist's practices cost him his life. For Chinese Buddhism, Daoism is a near other, a rival tradition whose existence is symbolically threatening.[24] It makes sense that Buddhist tellers and hearers enjoyed a story demonstrating Buddhism's superiority to Daoism. Moreover, the Buddhist tale demonstrates the narcissism of minor differences by framing Danzhi's death as a result of his failure to recognize how his suffering was the result of the specifically Buddhist idea of karma, an idea that distinguished Buddhism from Daoism.[25] If he had understood karma better and taken the actions the monk proscribed to ameliorate his karmic suffering, Danzhi might have survived.

Social-identity theory and the narcissism of minor differences conceptualize the appeal of such a story to a Buddhist audience, and this appeal provides one explanation for early Buddhists' composition and dissemination of this story. However, this story not only reminded Buddhists how superior Buddhism is to Daoism, but it could also persuade Daoists or those potentially drawn to Daoism to turn instead to Buddhism. If Danzhi had done so, he might have survived. The audience of such a tale could include both committed Buddhists and people the teller might convince to become Buddhists. The Buddhism represented by the stories of the *Minxiang ji* competes with alternative traditions, such as Daoism, for influence and adherence. Such narratives form part of the repertoire of religious actions and beliefs that adherents use to make sense of and navigate their world. These religious repertoires are also fields of contestation whereby people make claims and try to persuade others.[26] The amenability of miracle stories to these contests explains their telling and retelling.

MIRACLES IN THE ANCIENT MEDITERRANEAN

The stories of the *Minxiang ji* bear traces of the striving to create a group identity in a specific time and place: early medieval China. Likewise, the miracle stories of Mark and Q have a specific setting: the ancient Mediterranean world. Just as the cultural outlook of the late twentieth century shaped the Kentucky Fried Rat story, so too did the cultural milieu of the early Roman empire partially determine what authors could accomplish by telling stories of wonder workers. Fortunately, such stories from this epoch abound and provide ample material to understand what ancient audiences found appealing and disquieting about miracles and what ancient authors could accomplish by telling stories of miracle workers.

In the early Common Era, many stories presented their heroes as figures worthy of emulation and allegiance, and they often described these heroes working miracles. These stories share so many features that they form a pattern of hagiographical discourse. The stories adhering to this pattern depict human heroes who have some special connection to the divine, and the stories have the pretension of recording actual events in the style of ancient historiography.[27] This hagiographic discourse was a Jewish, Christian, and pagan phenomenon that developed in the first century of the Common Era and continued into late antiquity. Philo's *Life of Moses* represents the first complete development of this discourse, which continued among Christians in the Gospels and various acts of apostles and martyrs as well as among pagans, for instance in Philostratus's *Life of Apollonius of Tyana* of the early third century. This widespread discourse manifested the shared cultural environment of the Roman Empire.[28] In this setting, hagiographical discourse intended not merely to provide information about the protagonist, but also to defend the hero from rival interpretations, to create veneration of the hero, and to induce the hearers to live after the inspiring example of the protagonist.

Philostratus's *Life of Apollonius of Tyana* illustrates how miracles figured in such hagiographical discourse. When Apollonius travels to Rome, the following scene unfolds:

A girl seemed to have died at the hour of her marriage and her bridegroom followed the bier bitterly weeping over the unfinished marriage, and Rome wept with him too, for the girl belonged to a most highly accomplished family. But when Apollonius came upon this misfortune, he said, "Put down the bier, for I will put a stop to your tears over the girl." And then he asked what the girl's name might be. While the crowd supposed that he was going to give such an oration as belongs at a funeral and raises lamentations, he did nothing of the sort, but rather, touching her and speaking imperceptibly, he awoke the girl from seeming death, and the child spoke and returned to the house of her father, just as Alcestis was revived by Heracles. When the girl's relatives presented him with 150,000 sesterces, he said to give it to the child as a dowry. Now whether he found some spark of life in her that eluded those who attended her—for it is said how it was raining and steam was coming off from her face—or whether he rekindled her extinguished life and brought her back, the grasp of this has become unattainable not only for me, but even for those who were there. (*Vit.Apoll.* 4.45)

Philostratus carefully narrates the story to make the reader think the girl might be in a coma, rather than dead. He says the girl "seemed to have died," and that Apollonius "awoke the girl from seeming death." In his direct address to the reader at the end of this story, he makes this point explicit. Although he admits the possibility that the girl might actually have died, he also entertains the option that she was still alive and that only Apollonius noticed, perhaps seeing a clue in the vapor coming from her face due to her faint breathing. Throughout *Life*, the miraculous activities of Apollonius frequently stem from a similar diagnostic acumen. He averts a plague in Ephesus by having the citizens stone the demon who brought the plague and who was disguised as an old man (4.10); similarly, when the women of an Egyptian town are being raped and murdered by a mysterious force, Apollonius recognizes it as the work of a satyr and tells the townspeople how they can overcome the satyr with wine and stop his rampaging (6.27). His penetrating insight also allows Apollonius to predict the future or to know what is happening concurrently very far away.[29] Apollonius is a bit like Sherlock Holmes—his powers of observation allow him to do things that seem incredible to other people, even though his feats are, in principle, available to others if they had been able to see as clearly as Apollonius.[30]

Philostratus locates the source of these powers in Apollonius's tremendous wisdom. He writes *Life* to portray Apollonius accurately "with regard to the habits of wisdom (σοφίας) by which he gained god-like (δαιμόνιος) status and was considered divine (θεῖος)" (1.2). Apollonius's power flows from his wisdom. To be sure, this wisdom is supernatural, made possible by Apollonius's particular aptitude, but the same could be said of Pythagoras or Plato, those paragons of Greek philosophy with whom Philostratus counts Apollonius (1.1–2). Apollonius's wisdom is a divine endowment, traceable to his supernatural parentage. These divinely endowed proclivities, along with the moderate Pythagorean asceticism he practices, give Apollonius access to a special wisdom that provides penetrating insight into the way the world works.[31] Thus, Philostratus labors to make Apollonius's miracles result from the powers of observation his divinely endowed wisdom brings. In the case of the Roman girl, Philostratus explains that Apollonius saw what others had missed and recognized the life left in the girl.

In this story Philostratus also emphasizes the ease with which Apollonius moves among the rich and powerful, as the girl's relatives have sufficient influence to draw most of Rome for the funeral procession. Although Apollonius himself eschews riches and luxuries, he fits in with the wealthy. His reaction to the family's proffered gift makes this relation clear. This family has enough wealth to bestow a gift of 150,000 sesterces, equivalent to a farm laborer's daily wage for one hundred years and more than a third of the net worth required to attain equestrian rank.[32] Apollonius, a true philosopher, seeks not to acquire wealth, so he gives the money away. Nevertheless, his outlook aligns with the upper class. He does not give the money to the poor, but rather gives it as a dowry for the wealthy girl. Thus, Philostratus allows Apollonius to participate in the extravagant, reciprocal gift giving of the upper class while at the same time remaining a philosopher, indifferent to the accumulation of wealth.

Philostratus explicitly compares Apollonius's raising of this girl with Heracles's wresting Alcestis from death, as recounted in Euripides's play bearing her name. Throughout the *Life* Philostratus makes Apollonius the epitome and champion of Greek culture.[33] Apollonius resembles the great Greek heroes of mythology (e.g., Heracles) and the great Greek philosophers (e.g., Pythagoras). In another setting, Achilles's ghost recognizes Apollonius as a peer, and together they discuss obscurities about the Trojan War (4.15–16).[34] This connection to classical Greek culture also expressed itself in Apollonius's attention to the worship of the gods. Shortly before raising the Roman girl, Apollonius had so persuasively discussed the importance of piety that religious devotion spiked in Rome (4.41). This attention to proper cult worship marks Apollonius's travels as he restores shrines and corrects corrupt temple practices wherever he goes. Philostratus strives to connect Apollonius with traditional polytheism. Miracles, such as the raising of the Roman girl, show how Apollonius embodies the best aspects of Hellenic culture.

Philostratus's *Life* shares with other hagiographic discourses the performative purpose of creating veneration of the hero and inducing hearers to celebrate the intellectual and cultural tradition of which Apollonius is the epitome. Like many other such discourses it uses miracles to accomplish these goals. The miracles serve many purposes throughout the work. On one level, they help create an entertaining story that appeals to erudite readers' knowledge of literary traditions, along with mythology, geography, and history. The miracles of Apollonius further demonstrate the power and excellence of *paedeia,* for it is Apollonius's deep familiarity with and participation in the traditions of Greek learning, especially philosophy, that give him his power. In addition, the miracles of Apollonius demonstrate the virtues of a cultured man of learning—his devotion to Greek history, his piety and zeal for proper cult worship, his comfort with the upper class even as he eschews material gain. The miracles also show Apollonius to be divinely gifted, sharing a close connection with the gods, and thus to be worthy of veneration. Such miracle working was not a requirement for hagiographical literature, but it was a cultural idea available for authors to use to demonstrate the virtues and supernatural powers of their protagonists.

Although miracle stories served broadly similar purposes across hagiographical discourses of demonstrating power and virtue, authors used miracles to demonstrate different virtues and different conceptions of supernatural power at work in their heroes. Moreover, miracles did not appear only in stories about human miracle workers, for miracles could be the direct work of God or the gods. In the case of Philostratus's Apollonius, the miracles promote stability and maintain order by attesting to the divine approval of a leading figure in a religious tradition, which in Apollonius's case was classical polytheism. Christian apocryphal gospels and acts similarly promote stability as miracles attest the legitimacy of the leaders of the Jesus tradition. Miracle stories could also demonstrate the solicitude of a healing God, as in cult tales of Asklepios and Isis, or they could show how devotion to a god gave access to mystical union with the divine, as in the revelations that Aelius Aristides received from Asklepios or that Apuleius received from Isis. Miracles could appear as portents in stories that showed how the divine purposes operated in history, as in the historians Tacitus, Suetonius, Dio Cassius, and Josephus.[35]

Philostratus's *Life* thus provides an example of one way that miracle stories could positively characterize miracle working humans and deities. However, *Life* also evidences the negative way that ancient authors could construe miracle workers. Philostratus writes his account of Apollonius to refute those who "hold him to be a magician (μάγον) and libel him as an illegitimate sage (βιαίως σοφόν)" and who "take credit away from Apollonius for predicting things by virtue of wisdom (σοφίαν) and say that he did these things by craft (τέχνη) as a magician (μάγῳ)" (*Vit. Apoll.* 1.2). In one sense *Life* makes an apologia, rehabilitating Apollonius's reputation from detractors who labeled him a charlatan or a magician.[36] The wondrous deeds that Apollonius accomplishes are a double-edged sword for his reputation: to a supporter, they represent his divinely endowed power as a master of Greek wisdom, but to detractors they demonstrate his participation in the forbidden art of magic. To protect him from the charge of magic, Philostratus works assiduously to make clear that Apollonius' power comes from his wisdom.[37]

The story of his resuscitation of the Roman girl implicitly rejects the category of magic for Apollonius as his willingness to forego such a hefty reward demonstrates that he is no magician who performs miracles for his own enrichment.[38]

This category of illegitimate magic set against legitimate miracles proves very difficult to define and analyze. Ancient authors tend to use these categories as if they were well defined and objective, which can lead modern scholars to delineate the socially constructed features that differentiate miracle and magic. To a first approximation, the difference appears to be that miracles occur when a figure performs a feat in alliance with some divine purpose, while magic involves manipulation of supernatural power by human agents without particular attention to the will of the gods.[39]

However such distinct boundaries between miracle and magic do not stand up to scrutiny. The distinction between a magical incantation and a prayer for a miracle is not clear—both cases could be interpreted as attempts to manipulate divine power.[40] Moreover, there was not a unified concept of magic; even the terminology for magic is heterogeneous. Philostratus tells us that he writes to defend Apollonius from the charge of being a *magos* (μάγος), that is, one who practices *magia* (μαγεία). *Magia* referred to deeds accomplished by supernatural means and could carry both positive and negative connotations, although the negative valence was operative more often.[41] Philostratus also wishes to prove that Apollonius did not do his striking deeds through *techne* (τέχνη), that is, craft or trickery. The doer of wondrous deeds could be accused simultaneously of wielding illegitimate supernatural power and of fraudulently passing off magic tricks as supernatural accomplishments. Such an accusation could also take the form of the label *goes* (γόης), "sorcerer," a label Apollonius' opponents apply when accusing him before the emperor Domitian (7.17). The meaning of *goes* ranges from one who nefariously manipulates supernatural forces to a fraud performing tricks and passing them off as divine.[42] Magic was not a uniform concept with uniform meaning. Labeling one a *magos* or a *goes* is as much a matter of polemic as of applying a stable, well-defined category.

However, this lack of a firm boundary between miracle and magic does not mean that scholars should simply collapse the two into one underlying reality.[43] Ancient authors did recognize a distinction between legitimate and illegitimate exercises of supernatural power. Nor should magic be viewed as empty of substantive content, serving only to label practitioners as deviant. Such a view of magic cannot account for positive associations in conceptions of magic. For instance, one of the Greek Magical Papyri addresses its reader, "O blessed initiate of sacred magic (ὦ μα[κάρι]ε μύστα τῆς ἱερᾶς μαγείας)" (PGM 1.127), an address that makes little sense if magic is conceived as a category with only pejorative implications. Similarly, emptying "magic" of substantive content obscures how the accused could defend themselves from these charges by appealing to a substantive definition within the culture.

The second century CE *Apology* of Lucius Apuleius illustrates the problems that arise when magic is viewed as a pejorative empty of content. Apuleius marries a wealthy older widow named Pudentia; Pudentia's family, upset at the marriage and the subsequent loss of their inheritance to a man they viewed as an upstart, accuses Apuleius of practicing magic.[44] Apuleius's esoteric interests in biology and philosophy make him a target of the accusation that he is a magician, and the accusation suggests that he has crossed beyond the bounds of social acceptability.[45] If the accusers cannot achieve a legal sanction against Apuleius, they can at least impugn his character and oust him from the realm of respectable society. As part of his rhetorical strategy to defend himself, Apuleius brings up the positive associations of magic, its derivation from Persian wisdom and religious practice, and Plato's approval of this Persian custom (*Apol.* 26). The defense here relies on the ambiguity of *magia*; while his opponents use it to label him a deviant, Apuleius can draw on positive connotations to counter this pejorative use.[46]

However, the bulk of Apuleius's defense depends not on emphasizing the positive aspects of magic, but on rejecting the label of *magia* for his deeds altogether. His defense primarily focuses on relabeling as "philosophy" those deeds which his accusers have labeled "magic" and on showing that his actions lie within the bounds of social acceptability.[47] For instance, one of the specific accusations is that Apuleius tried to procure unusual fish to make magical charms. Apuleius's first refutation of this charge is that fish have nothing to do with making magic charms; other material, such as herbs and wax, are well known to be the material from which charms are constructed (30–31). Second, he tells his accusers that his interest in the fish was to examine it for his work as an ichthyologist, and that they can read the treatise which he was composing to verify his claim (36). Both defenses rely on the presupposition that magic is more than just an accusation; for Apuleius, magic is a category with definable characteristics against which certain actions can be measured to determine whether or not they belong. If this were not the case, if magic were simply a label empty of content besides polemical intent, Apuleius would have had no means to rebut the accusation.

Thus, while magic in the ancient world certainly was not a sharply defined construct conducive to objective categorization, neither was it completely devoid of meaning beyond its deviance labeling function. There were conventional ways of distinguishing magic from more legitimate practices: magic involved manipulating spirits, magic was used for selfish or trivial purposes, magic was secretive and not associated with the civic cult, or magic involved injuring people.[48] None of these criteria were used with absolute consistency, which makes the definition of magic very nebulous, but not completely empty of content. Along with the instability of meaning lies a contradiction in the evaluation of magic. Officially, magic was treated as a threat to the social order and was forbidden, yet there is evidence of magical practices in all levels of Roman society, evidence that it was, in fact, condoned even as it was forbidden and that suppression of these practices was sporadic.[49] That magic lacks a stable definition and status in ancient Mediterranean society does not imply that it is a vacuous concept. Such a lack of a fixed meaning potentially makes a concept useful within a society. As anthropologist Ernest Gellner observed, for a native concept, "its use may depend on its lack of meaning, its ambiguity, its possession of wholly different and incompatible meanings in different contexts, *and* on the fact that, at the same time, it as it were emits the impression of possessing a consistent meaning throughout."[50] Magic in the ancient world is just such a concept; it has a definite enough meaning to function as a coherent label but enough ambiguity to allow accusers to deploy it to suit their interests.[51]

Descriptions of wonder workers in the ancient world thus represent two simultaneous contests: a contest to place the wonder worker in the author's preferred category (a preference that depends on the author's stance toward the wonder worker) and a contest to define the parameters of the chosen category. This book will examine Mark and Q as two ways that early Jesus followers engaged in this double contest to define who Jesus was and illustrate the import of his deeds.

CONCLUSION

The last chapter used the Kentucky Fried Rat story and its analysis by folklorists to illustrate how one can examine variant forms of stories to gain insight into the situation of their telling and retelling. Compared with the folkloristic approach discussed there, the approaches discussed in this chapter presuppose contestation in the actions they study. The first section viewed Danzhi's story through the lens of the rivalry between different religious groups, and the second section showed Apollonius's story to be a contest to portray his miracles as the results of *paideia* rather than of magic. The folkloristic approach to the Kentucky Fried Rat, on the other hand, did not view the variants as evidence of a contest. The story reflects anxiety about certain aspects of twentieth century change, but does not necessarily contest this change, nor do the variants reflect a contest to control the shape of the narrative, to produce the definitive version of the Kentucky Fried Rat story.

Looking at the differences in how the miracle overlaps construct the relationships of miracles, Jesus, and the kingdom of God, we could adopt either approach: viewing the differences as reflecting diverse views of miracles that co-existed (as folklorists tend to view stories) or as reflecting a competition to define the group against others (as the approaches reviewed in this chapter would suggest). Therefore, as this book examines these overlaps, it will attend to which approach does the most justice to the data at hand. This issue of contestation will come to the fore especially in the chapter on the Temptation. The Inquisitor claimed that in this story Jesus repudiated the use of miracles that the Church ultimately adopted. We will examine whether the Q Temptation story repudiates the view that miracles signify Jesus' divine identity or if it simply provides a different construction of the significance of miracles.

NOTES

1. Henri Tajfel, "Experiments in Intergroup Discrimination," *Scientific American* 223.2 (1970): 96–102.
2. Maurice Halbwachs, *The Collective Memory,* trand. Francis J. Ditter, Jr. and Vida Yazdi Ditter (New York: Harper & Row, 1980); Paul Connerton, *How Societies Remember* (Cambridge: Cambridge University Press, 1989).
3. Aleida Assmann, "Canon and Archive," in *Cultural Memory Studies: An International and Interdisciplinary Handbook,* ed. Astrid Eril, Ansgar Nünning, and Sara B. Young (Berlin: Walter de Gruyter, 2008), 97–108.
4. Thomas J. Anastasio et al., *Individual and Collective Memory Consolidation: Analagous Processes on Different Levels* (Cambridge, MA: MIT Press, 2012).
5. Jan Assmann, "Collective Memory and Cultural Identity," trans. John Czaplichka, *New German Critique* 65 (1995): 126–28; Jan Assmann, "Communicative and Cultural Memory," in Eril, Nünning, and Young, *Cultural Memory Studies,* 109–18.
6. Bernd Steinbock, *Social Memory in Athenian Public Discourse: Uses and Meanings of the Past* (Ann Arbor: University of Michigan Press, 2012), 12–13; Barbara A. Misztal, *Theories of Social Remembering* (Philadelphia: Open University Press, 2003), 120.
7. Ilja Srubar, "Lifeworld and Trauma: Selectivity of Social Memories," in *Theorizing Social Memory: Conepts and Contexts,* ed. Gerd Sebald and Jutin Wagle (London: Routledge, 2016), 17–31.
8. Steinbock, *Social Memory,* 11.
9. Assmann, "Collective Memory," 130; Allison, *Constructing Jesus,* 5–6.
10. Mary B. Spaulding, *Commemorative Identities: Jewish Social Memory and the Johannine Feast of Booths* (London: T&T Clark, 2009), 10–14. Misztal, *Theories,* 50–74.
11. István Czachesz, "Explaining Magic; Earliest Christianity as a Test Case," in *Past Minds: Studies in Cognitive Historiography,* ed. Luther H. Hartin and Jesper Sørensen (London: Equinox, 2011), 151–55.
12. Allison, *Constructing Jesus,* 2–3.
13. Gerald Echterhoff, "Languange and Memory: Social and Cognitive Processes," in Eril, Nünning, and Young, *Cultural Memory Studies,* 263–74.
14. Nina Leonhard, "Memory as a Means of Social Integration," in Sebald and Wagle, *Theorizing Social Memory,* 109–21; Spaulding, *Commemorative Identities,* 8–10; Misztal, *Theories,* 2003; Assmann, "Collective Memory," 128.
15. For an application of these social scientific approaches to a Gospel miracle (the raising of Lazarus in John 11) see Esler and Piper, *Lazarus,* 23–44, 104–30.
16. Marilynn B. Brewer, "Ingroup Bias in the Minimal Intergroup Situation: A Cognitive-Motivational Analysis," *Psychological Bulletin* 86.2 (1979): 307–24; J. A. Cameron, J. M. Alverez, D. N. Ruble, and A. J. Fullgni, "Children's Lay Theories about Ingroups and Outgroups: Reconceptualizing Research on Prejudice," *Personality and Social Psychology Review* 5.2 (2001); 118–28; Naomi Struch and Shalom H. Schwartz, "Intergroup Aggression: Its Pre-

dictors and Distinctness from In-group Bias," *Journal of Personality and Social Psychology* 56 (1989): 364–73.

17. Marilynn B. Brewer, "The Social Psychology of Intergroup Relations: Social Categorization, Ingroup Bias, and Outgroup Prejudice," in *Social Psychology: Handbook of Basic Principles,* 2nd Ed., eds. Arie W. Kruglanski and Tory E. Higgens (New York: Guilford Press, 2007), 702.

18. W. G. Stephan and C. W. Stephan, "An Integrated Threat Theogy of Prejudice," in *Reducing Prejudice and Discrimination*, ed. S. Oskamp (Mahwah, NJ: Erlbaum, 2000), 23–45.

19. J. Jetten, R. Spears, and T. Postmes, "Intergroup Distinctiveness and Differentiation: A Meta-Analytic Integration," *Journal of Personality and Social Psychology* 86.6 (2004): 862–79.

20. Brewer "Social Psychology," 703.

21. Sigmund Freud, *Group Psychology and the Analysis of Ego,* trans. James Strachey (New York: W.W. Norton, 1959), 42–43 and *Civilization and Its Discontents,* trans. James Strachey (New York: W.W. Norton, 1961), 61.

22. Jonathan Z. Smith, "Differential Equations: On Constructing the Other," in Idem, *Relating Religion: Essays in the Study of Religion* (Chicago: University of Chicago Press, 2004), 242–46; Jonathan Z. Smith, "What a Difference a Difference Makes," in Idem, *Relating Religion,* 276.

23. Robert Ford Campany, "Religious Repertoires and Contestation: A Case Study Based on Buddhist Miracle Tales," *HR* 52.2 (2012): 115.

24. For the rivalry and interactions between Buddhism and Daoism in early Medieval China, see Christine Mollier, *Buddhism and Taoism Face to Face: Scripture, Ritual, and Iconographic Exchange in Medieval China* (Honolulu: University of Hawaii Press, 2009).

25. Karma, and the recognition of its consequences, recurs as a theme throughout the *Minxiang ji* in stories that show the superiority of Buddhism to indigenous Chinese traditions (Campany, "Religious Repertoires," 112–14).

26. Campany, "Religious Repertoires," 109.

27. Marc van Uytfanghe, "La *Vie d'Apollonius de Tyane* et le discours hagiographique," in *Theios Sophistes: Essays on Flavius Philostratus' Vita Apollonii*, eds. Danny Praet and Kristoffel Demoen (Leiden: Brill, 2008): 354–61.

28. Ibid., 347–50.

29. He predicts Nero's unsuccessful attempt to dig a canal on the isthmus of Corinth (4.24), and he recognizes an omen of the year of the four emperors (5.13). He understands strange tidal phenomenon as the signs of a distant earthquake (4.34), and while in Greece he recognizes the moment when Domitian is murdered in Rome (8.25–27).

30. Apollonius's power of correct interpretation extends also to literature, art, and religious practices, and throughout the work Philostratus presents him providing the correct and persuasive interpretation of the phenomena he encounters. See Graeme Miles, "Reforming the Eyes: Interpreters and Interpretation in the *Vita Apollonii*," in *Theios Sopheistes: Essays on Flavius Philostratus' Vita Apollonii,* eds. Danny Praet and Kristoffel Demoen (Leiden: Brill, 2008), 130-39.

31. Graham Anderson, *Philostratus: Biography and Belles Lettres in the Third Century A.D.* (London: Croom Helm, 1986), 138–39; Erkki Koskenniemi, "The Function of the Miracle Stories in Philostratus's *Vita Apollonii Tyanensis*," in *Wonders Never Cease: The Purpose of Narrating Miracle Stories in the New Testament and its Religious Environment,* eds. Michael Labahn and Bert Jan Lietaert (London: T&T Clark, 2006), 76.

32. Taking a denarius (which is the equivalent of 4 sesterces) as a typical daily wage for a laborer as in Matt 20:2, 150,000 sesterces would be 37,500 times a daily wage. 400,000 sesterces was the minimum net worth required for equestrian status in first-century Rome. Susan Treggiari, "Social Status and Social Legislation," in *The Cambridge Ancient History Volume 10: The Augustan Empire, 43 BC–AD 69,* 2nd Ed., eds. Alan K. Bowman, Edward Champlin, and Andrew Lintott (Cambridge: Cambridge University Press, 1996), 879–80.

33. Simon Swain, *Hellenism and Empire: Language, Classicism, and Power in the Greek World AD 5–250* (Oxford: Clarendon, 1996), 381–95.

34. Philostratus may have modeled the meeting with Achilles's ghost on a similar story of Homer meeting Achilles's ghost and thus have intended further to link Apollonius to Homer and further to cement Apollonius's connection with Greek culture. See Peter Grossardt, "How to Become a Poet? Homer and Apollonius Visit the Mound of Achilles," in Demoen and Praet, *Theios Sophistes,* 76–80.

35. Howard Clark Kee, *Miracle in the Early Christian World: A Study in Sociohistorical Method* (New Haven, CT: Yale University Press, 1983), 1–42, 293–95.

36. Although we do not have access to the other accounts of Apollonius to which Philostratus had access, it is clear that Apollonius's miracles made him disreputable in some literary circles. D. H. Raynor, "Moeragenes and Philostratus: Two Views of Apollonius of Tyana," *The Classical Quarterly* 34.1 (1984): 222–26; Francis, *Subversive Virtue,* 90–98.

37. Anderson, *Philostratus,* 139–42.

38. Andy M. Reimer, *Miracle and Magic: A Study in the Acts of the Apostles and the Life of Apollonius of Tyana* (London: Sheffield Academic Press, 2002), 137.

39. Howard Clark Kee, *Medicine, Miracle, and Magic in New Testament Times* (Cambridge: Cambridge University Press, 1986).

40. Fritz Graf, "Prayer in Magic and Religious Ritual," in *Magika Hiera: Ancient Greek Magic and Religion,* eds. Chrisopher A. Faraone and Dirk Obbink (New York: Oxford University Press, 1997), 188–213.

41. Naomi Janowitz, *Magic in the Roman World: Pagans, Jews, and Christians* (London: Routledge, 2001), 10.

42. Georg Luck, "Witches and Sorcerers in Classical Literature," in *Witchcraft and Magic in Europe: Ancient Greece and Rome,* eds. Bengt Ankarloo and Stuart Clark (Philadelphia: University of Pennsylvania Press, 1999), 99.

43. This is the error of Morton Smith, *Jesus the Magician* (New York: Harper & Row, 1978). A critique along these lines occurs in Susan R. Garrett, *The Demise of the Devil: Magic and the Demonic in Luke's Writings* (Minneapolis: Fortress, 1989), 23–25.

44. Vincent Hunink, *Apuleius of Madauros Pro Se De Magia (Apologia) Edited With a Commentary* (Amsterdam: J. C. Gieben, 1997), 2.9–10.

45. James A. Francis, *Subversive Virtue: Asceticism and Authority in the Second-Century Pagan World* (University Park: Pennsylvania State University Press, 1995), 92–94.

46. Janowitz, *Magic in the Roman World,* 10.

47. James B. Rives, "Magic in Roman Law: The Reconstruction of a Crime," *Classical Antiquity* 22.3 (2003): 322–28.

48. Craig Keener, *Miracles: The Credibility of the New Testament Accounts* (Grand Rapids, MI: Baker Academic, 2011), 1:47–48.

49. Ramsay MacMullen, *Enemies of the Roman Order: Treason, Unrest and Alienation in the Empire* (Cambridge, MA: Harvard University Press, 1966), 126–27; C. R. Phillips III, "*Nullum Crimen sine Lege:* Socioreligious Sanctions on Magic," in *Magika Hiera: Ancient Greek Magic and Religion,* eds. Chrisopher A. Faraone and Dirk Obbink (New York: Oxford University Press, 1997), 260–76; Rives, "Magic," 334–36; Francis, *Subversive Virtue,* 90–92.

50. Ernest Gellner, "Concepts and Society," in *Selected Philosophical Themes,* Vol. 1, *Cause and Meaning in the Social Sciences* (London: Routledge, 2003), 41.

51. Garrett, *Demise,* 18.

Chapter Three

The Kingdom of God and the Kingdom of Satan

According to the Inquisitor, by rejecting Satan's temptations to adopt miracle, mystery, and authority Jesus wasted the opportunity to establish a universal kingdom that would usher in universal peace.[1] The idea of a universal kingdom appears also in the biblical texts. The Q version of each overlap brings up either the kingdom of God or the kingdom(s) of Satan, or both. Although Mark's versions of these stories do not mention either of these kingdoms, the kingdom of God appears elsewhere in that Gospel, and Mark makes mention of Satan without reference to Satan's kingdom in both the Testing and the Beelzebul Controversy. To assess how Mark and the Double Tradition each relate the kingdoms of God and Satan to Jesus and his miracles requires first determining what the kingdom of God and Satan could have meant to the audience of these texts. The previous chapter looked to Greek and Latin literature of the early Common Era to provide the background for miracles in Mark and the Double Tradition. Miracles were widely enough attested to allow such a broad basis of comparison. In contradistinction, the concepts of the kingdom of God and Satan draw on a particularly Jewish idiom. This chapter will therefore explore the background of these ideas in Jewish literature to illuminate their use in Mark and Q.[2]

The nature of the kingdom of God in Jesus' proclamation has been a vexed one in biblical scholarship. Does it represent an eschatological occurrence that interrupts history, or a transcendental state of ethical or spiritual awareness available within history, or both? If it is eschatological, is it an event in the future, or is it a realized eschatology present now, or both?[3] Is it a state of God's rule that can coexist alongside other rulers, or is it a space of God's rule that displaces other political powers?[4] Nor are these distinctions always clear. If the kingdom is a realized eschatological experience, how is that different from it being a transcendental state expressed in eschatological metaphors? If it is a political entity that only symbolically displaces other political powers, is it anything else than a state of recognizing the sovereignty of God? Scholars who argue over such questions do so on the basis of the polysemy inherent in the phrase, a polysemy that allowed Jesus and his hearers to attach multiple levels of meaning to the term.[5] The last chapter cited Ernest Gellner's observation that a concept's use in a society can be based on its bearing different and sometimes contradictory meanings while it gives the impression of having a stable meaning, and that magic in the ancient Mediterranean was such a concept. The kingdom of God is another such concept.

Fortunately, the task of this book does not require an exhaustive exploration of the possible nuances of the kingdom of God concept. The question to be answered is why the Q miracle overlaps link Jesus' miracles with the kingdom of God while Mark's do not. One possible answer, which this chapter rejects, is that for Q the kingdom of God is a non-eschatological state of living in the world that the healing miracles symbolize, while for Mark the kingdom of God is the future eschatological fulfillment and is therefore not present in Jesus' miracles.[6] This chapter will instead argue that both Mark and the Double Tradition associate the kingdom of God with the irruptive emergence of God's eschatological reign in the future and with the foreshadowing of this irruption in Jesus' work. The difference lies in the extent to which each text emphasizes Jesus' unique role in the future emergence of the kingdom of God.

This chapter examines the deployment of kingdom of God language in Mark and Q, along with its use in other Jewish literature, to examine the eschatological connotation of the term in both texts. Next, the chapter will examine the development of the idea of Satan in Jewish literature to argue that in both Mark and Q, Satan serves as the eschatological opponent that God has promised to overcome.

THE KINGDOM OF GOD: BACKGROUND

The exact phrase "kingdom of God" never appears in the Hebrew or Aramaic documents that would become the Tanakh.[7] Nevertheless, biblical authors do occasionally speak of kingship or a kingdom that belongs to God, and even more frequently the biblical authors speak of God reigning as king. Several times does the Psalmist speak of God's kingdom or kingship (e.g., 22:28, 103:19, 145:11) or of God as a king who reigns over the earth (e.g., 47:2, 97:1, 99:1). God's kingdom in the Psalms indicates the divine sovereignty over the earth that God has exercised since creation, but at the same time God's kingship is specially connected with God's special relationship with

Israel.[8] Similarly, the canticle of Moses (Exod 15:1–18) describes the events of the Exodus from Egypt and conquest of the Promised Land and then closes with, "The Lord will reign forever and ever" (Exod 15:18). In the poetry of ancient Israel, the concept of God reigning as king indicates both God's universal sovereignty as well as the special exercise of this universal sovereignty in God's election of Israel.

The Chronicler similarly uses God's kingship to indicate both God's universal power and God's special relationship with Israel, specifically with the Davidic line. Much as in the Psalms, the Chronicler extols God's kingdom as extending throughout all creation (1 Chr 29:11). At the same time, the Chronicler conflates God's kingdom with the kingdom of Israel ruled by a Davidic king (e.g. 1 Chr 17:14, 1 Chr 28:5).[9] The throne of David becomes virtually synonymous with the throne of the kingdom of God.[10]

Just as the concept of God's kingdom can operate on different spatial registers, from the cosmic to the national, so can the concept take on various temporal implications, including an eschatological dimension. Daniel notes that God's sovereignty is eternal and has existed forever (Dan 4:3, 4:34), but the kingdom also has a decidedly future dimension (Dan 7:27). For Daniel, God's kingdom becomes especially manifest in the eschatological vindication of God's people. Obadiah similarly connects God's kingdom with eschatological fulfillment: "Those who have been saved will go up to Mount Zion to rule Mount Esau, and the kingdom will be the Lord's" (Obad 21).[11]

God's reigning as king became a favorite way for prophets to speak of God's promised restoration of Israel. God commits to bring Israel out of exile with the promise, "I will be king over you" (Ezek 20:33). In Micah, God promises to gather a remnant of Israel and to lead them as king (Mic 2:12–13).[12] Zephaniah assures his hearers, "The king of Israel, the Lord, is in your midst; you shall fear disaster no more. On that day it shall be said to Jerusalem: 'Do not fear, O Zion, do not let your hands grow weak. The Lord, your God, is in your midst, a warrior who gives victory'" (Zeph 3:15–17). The future culmination of God's kingship will extend beyond the restoration of Israel, as Zechariah avers, "the Lord will become king over all the earth; on that day the Lord will be one and his name one" (Zech 14:9). Isaiah extends this domination to the heavenly bodies: "On that day the Lord will punish the hosts of heaven in heaven and the kings of the earth on earth . . . then the moon will be abashed, and the sun ashamed; for the Lord of hosts will reign on Mount Zion and in Jerusalem" (Isa 24:21, 23).[13] Although God always has been king of all creation, in the eschaton this kingship will become particularly manifest.

In the Targumim, the Aramaic translations of the Tanakh that emerged in the early Common Era, God's kingdom appears in many places where the MT speaks of God as king. For instance, where Exodus 15:18 in the MT says that God will reign, Targum Onkelos says, "The Lord's kingdom is eternal, forever and ever." Targum Pseudo-Jonathan interprets this verse with a stronger eschatological thrust: "And God is the king of kings in this age and God's is the kingdom in the age to come, and it is God's and will be forever and ever." The eschatological predictions of God's reigning as king from the Prophets often come into Targum Pseudo-Jonathan as predictions that God's kingdom will be revealed. While Zechariah 14:9 (MT) predicts God becoming king, Targum Pseudo-Jonathan renders the corresponding verse, "the kingdom of the Lord shall be revealed over all the inhabitants of the earth." Similarly, where the MT of Isaiah 24:23 speaks of God reigning on Zion and in Jerusalem, Targum Pseudo-Jonathan has, "the kingdom of the Lord of Hosts shall be revealed on the mountain of Zion and in Jerusalem."[14] The Targumim preserve and expand the idea of God's kingdom and its particular eschatological orientation developed in the MT.[15]

The kingdom of God's presence and futurity find expression also in the Wisdom of Solomon. This book contains the only mention of the βασιλεία θεοῦ in the Septuagint.[16] The author conceptualizes this kingdom as the teaching of personified Wisdom: "She [i.e., Wisdom] guided him [i.e., the righteous man] on straight paths; she showed him the kingdom of God, and gave him knowledge of holy things; she prospered him in his labors and increased the fruit of his toil" (Wis 10:10). Here, the kingdom of God points to a life lived in the present according to the precepts of divine Wisdom. While this βασιλεία θεοῦ appears here as a present reality, the kingdom brought by divine Wisdom also has an eternal dimension: "The desire for Wisdom leads to a kingdom. Therefore, if you delight in thrones and scepters, O monarchs over the peoples, honor wisdom, so that you may reign forever" (Wis 6:20–21). This eternal kingdom is the lot of the just who will govern the world, "and the Lord will reign over them forever" (Wis 3:8). For the author of Wisdom, God's kingship/kingdom indicates both a present blessedness in a life lived consistent with God's Law and the future blessed state where the just will be rewarded.[17]

The promise of this eschatological kingdom surfaces in several other works from around the turn of the Common Era. The *Psalms of Solomon* (ca. 63 BCE) speak of the "kingdom of our God" (17.3) being forever over the nations, and then connect this perpetual kingship with God's promise to raise a Davidic king who will rule over all the earth with justice (17.4). The third book of the *Sibylline Oracles*, thought to date from approximately the second century BCE, contains the promise that God will "raise up a kingdom for all ages among men," in which peace and blessedness will reign eternally (3.767–69).[18]

In the *Testament of Moses*, likely written in the first century CE, the author links the emergence of God's eschatological kingdom with the defeat of the devil, the end of sorrow, and the judgment of the wicked: "Then God's kingdom will appear throughout God's whole creation. Then the devil will have an end, and sorrow will be led away with him. . . . The Heavenly One will arise from the throne of God's kingdom and will go out from God's holy habitation with indignation and wrath on account of God's children, and the earth will tremble" (10.1–4).[19] The link between God's kingdom and the eschatological defeat of evil appears also in the *War Scroll* of Qumran, which describes how the Sons of Light will defeat the Sons of Darkness in battle: "So the kingship shall belong to the God of Israel, and by the holy ones of His people He shall act powerfully" (1QM 6.6).[20]

In Jewish literature, God's kingdom/kingship evokes a wide-ranging story of God's sovereignty that stretches from creation to the last days and that is simultaneously universal and specially present in the history of Israel.[21] An author can use kingship language to emphasize one or more aspects of this wide-ranging story of God's powerful rule over creation. For instance, when Philo talks about God reigning as king, he does so to emphasize the sovereignty God exercises as creator of all.[22] The Mishnah, similarly, uses the kingdom of Heaven to describe God's universal sovereignty.[23]

Despite the ubiquity and eternity of God's kingship, the concept of God's kingdom takes on a particularly eschatological focus in the prophets and in much Jewish literature near the turn of the Era.[24] Therefore, when Mark or the Double Tradition speaks of the kingdom of God, the reader should be alert for eschatological dimensions. For Mark and Q, the kingdom of God indicates a state of future eschatological blessedness for God's faithful and punishment for God's enemies just as the concept does in so much other Jewish literature.

THE KINGDOM OF GOD: Q

In several places the Double Tradition leaves the nature of the kingdom of God amorphous. Jesus instructs his followers to seek first the kingdom of God (Matt 6:33//Luke 12:31) without specifying the nature of this kingdom, whether it is a present reality or a future aspiration, or both. Similarly, Jesus assures that the least in the kingdom of God is greater than John the Baptist (Matt 11:11//Luke 7:28), but again Jesus leaves vague what this kingdom represents and who the least in it would be. In an even more cryptic statement, Jesus claims that some are attempting to enter the kingdom by violence (Matt 11:12//Luke 16:16).

The use of the phrase "kingdom of God" elsewhere in the Double Tradition confirms the eschatological dimension of the concept. The first beatitude promises the kingdom of God/heaven to the poor (Matt 5:3//Luke 6:3). Both Matthew and Luke frame this beatitude in the present tense, but the following beatitudes speak of future states of blessedness. The kingdom of God is a present reality that also connects to the future rewards awaiting those who suffer in the present.[25]

The second petition in the Lord's Prayer, "your kingdom come" (Matt 6:10//Luke 11:2) emphasizes the futurity of the kingdom. The prayer makes no mention of the presence of God's kingdom; rather, it pictures the kingdom as a reality that is yet to come. While prophetic and apocalyptic literature does not specifically speak of God's kingdom as coming, the idea that God would come on the last day was well established (e.g., Ps 96:13; Isa 35:4, 40:10, 59:19, 66:15; Zech 14:5). The petition for God's kingdom to come in the Lord's Prayer expresses the hope that God will come to judge the world and save God's people.[26]

The eschatological nature of the kingdom of God in Q comes to fullest expression in the logion of many coming from east and west to dine with the patriarchs in the kingdom:

> I tell you, many will come from east and west and will recline at table with Abraham and Isaac and Jacob in the kingdom of the heavens, but the children of the kingdom will be thrown into the outer darkness, where there will be weeping and gnashing of teeth. (Matt 8:11–12)

> There will be weeping and gnashing of teeth when you see Abraham and Isaac and Jacob and all the prophets in the kingdom of God, and you yourselves thrown out. Then people will come from east and west, from north and south, and will recline at table in the kingdom of God. (Luke 13:28–29)

In this statement, Jesus links the kingdom of God with an eschatological banquet and the judgment of the unfaithful.[27]

Although the kingdom of God refers to this future state, the Double Tradition makes clear that Jesus' activities somehow foreshadow this irruptive eschatological fulfillment and make the kingdom of God partially present. The presence of the kingdom of God comes out in Q's parables of the Mustard Seed and Leaven (Matt 13:31–33//Luke 13:18–21). In these parables Jesus compares the kingdom of God to items (a mustard seed, leaven) that are small but that have tremendous results. The parables indicate that the kingdom of God, though inconspicuous, is at work in the world and will manifest itself fully in the future.[28] The kingdom of God for Q represents God's eschatological rule that is incipiently present in history.

The Double Tradition thus draws on the multivalent symbol of God's kingdom to speak of God's eschatological consummation that is present, at least embryonically, in Jesus' activity. These appearances of kingdom of God language in Q provide cotexts to help interpret the miracle overlaps. When the study turns to each of the overlaps, it will show how the Beelzebul Controversy, the Commissioning, and the Temptation depict the eschatological reality of the kingdom of God being present in Jesus' miracles—with the miracles as foretastes of the eschatological blessing to come.

THE KINGDOM OF GOD: MARK

Mark makes the kingdom of God a major theme of Jesus' preaching throughout the Second Gospel. Early in the Gospel, Mark offers a summary of Jesus' proclamation: "The time is fulfilled, and the kingdom of God has come near (ἤγγικεν). Repent and believe in the good news" (Mark 1:15). Because ἐγγίζω denotes approach,[29] scholarly debate has arisen over whether the perfect form ἤγγικεν in Mark 1:15 refers to the kingdom of God as having drawn near, but not yet arrived, or as having already arrived.[30] Despite the scholarly insistence that ἤγγικεν be taken either as "has drawn near" or as "has arrived," Mark's phrasing likely indicates a purposeful vagueness as to whether the kingdom of God is imminent, yet still in the future, or is already present in Jesus' ministry.

Indeed, throughout the Gospel, Mark's Jesus speaks of the kingdom of God as both present and future. Mark's Jesus depicts the kingdom of God as a future reality when he instructs his followers to pluck out the offending eye because "it is better to enter into the kingdom of God with one eye then to have two eyes and be thrown into Gehenna" (Mark 9:47). Here the kingdom of God is a future reward, contrasted with the future punishment of Gehenna.[31] Similarly, when Jesus speaks of the difficulty of the rich entering the kingdom of God, he speaks of it in the future: "With such great difficulty will those having wealth enter into the kingdom of God" (Mark 10:23). Again, the kingdom of God refers to salvation in the age to come.[32] Jesus' final reference to the kingdom of God in Mark's Gospel similarly uses the kingdom as shorthand for future reward. At the last supper, Jesus promises his disciples, "Amen I say to you that no longer will I drink from the fruit of the vine until that day when I drink it anew in the kingdom of God" (Mark 14:25). This prophecy announces both Jesus' imminent death and the eschatological reward that will follow.[33]

While Mark's Jesus uses the term "kingdom of God" to indicate future blessings, he also speaks about the kingdom of God as already present. The kingdom of God is a repeated theme in the parable chapter, Mark 4. After a brief introduction (4:1–2), the chapter begins with the lengthiest parable, that of the sower sowing seed among the different types of soil (4:3–9). Jesus gives the disciples a lengthy interpretation of the parable, in which he explains that the growth of the seeds in the various soils represents differing responses to the proclamation (4:13–20). Between the parable and its explanation, Mark has Jesus tell his disciples, "To you the mystery of the kingdom of God has been given, but to those outside, everything comes in parables"

(4:11). The mystery of the kingdom of God involves understanding that the way people in the present respond to the word of God as proclaimed by Jesus will determine their ultimate fate. [34]

The fourth chapter of Mark contains two other parables that link seeds with the kingdom of God. After explaining the parable of the Sower, Jesus likens the kingdom of God to a seed growing:

> The kingdom of God is like a man who scattered seed on the ground, and he would sleep and rise night and day, and the seed would sprout and grow even as he does not know; by itself the earth produces fruit, first the stalk then the ear, then the full grain in the ear, but when the grain is ripe, immediately he sends out the sickle, because the harvest is present. (Mark 4:26–29)

Jesus here indicates that the kingdom of God will come to fruition in time (at the harvest) and without human intervention, but at the same time the kingdom of God is incipiently present in the form of the seeds. [35]

Mark's Jesus, like Q's Jesus, further stresses the incipient presence of the kingdom of God in the parable of the Mustard Seed (4:30–32). [36] Again, the kingdom of God will become fully manifest in the future, just as the mustard seed will grow into a tree in which the birds can nest, but the kingdom is also inconspicuously present now. [37] For Mark, the full manifestation of the kingdom belongs to the future, but the kingdom also exists in the present, just in a hidden form. [38]

Mark shares with Q the idea of the kingdom of God as a state of eschatological blessing that is already somehow present in Jesus' ministry but whose full manifestation lies in the future. Therefore, the absence of the kingdom of God from Mark's version of the miracle overlaps cannot be due to Mark's disinterest in demonstrating how God's kingdom came to expression in Jesus' ministry. Rather, it seems that Mark was not interested in linking the healing and exorcistic miracles of Jesus with the kingdom.

Nevertheless, Mark does link the kingdom of God with one of Jesus' miracles: the Transfiguration. [39] For Mark, the miracle that reveals the incipient presence of the kingdom of God is the Transfiguration, not the exorcisms or healings. Jesus tells his disciples, "Amen I say to you that there are some standing here who will not taste death until they see the kingdom of God having *come* in *power*" (Mark 9:1). This verse parallels 13:30, which concludes the apocalyptic discourse of chapter 13: "Amen I say to you that this generation will not pass until all these things [i.e., the predictions Jesus has made in chapter 13] have happened." Both verses share the "Amen I say to you" formula, followed by a promise that people will not die before witnessing an event. Among the things Jesus predicts in the apocalyptic discourse is "the son of man *coming* on the clouds with great *power* and glory." These verbal similarities tie 9:1 to the prediction of the coming son of man in chapter 13 and indicate that 9:1 refers to the coming of the son of man in glory as the manifestation of the kingdom of God.[40] The preceding verse further strengthens the association between the kingdom of God in 9:1 and the parousia by speaking of the Son of Man "when he *comes* in the glory of his Father with the holy angels" (8:31).[41] Mark makes the coming of the Son of Man in glory synonymous with the coming of the kingdom of God.[42]

However, the promise in 9:1 also has a more proximate referent. The following verse reads, "And after six days Jesus took Peter and James and John and took them up a high mountain by themselves. And he was transfigured before them" (9:2). Through this narrative sequence Mark connects the promise of seeing the kingdom of God with Peter, James, and John witnessing the Transfiguration.[43] The Transfiguration demonstrates the divine power emanating from Jesus, his connection with Israel's ancient heroes, and his status as God's son:

> And his clothes became radiantly white, such as no fuller on earth could bleach them, and then Elijah with Moses appeared to them and they were talking with Jesus. And Peter replied to Jesus, "Rabbi, it is good for us to be here. Let us make three tents, one for you and one for Moses and one for Elijah," for he did not know what to say, for they were terrified. Then a cloud came, casting a shadow over them and a voice came from the cloud: "This is my beloved son, listen to him." Suddenly, looking around they no longer saw anyone there except Jesus alone with them. (Mark 9:3–8)

The Transfiguration narrative closes with Jesus charging the three witnesses not to tell what they had seen, "until the Son of Man had risen from the dead" (Mark 9:9), a phrase that links the Transfiguration to Jesus' resurrection as well. The promise in 9:1 that some would see the kingdom of God connects to several points in Mark's narrative, so Mark's audience would see the kingdom of God come in power as a reference to Jesus' post-resurrection glory which the Transfiguration prefigured and which the parousia would soon demonstrate publicly.[44] Mark views the kingdom of God as the eschatological reality to be revealed when Jesus comes again in glory to execute God's judgment on the earth.[45] The kingdom is incipiently present in Jesus' ministry to the extent that Jesus' power and future role as eschatological judge manifest themselves in his earthly activities.

SATAN AND HIS KINGDOM

The coming of the kingdom of God was one way to express the widespread idea that God would win the definitive victory over evil. The opponents over whom God would win this victory could be various. Zechariah, for instance, describes God's becoming king in a victory over all the nations that war against Judah (Zech 14:1–20). Isaiah envisions God's future victory not only over Israel's human opponents, but also over abstract entities, such as death and sorrow: "God will swallow up death forever. Then the Lord God will wipe away the tears from all faces, and the disgrace of God's people God will take away from all the earth" (Isa 25:7–8). Such abstract forces of evil can also be joined to a personified, supernatural opponent whom God will conquer, as in the *Testament of Moses*: "Then God's kingdom will appear throughout God's whole creation. Then the devil will have an end, and sorrow will be led away with him" (10.1–2). This supernatural opponent of God, known by many names, appears also in the Beelzebul Controversy and the Temptation, and Mark and the Double Tradition both presume their audiences are familiar with this figure.

This evil supernatural figure entered the Jewish worldview through a long process of development. Satan, one of the more common names for this figure, traces its origin in the Hebrew word *satan* (שטן), adversary. A supernatural *satan* appears but rarely in the books that would become the Scriptures of Israel. The angel of the Lord acts as a *satan* in blocking the path of Balaam's donkey (Num 22:22). In other instances, the *satan* appears as a supernatural entity distinct from the angel of the Lord. It is the *satan* who, as one of the members of God's heavenly court, receives permission from God to inflict calamities on Job (Job 1–2). In Zech 3:1, the *satan* stands before the Lord to accuse the high priest Joshua. In these cases, the *satan* is a divine functionary who tests and accuses humans in the exercise of divine justice. In 2 Samuel 24:1, God influences David to undertake a census because God is angry with Israel. In the Chronicler's retelling of David's census, *satan* appears outside the context of a heavenly court and without the definite article: "Satan [or a satan] stood up against Israel, and incited David to count the people of Israel" (1 Chr 21:1). The Chronicler declines to clarify whether the anarthrous *satan* here indicates the name of a character or merely identifies an adversary.

In other literature of the Second Temple period, the character of this superhuman adversary of God's people develops as does the idea of a host of demons under his command.[46] Whereas the Tanakh tends to assign most supernatural causation to God (such as God's sending of the evil spirit to torment King Saul in 1 Sam 16:14), post-exilic Judaism adopted dualistic systems that separated God's good purposes from those of hostile supernatural agents.[47] In Second Temple Jewish literature, authors inserted these agents into their retellings of biblical stories. The author of *1 Enoch*, for instance, expands on a brief story that precedes the account of Noah in Genesis:

> When people began to multiply on the face of the ground, and daughters were born to them, the sons of God saw that they were fair; and they took wives for

themselves of all that they chose. . . . The giants were on the earth in those
days when the sons of God went in to the daughters of humans, who bore
children to them. These were the heroes that were of old, warriors of renown.
(Gen 6:1–4)

The Genesis story does not indicate that the sons of God erred or sinned in
mating with human women. In the retelling of this story in *1 Enoch*, this
conduct of the "Watchers" is described as sinful by their leader Semyaz, who
nevertheless consents to it (6.3). The offspring of the Watchers and the
human women are bloodthirsty giants who prey on humans and despoil the
land (7:1–6). One of the most devious of the Watchers, Azazel, teaches
human beings the corrupting skills of warfare, which instigates conflict
among the peoples on earth (8.1). In response to the carnage that Semyaz,
Azazel, and their compatriots cause, God sends the angels Raphael, Michael,
and Gabriel to destroy the giants and to bind the Watchers until the final
judgment, when they will be imprisoned forever (10.1–22). The Epistle of
Jude alludes to this host of fallen angels bound until the final judgment: "The
angels who did not keep their authority but left their own dwelling place he
has kept in eternal chains under darkness for the judgment of the great day"
(Jude 6).

Jubilees tells a similar story of how the Watchers caused corruption on
the earth when they mated with human women (5.1–2). In *Jubilees*, the
offspring of the Watchers and the women become demons who torment and
kill human beings. After the flood, Noah asks God to restrain these demons
(10.1–6). Before God can grant Noah's prayer, Mastema, "the chief of the
spirits," importuned God, "O Lord, Creator, leave some of them before me,
and let them obey my voice. And let them do everything which I tell them,
because if some of them are not left for me, I will not be able to exercise the
authority of my will among the children of men" (10.7–8). God agrees to
leave one tenth of the demons free "so that they might be subject to Satan
upon the earth" (10.11). In *Jubilees*, Mastema does not act contrary to God's
will, but rather he serves as a divine functionary who tests God's people,
much as the *satan* does in Job. However, unlike the *satan* in Job, Mastema
has a retinue of demonic underlings.

In the Qumran literature, yet another name for the leader of the forces
opposed to God appears. The War Scroll describes the final battle between
the Sons of Light and the Sons of Darkness. The author also refers to "The
Sons of Darkness" as "the army of Belial" (1QM 1.1). Although the *War
Scroll* describes Belial's army as a human force made up of Israel's neighbors and apostate clans from the twelve tribes of Israel, it also refers to God
driving away Belial's "spirits of destruction" (14.10). Another Qumran frag-
ment mentions Belial alongside the spirits under him: " [t]he[y] shall de-
nounce Belial and all his guilty lot. And they shall say in response: 'Cursed is

[B]elial because of his malevolent [pu]rposes, and he is damned for his guilty dominion. Cursed are all the spirits of his [lo]t for their wicked purpose'" (4Q286 7.2.1–3).[48] The Belial of the Qumran literature, like Mastema in *Jubilees* and Azazel in *1 Enoch*, leads hostile spiritual forces against God's people.

Beelzebul, the prince of the demons, appears in the *Testament of Solomon*, a work of the early Common Era. This *Testament* tells of Solomon summoning, interrogating, and enslaving a number of demons during the construction of the Temple. Among Solomon's demonic interlocutors is "Beelzebul, the ruler (ἔξαρχος) of the demons" (3.6). Beelzebul tells Solomon, "I bring destruction by means of tyrants; I cause the demons to be worshipped alongside men; and I arouse desire in holy men and select priests. I bring about jealousies and murders in a country, and I instigate wars" (6.4). Beelzebul's role in instigating human strife recalls Azazel's troublemaking activities in *1 Enoch*.

With the idea of a chief demon that functions as God's cosmic opponent came the belief that God's definitive eschatological actions would include vanquishing this opponent.[49] Belial is one such opponent, destined for defeat, in 1QM's war of God's Sons of Light against the Sons of Darkness. Similarly, God's temporary binding of Azazel and the other Watchers will be made permanent in the end time (*1 Enoch* 10.1–22). *Jubilees* likewise predicts a glorious future of life and abundance when Satan shall be no more (23.29, 50.5). The *Testaments of the Twelve Patriarchs*, another work of the early Common Era, predicts the defeat of Beliar, a variant of Belial, at the end of time (*T. Levi* 18.12, *T. Zeb.* 9.8, *T. Dan.* 5.11, *T. Benj.* 3.8).

Revelation similarly predicts the conquest of Satan and his host. At one point in the vision, a dragon appeared in the sky, "and a war occurred in heaven so that Michael and his angels waged war against the dragon, both the dragon and his angels waged war" (12:7). A little later the author reveals that the dragon "is called the Devil and Satan" (12:8). Michael succeeded in throwing this dragon out of heaven down to earth, where the dragon gave power to the two beasts (13:1–18). Although this dragon made mischief for a while, eventually an angel came down from heaven, "and seized the dragon, who is the ancient serpent, who is the Devil and Satan, and bound him for a thousand years and cast him into the abyss and shut and sealed it over him" (20:2–3). Like the Watchers in *1 Enoch*, the dragon, suffers bondage at the hands of God's angel. Revelation envisions a two-stage conquest of the Devil, first in heaven and then on earth. In the heavenly contest, the angels under the leadership of Michael fight the angels following the dragon. In the subsequent fight on earth, it is a single angel who meets the dragon and binds him.

A one-on-one combat with the eschatological opponent features also in 2 Thessalonians. This letter claims that the appearance of "the person of lawlessness (ὁ ἄνθρωπος τῆς ἀνομίας)" will precede the day of the Lord (2:3). The author leaves the identity of this person of lawlessness ambiguous, and it is not clear whether this figure is a human being or some supernatural opponent. Whoever this ἄνθρωπος is, he is clearly connected with Satan: "his coming is by the activity of Satan" (2:9). The author assures the readers that once this ἄνθρωπος appears Jesus will destroy him by the breath of his mouth (2:8). Here the eschatological victory again appears as single combat between God's agent and an eschatological opponent connected with Satan.

The literature here reviewed shows that the concept of a supernatural adversary to God had widespread currency in Second Temple Judaism, but a tremendous amount of variability existed in how authors depicted this figure. The most obvious index of variability is the sheer number of names for this figure: the devil, the dragon, Satan, Mastema, Azazel, Belial/Beliar, Beelzebul. Moreover, the relationship of this figure to God can vary from that of a divine functionary who puts the faithful to the test (e.g., Mastema in *Jubilees*), to a figure fighting against God (e.g., Belial in the War Scroll). This figure also frequently appears in the final confrontation between good and evil, but his role in this confrontation can take many forms. He can appear as the leader of a demonic host that God defeats with his army of angels, as in Revelation's war in heaven (12:7–9) or in the War Scroll. These texts do not speak of a kingdom of Satan, but many of them speak of Satan as the leader of a band of demons. It would not be a far leap to describe this evil host as Satan's kingdom, as occurs in the Q version of the Beelzebul Controversy (Matt 12:26//Luke 11:18). However, the eschatological victory can also appear as the vanquishing of Satan without reference to his retinue, as in *Jubilees*'s promise of a time when Satan will be no more (23.29, 50.5) or in the kingdom of God's appearance in the *Testament of Moses* (10.1–2). When Mark and the Double Tradition told stories about Jesus and Satan, they could draw on the idea of God (or God's agent) vanquishing Satan alone or of the forces of God overcoming the forces of Satan. Mark chooses imagery of Satan acting individually, while the Double Tradition chooses the group imagery of the kingdom of Satan arrayed against the kingdom of God.

CONCLUSION

Both Satan and the kingdom of God were concepts alive within the thought world of Second Temple Judaism, and early Jesus followers seized upon these concepts to help articulate the importance of what Jesus did and who he was. Each term provides a way to refer to aspects of the story of Israel's God. The kingdom of God conjures up God's sovereignty enacted in creation, the election of Israel, and the final conquest over evil that is to come. The mention of Satan evokes the forces of evil that seem to thwart God's purposes in the short term but that will ultimately come to an end in the eschaton. Although both terms stood in for a larger story, there was enough flexibility in how that story was told that neither term had a single meaning. There was no one conception of God's kingdom to which every author who used the term referred. The contours of the story of how God's sovereignty came to expression through history were stable enough, but authors had freedom in painting the details. Much less was there any singular conception of Satan's role in God's story, especially in how Satan figured in God's eschatological victory over evil. Both Mark and the Double Tradition can speak of Satan and the kingdom of God within the same conceptual background, but they do so in ways that draw on different aspects of the stories to relate Satan and the kingdom of God in two distinct ways to Jesus and his miracles. In the miracle overlaps we see this difference most clearly.

NOTES

1. Dostoyevsky, *Brothers*, 296.
2. In this category I am including literature that may have been composed by early Jesus followers, who may not have been ethnically Jewish, since these works share a worldview shaped by the history of the God of Israel.
3. This scholarly debate was inaugurated by Johannes Weiss's advocacy for an eschatological interpretation of the kingdom in his 1892 publication, *Die Predigt Jesu vom Reiche Gottes*, available in English translation as *Jesus' Proclamation of the Kingdom of God*, trans. Richard Hyde Hiers and David Larrimore Holland (Chico, CA: Scholars Press, 1971). The translators' introduction to this work surveys the debates up to the middle of the twentieth century. See also Wendell Willis, ed., *The Kingdom of God in 20th Century Interpretation* (Peabody, MA: Hendrickson, 1987); H. Leroy Metts, "The Kingdom of God: Background and Development of a Complex Discourse Concept," *CTR* 2.1 (2004): 51–82. For non-eschatological interpretations of the kingdom of God, see Michael L. Humphries, *Christian Origins and the Language of the Kingdom of God* (Carbondale, IL: Southern Illinois University Press, 1999), 57–60; Leif Vaage, "Q: The Ethos and Ethics of an Intinerant Intelligence" (Ph.D. Dissertation, Claremont Graduate School, 1987), 403–14; John Dominic Crossan, *Jesus: A Revolutionary Biography* (San Francisco: Harper, 1994), 121; Marcus Borg, "Jesus and Eschatology: A Reassessment," in *Images of Jesus Today,* eds. James H. Charlesworth and Walter P. Weaver (Valley Forge, PA: Trinity Press International, 1994), 42–67; Burton L. Mack, "The Kingdom Sayings in Mark," *Foundations and Facets Forum* 3.1 (1987): 16
4. Gustaf Dalman, *The Words of Jesus Considered in the Light of Post-biblical Jewish Writings and the Aramaic Language* (Edinburgh: T&T Clark, 1902), 134–35, 148. Halvor Moxnes, *Putting Jesus in His Place: A Radical Vision of Household and Kingdom* (Louisville, KY: Westminster John Knox, 2003); Alan Storkey, *Jesus and Politics: Confronting the Powers* (Grand Rapids, MI: Baker Academic, 2006), 111–32; Mary Ann Beavis, *Jesus and Utopia: Looking for the Kingdom of God in the Roman World* (Minneapolis: Fortress, 2006).
5. Norman Perrin, *Jesus and the Language of the Kingdom: Symbol and Metaphor in New Testament Interpretation* (Philadelphia: Fortress, 1980).
6. This corresponds roughly with the formulation of Humphries, *Christian Origins,* 39–44, 57–60.
7. Meier, *Marginal Jew*, 2.241.
8. Karl Allen Kuhn, *The Kingdom According to Luke and Acts: A Social, Literary, and Theological Introduction* (Grand Rapids, MI: Baker, 2015), 27. Robert D. Rowe, *God's Kingdom and God's Son: The Background to Mark's Christology From Concepts of Kinship in the Psalms* (Leiden: Brill, 2002), 17–20; Meier, *Marginal Jew,* 2:245

9. Gary N. Knoppers, *1 Chronicles 10–29: A New Translation with Introduction and Commentary* (New York: Doubleday, 2004), 673, 893, 928.

10. Raymond Kuntzmann, "Le Trône de Dieu dans l'Oeuvre du Chroniste," in *Le Trône de Dieu,* ed. Marc Philonenko (Tübingen: Mohr, 1993), 19–27; Sara Japhet, *The Ideology of the Book of Chronicles and Its Place in Biblical Thought* (Frankfurt am Main: Lang, 1989), 403.

11. Paul R. Raabe, *Obadiah: A New Translation with Introduction and Commentary* (New York: Doubleday, 1996), 271.

12. Francis I. Andersen and David Noel Freedman, *Micah: A New Translation with Introductaion and Commentary* (New York: Doubleday, 2000), 341.

13. Joseph Blenkinsopp, *Isaiah 1–39: A New Translation with Introduction and Commentary* (New York: Doubleday, 2000), 355.

14. Rowe, *God's Kingdom,* 112.

15. Klaus Koch, "Offenbaren wird sich das reich Gottes," *NTS* 25.2 (1979): 158–65; Geert Wouter Lorein, "מלכותא in the Targum of the Prophets," *AS* 3.1 (2005): 15–42.

16. Meier, *Marginal Jew,* 2:243.

17. Rowe, *God's Kingdom,* 106–6; Meier, *Marginal Jew,* 2:250.

18. For the dating, see J. J. Collins' introduction in *OTP* 1:355.

19. For dating, see J. Priest's introduction in *OTP* 1:921. The text is extant only in a single Latin palimpsest, but it is likely a translation of Greek, which itself is likely a translation of a Semitic original.

20. Rowe, *God's Kingdom,* 102–3.

21. Meier, *Marginal Jew,* 2:241.

22. Cf. *Plant.* 47, 51; *Mut.* 28; *Somn.* 2.100, 2.289; *Spec.* 1.207.

23. As in *m. Ber.* 2:1–2, where accepting the yoke of the kingdom of Heaven precedes accepting the specific yoke of the commandments. For the relatively minor role the kingdom of God/heaven plays in Rabbinic thought, see Jacob Neusner, "The Kingdom of Heaven in Kindred Systems, Judaic and Christian," *BBR* 15.2 (2005): 279–305.

24. James D. G. Dunn, "Jesus and the Kingdom: How Would His Message Have Been Heard?" in *Neotestamentica et Philonica: Studies in Honor of Peder Borgen,* eds. David E. Aune, Torrey Seland, and Jarl Henning Ulrichsen (Leiden: Brill, 2003), 3–7; Meier, *Marginal Jew,* 2:269.

25. George Raymond Beasley-Murray, *Jesus and the Kingdom of God* (Grand Rapids, MI: Eerdmans, 1986), 162; Mark Allan Powell, "Matthew's Beatitudes: Reversals and Rewards of the Kingdom," *CBQ* 58 (1996): 465; Meier, *Marginal Jew,* 2:331.

26. Giovanni B. Bazzana, *Kingdom of Bureaucracy: The Political Theology of Village Scribes in the Sayings Gospel Q* (Leuven: Peeters, 2015), 165–201; Meier, *Marginal Jew,* 2:299; Beasley-Murray, *Kingdom,* 151.

27. Whether the many from east and west are the gathered Gentiles (as in Isa 25:6–8) or the lost tribes of Israel (as in Zech 8:7–8) divides scholars. For arguments in favor of Gentiles, see Beasely-Murray, *Kingdom,* 173–74; Meier *Marginal Jew* 2:314. For lost tribes, see George Wesley Buchanan, *Jesus: The King and His Kingdom* (Macon, GA: Mercer University Press, 1984), 34–35; Dale C. Allison, Jr., *The Jesus Tradition in Q* (Harrisburg, PA: Trinity Press International, 1997), 177–79. Whoever the many from east and west are, it is clear that an eschatological banquet is imagined; see Barry D. Smith, *Jesus' Twofold Teaching about the Kingdom of God* (Sheffield, UK: Sheffield Phoenix, 2009), 128–31.

28. Kyle Snodgrass, *Stories with Intent: A Comprehensive Guide to the Parables of Jesus* (Grand Rapids, MI: Eerdmans, 2008), 226–27; W. G. Kümmel, *Promise and Fulfillment: The Eschatological Message of Jesus,* trans. Dorthea M. Barton (Naperville, IL: Allenson, 1957), 130-31; Nils Dahl, "The Parables of Growth," in Idem, *Jesus in the Memory of the Early Church* (Minneapolis: Augsburg, 1976), 155; C. H. Dodd, *The Parables of the Kingdom* (New York: Scribner, 1961), 190–91; W. D. Davies and Dale C. Allison, *Matthew 8–18* (London: T& T Clark, 1991), 417; Smith, *Twofold Teaching,* 29–36; Beasley-Murray, *Kingdom,* 123–25.

29. *BDAG* 213, ἐγγίζω.

30. For arguments in favor of "has arrived," see Smith, *Twofold,* 5; Beaseley-Murray, *Kingdom,* 72–73; Dodd, *Parables,* 36–37. For "has come near, see Rowe, *God's Kingdom,* 120–21;

Joel Marcus, *Mark 1–8: A New Translation with Introduction and Commentary,* The Anchor Bible (New Haven: Yale University Press, 2000), 173.

31. Beasley-Murray, *Kingdom,* 175; Adela Yarbro Collins, *Mark: A Commentary* Hemeneia—A Critical and Historical Commentary on the Bible (Minneapolis: Fortress, 2007), 454.

32. Beasley-Murray, *Kingdom,* 177.

33. Marinus De Jonge, "Mark 14:25 among Jesus' Words about the Kingdom of God," in *Sayings of Jesus Canonical and Non-Canonical: Essays in Honour of Tjitze Baarda,* eds. William L. Petersen, Johan S. Vos, Henk J. De Jonge (Leiden: Brill, 1997), 130–35; Beasley-Murray, *Kingdom,* 263; Collins, *Mark,* 657.

34. Aloysius M. Ambrozic, *The Hidden Kingdom: A Redaction Critical Study of the References to the Kingdom of God in Mark's Gospel* (Washington, DC: Catholic Biblical Association of America, 1972), 106; Madeline Boucher, *The Mysterious Parable* (Washington, DC: The Catholic Biblical Association, 1977), 83–84; Rowe, *God's Kingdom,* 133; Snodgrass, *Stories,* 164.

35. Ernst Fuchs, *Studies in the Historical Jesus,* trans. Andrew Scobie (Naperville, IL: Allenson, 1964), 134, 180; Snodgrass, *Stories,* 186–87; Beasley-Murray, *Kingdom,* 196; Smith, *Twofold,* 31.

36. See the note on the Q version above; additionally, R. T. France, *The Gospel of Mark: A Commentary on the Greek Text* (Grand Rapids, MI: Eerdmans, 2002), 216.

37. Smith, *Twofold,* 35.

38. Ambrozic, *Kingdom,* 135.

39. Rowe, *God's Kingdom,* 134.

40. Collins, *Mark,* 413.

41. Ernest van Eck, "Eschatology and Kingdom in Mark," in *Eschatology of the New Testament and Some Related Documents,* ed. Jan G. van der Watt (Tübingen: Mohr Siebeck, 2011), 81; Marcus, *Mark,* 2:622

42. Kuhn, *Kingdom,* 46–47.

43. Beasley-Murray, *Kingdom,* 188; Collins *Mark* 412.

44. Joel Marcus, *Mark 8–16: A New Translation and Commentary,* The Anchor Bible (New Haven, CT: Yale University Press, 2009), 622. For other treatments that have detailed the connections Mark's Transfiguration has with Jesus' parousia, resurrection, and status as God's son, see Howard Clark Kee, "The Transfiguration in Mark: Epiphany or Apocalypic Vision?" in *Understanding the Sacred Text: Essays in honor of Morton S. Enslin on the Hebrew Bible and Christian Beginnings,* ed. J. Reumann, 135–52 (Valley Forge, PA: Judson Press, 1972); H. P. Müller, "Die Verklärung Jesu: Ein motivgeschichtliche Studie" *ZNW* 51 (1960): 61–62; F. R. McCurley, Jr., "And After Six Days (Mark 9:2): A Semitic Literary Device," *JBL* 93 (1974): 67–81; G. H. Boobyer, *St Mark and the Transfiguration Story* (Edinburgh: T&T Clark, 1942); Candida R. Moss, "The Transfiguration: An Exercise in Markan Accomodation," *Biblical Interpretation* 12.1 (2004): 70–73.

45. Rowe, *God's Kingdom,* 160.

46. For the development of Jewish demonology, see Andrei A. Orlov, *Dark Mirrors: Azazel and Satanael in Early Jewish Demonlogy* (Albany: State University of New York Press, 2011); Bernard J. Bamberger, *Fallen Angels: Soldiers of Satan's Realm* (Philadelphia: Jewish Publication Society, 2006), 1–59; Angela Kim Harkins, Kelley Coblentz Bautch, and John C. Endres (eds.), *The Watchers in Jewish and Christian Traditions* (Minneapolis: Fortress, 2014); Idem, *The Fallen Angels Traditions: Second Temple Developments and Reception History* (Washington, DC: Catholic Biblical Association, 2014); Archie T. Wright, *The Origin of Evil Spirits: The Reception of Genesis 6.1–4 in Early Jewish Literature* (Tübingen: Mohr Siebeck, 2005); Armin Lange, Hermann Lichtenberger, and Diethard Römheld (eds.), *Die Dämonen Demons: die Dämonologie der israelitisch-jüdischen und frühchristlichen Literatur im Kontext ihrer Umwelt* (Tübingen: Mohr Siebeck, 2003).

47. T. J. Wray and Gregory Mobley, *The Birth of Satan: Tracing the Devil's Biblical Roots* (Gordonsville, VA: Palgrave Macmillan, 2005), 165.

48. The reconstruction is that of Michael Wise

49. Dunn, "Jesus and the Kingdom," 6.

Chapter Four

The Beelzebul Controversy

The Grand Inquisitor unabashedly claims that the Church has allied itself with Satan by accepting miracles as a means of exercising power. The idea that miracles result from a pact with the devil surfaces in the Gospel narratives when Jesus faces the accusation in the Beelzebul Controversy that his exorcisms prove that he is in league with Satan (Mark 3:22–30; Matt 12:22–31; Luke 11:14–23). Beginning with the common elements in the two versions, this chapter will demonstrate that both Mark and the Double Tradition portray Jesus disputing with other Jews about how Jesus fits into the Second Temple eschatological scheme of God's ultimate victory over evil. Based on the concepts of identity formation discussed in chapter 2, this chapter will argue that the depiction of Jesus in conflict with other Jews about his eschatological significance helped early Jesus followers to distinguish themselves from non-Jesus followers and, in so distinguishing themselves, create a positive identity for their group. The differences between the Mark and Q versions evince two similar, but distinct, ways of making such delineations between Jesus followers and non-Jesus followers: for the Double Tradition the crucial distinction is recognizing that God's eschatological victory is present in Jesus' ministry, while for Mark that distinction lies in recognizing that Jesus himself will realize God's eschatological victory. Thus, the Double Tradition depicts Jesus as a participant alongside others in God's victory, whereas Mark depicts Jesus alone accomplishing God's victory.

Performing these tasks requires first looking at the texts from Mark, Matthew, and Luke to determine what elements the Double Tradition version of this story contains, what the Double Tradition version has in common with Mark's, and how Mark and the Double Tradition differ. The comparison will show that Q depicts God's victory in corporate terms that envision participa-

tion by Jesus and Jesus' followers, while Mark depicts this victory in terms
of Jesus' single combat with the devil.

Mark's version goes as follows:

> And the scribes coming down from Jerusalem were saying, "He has Beelze-
> bul," and "By the prince of the demons he casts out demons." And calling
> them together he was speaking to them in parables: "How is Satan able to cast
> out Satan? And if a kingdom were divided against itself, that kingdom cannot
> stand, and if a house were divided against itself, that house could not stand,
> and if Satan rose up against himself and is divided, he cannot stand but has his
> end. But no one is able to enter the house of a strong man to steal his property
> unless he first binds the strong man and then he can plunder his house. Amen I
> say to you that all sins will be forgiven to the sons of men and whatever
> blasphemies they may have blasphemed, but whoever blasphemed against the
> Holy Spirit will not have forgiveness eternally, but is guilty of an eternal sin."
> Because they were saying, "He has an unclean spirit." (Mark 3:22–30)

Mark begins with an accusation that Jesus performs exorcisms by the power
of Beelzebul, the prince of demons. Jesus denies this charge with two arguments. First, he uses the parables of the divided house and divided kingdom
to argue that if the accusation were true, then Satan would be divided against
himself and would fall. The second argument comes in the form of the
parable of the strong man: Jesus' exorcisms are akin to plundering a strong
man's house, an action possible only if the strong man has been overpowered. By implication, Jesus cannot be in league with Satan; Jesus must have
overpowered him. Jesus concludes with the condemnation of those who blaspheme against the Holy Spirit, which Mark explains is due to the opponents'
charge that Jesus has an unclean spirit.

The Q version contains many of the same elements, with a few notable
additions and deletions. Matthew's and Luke's versions are reproduced below. Elements common to Matthew and Luke but different from Mark (i.e.,
the Double Tradition) are underlined:

Then a demon possessed man, blind
and deaf, was brought to him, and he
healed him so that the deaf man spoke
and saw, and the whole crowd were
beside themselves and were saying,
"Is this not the son of David?" But the
Pharisees hearing this said, "This man
does not cast out demons except by
Beelzebul the prince of demons."

And he was casting out a demon
that was deaf. And it happened that
as the demon went out the deaf man
spoke, and the crowd was amazed.

But some of them said, "By
Beelzebul the prince of demons he
casts out demons." And others

But Jesus, <u>knowing their</u> thoughts, <u>said to them, "Every kingdom divided against itself is laid waste</u>, and every city or house divided against itself will not stand. And if Satan casts out Satan, he has been divided against himself. <u>How</u> then <u>will his kingdom stand?</u>

<u>And if I cast out demons by Beelzebul, by whom do your sons cast them out? Because of this they will be your judges. But if by the</u> spirit <u>of God I cast out demons, then the kingdom of God has come upon you.</u> Or how is someone able to enter the house of a strong man and steal his property unless he first should bind the strong man? Then he plunders his house.

<u>Whoever is not with me is against me, and whoever does not gather with me scatters.</u> Because of this I say to you, every sin and blasphemy will be forgiven for humans except the blasphemy of the holy spirit will not be forgiven." (Matt 12:22–31)

testing him were asking for a sign from heaven from him.
But Jesus, <u>knowing their</u> minds, <u>said to them, "Every kingdom divided against itself is laid waste</u> and house falls upon house.

And if Satan has been divided against himself, <u>how will his kingdom stand?</u> Because you said that by Beelzebul I cast out demons.
<u>And if I cast out demons by Beelzebul, by whom do your sons cast them out? Because of this, they will be your judges. But if by the</u> finger <u>of God I cast out demons, then the kingdom of God has come upon you.</u> Whenever a strong man, fully armed, guards his castle, his possessions are at peace. But if a stronger man comes near and should conquer him, he takes away the armor on which he relied and will distribute his booty. <u>Whoever is not with me is against me, and whoever does not gather with me scatters.</u> (Luke 11:14–23)

Common elements in the Mark and Q versions include:

1. an accusation that Jesus exorcises by the power of Beelzebul, the prince of demons
2. Jesus' rebuttal of this accusation with an analogy of the destruction of a divided kingdom
3. Jesus' assertion that if Satan were divided against himself he would be playing a part in his own downfall.

Luke and Matthew do not agree against Mark with regard to the sayings about a divided house or the binding of the strong man. Thus, I do not assign these elements to the Double Tradition, although if Q existed as an independent document, it could very well have contained these elements.

The major differences between the Markan and Q versions are as follows:

1. Q introduces the Controversy by having Jesus exorcise a deaf demon to the amazement of the crowd (Matt 12:22–23//Luke 11:14), while Mark does not introduce the story with an immediately preceding exorcism.
2. The accusation in Q lacks the statement that Jesus "has" (ἔχει) Beelzebul and the resulting linking of this wording of the accusation with the sin against the Holy Spirit as in Mark (3:22, 29–30).
3. Q does not use "parables" (παραβολαῖς) to describe Jesus' response as Mark (3:23) does.
4. In Q, Jesus knows what his opponents are thinking (Matt 12:25//Luke 11:17), while Mark does not credit this insight to Jesus.
5. Q's analogy about the divided kingdom speaks of the kingdom being "laid waste" (ἐρημοῦται) (Matt 12:25//Luke 11:17) rather than simply unable to stand, as in Mark 3:24.
6. According to Mark, because Satan is divided against Satan, Satan cannot stand (Mark 3:26); the Q version states that Satan's *kingdom* cannot stand (Matt 12:26//Luke 11:18).
7. Q has Jesus ask the rhetorical question about the exorcisms performed by the sons of his opponents (Matt 12:27//Luke 11:19), while Mark's Jesus does not recognize other exorcists in this story.
8. In Q, Jesus asserts that his exorcisms indicate the coming of the kingdom of God (Matt 12:28//Luke 11:20); this assertion has no parallel in Mark.
9. Unlike in Mark, Q's Jesus asserts after the saying about binding the strong man that whoever is not for him is against him (Matt 12:30//Luke 11:23).

CONTROVERSY AND IDENTITY

The Beelzebul Controversy, as told in both in Mark and Q, likely satisfied the need of Jesus followers to distinguish themselves from non-Jesus following Jews. To demonstrate that the story would serve such differentiation, this section will proceed by 1) demonstrating that the Beelzebul Controversy depicts Jesus and his opponents disputing on the basis of a specifically Jewish conception of demonic forces; 2) arguing that early Jesus followers felt a need to distinguish themselves from non-Jesus following Jews; and 3) concluding that depicting Jesus arguing with opponents on the basis of their shared Jewish conception of demonic forces would have helped satisfy the need of early Jesus followers to distinguish themselves from non-Jesus following Jews.

The Jewish Outlook of the Beelzebul Controversy

The last chapter showed how the idea of Satan as the head of a legion of demons developed in Jewish literature. Jesus and his opponents in the Beelzebul Controversy all assume that such an array of evil demonic forces under Satan's command exists, that these forces are active in demonic possessions, and that Jesus' exorcisms truly represent the expulsion of these demons. To demonstrate the specifically Jewish character of a controversy in which the disputants share these presuppositions, we will look to other literature of the turn of the Era as well as to a cross-cultural anthropological model of demon possession to see other ways of construing the nature of demons and the reality of exorcisms, ways that neither Mark nor the Double Tradition adopts.

Both Jesus and his opponents accept that Jesus accomplishes his exorcisms by supernatural power, so at issue in the dispute is whether Jesus' power is legitimate or illegitimate. Chapter 2 examined the accusations that a miracle worker such as Apollonius or Jesus could face, and that a challenge to the propriety of miracle working could take the form of accusations of illegitimacy or of fraud. Several examples from Jewish retellings of the contest between Moses and the Egyptian magicians illustrate the different ways that the evangelists could have framed a controversy about the propriety of Jesus' miracles.

In the biblical version of the story, to prove the power of God before Pharaoh, Moses has Aaron throw down his staff, which transforms into a snake. Pharaoh's magicians are able perform a similar feat, but Aaron's snake devours these other snakes and demonstrates the superior power of Israel's God (Exod 7:10–12). The biblical version does not give much detail as to the nature of the magicians' power. Both Philo and Josephus retell this story in Greek to a cosmopolitan Hellenistic audience, whereas *Jubilees* and the *Damascus Document* retell the story to a more specifically Jewish audience. Notably, Philo and Josephus express the superiority of Moses to the magicians as that of authentic divine power to human fraud, while *Jubilees* and the *Damascus Document* express the difference as one between divine and demonic power, much as the Beelzebul Controversy is framed.

In *Antiquities,* Josephus has Moses explain the difference between the magicians' power and that which he and Aaron wield: "the good things accomplished by me differ so strongly from those accomplished by their magic and craft (μαγείας καὶ τέχνης), as divine things differ from human things (τὰ θεῖα τῶν ἀνθρωπίνων): but I will demonstrate that what I do is not done by sorcery or counterfeit of the truth (κατὰ γοητείαν καὶ πλάνην τῆς ἀληθοῦς), but that what I do appears by the foreknowledge and power of God (κατὰ δὲ θεοῦ πρόνοιαν καὶ δύναμιν)" (2.286). Although Moses and Aaron do similar deeds as the Egyptian magicians, the magicians use human artifice (τέχνη) and deceit (πλάνη) while Moses and Aaron use divine power.

Philo similarly differentiates the divine power of Moses and Aaron from the tricks of the Egyptian magicians. In his *Life of Moses*, Philo gives the reaction of the Egyptian magicians when Aaron's snake swallows all of theirs: "they no longer fancied that what was done was the sophistry or craft of men (ἀνθρώπων σοφίσματα καὶ τέχνας), devised merely for deceit (ἀπάτην); but they saw that it was a more divine power (δύναμιν θειοτέραν) which was the cause of these things" (1.94). Like Josephus, Philo presents the magicians working through artifice (τέχνη) and deceit (ἀπάτη), while Moses wields authentic divine power. Both Josephus and Philo present Moses as a cultural hero of the Jews in a cosmopolitan Hellenistic intellectual climate that included a skeptical tradition. They therefore had to demonstrate how Moses was not a fraud, while his Egyptian opponents who did similar, but inferior deeds, belonged to the class of charlatans.

In contrast to these works addressed to Greek audiences, *Jubilees* and the *Damascus Document* distinguish Moses from the magicians in a specifically Jewish idiom. In *Jubilees,* an angel recalls to Moses how "Prince Mastema stood up before you and desired to make you fall into the hand of Pharaoh. And he aided the magicians of the Egyptians, and they stood up and acted before you" (48.9). The Damascus Document gives a similar account of the difference between Moses and the Egyptian magicians: "For in ancient times, Moses and Aaron arose by the hand of the Prince of Lights and Belial in his cunning raised up Jannes and his brother when Israel was first delivered" (5.17–19).[1] Like Jesus' opponents in the Beelzebul Controversy, these Jewish authors attribute the activity of opposing miracle workers to the malevolent leader of the demons.

The Synoptics betray no such awareness of the skeptical tradition that would label some miracle workers frauds, as Josephus and Philo do. Mark and the Double Tradition could have had Jesus' opponents challenge the reality of his miracles; the Gospel of John gives one example of how to do so. John's Jesus heals a man born blind, and the reaction of Jesus' opponents, whom John labels "the Jews," is incredulity: "The Jews did not believe that he had been blind and received his sight until they called the parents of the man who received his sight" (9:18). In this story, Jesus' opponents begin by doubting the reality of Jesus' miracle and must have it proven to them. Early Jesus followers who wanted to tell a story about opponents accusing Jesus of malfeasance in performing his miracles could frame the dispute over the reality of Jesus' miracles. Both Jewish and non-Jewish authors in antiquity sought to delineate true miracle workers from charlatans. In both versions of the Beelzebul Controversy, the storytellers instead choose to frame the dispute around what the exorcisms prove about Jesus' relationship to the prince of demons.

Another way of conceptualizing a dispute over the legitimacy of those who manipulate possessing spirits comes from the cross-cultural model of spirit-possession developed by I. M. Lewis.[2] Lewis' theory views exorcisms as expressions of resistance to the hegemony of societal elites. The conflict around exorcisms in Lewis' model shows another way that societies can frame disputes over the legitimacy of exorcists, another way that neither Mark nor the Double Tradition adopt.

Based on his fieldwork with several sub–Saharan African peoples, Lewis observed that spirit possession and the manipulation of possessing spirits allowed the socially downtrodden to protest their plight. Lewis noted that in these societies possession phenomena tended to occur among women and low-status men. He further noted that possession gave these oppressed people a way to inconvenience and challenge their oppressors without fear of repercussions, since the behavior was attributed to the possessing spirit.[3] The sub-Saharan societies Lewis studied often identified these afflicting spirits as the gods of their neighbors, gods who opposed their own central pantheon. This observation led Lewis to label this type of spirit possession "peripheral."[4]

Lewis also observed that in societies in which these possessions occurred there frequently existed a group of people with the shamanistic ability to control these spirits. He further observed that these shamans tended to be drawn from the same oppressed groups that suffered spirit possession. Usually these shamans would have experienced possession by these spirits themselves. Although the powerful men in the society would seek the services of these shamans in order to expel the spirit from the possessed subordinate, usually such exorcisms were not possible and the possession could only be mitigated or controlled. Thus, the possessed person would need the shaman's repeated services and would also need to participate in rituals with others who suffered from such chronic possession. From the perspective of the dominant males, these activities were viewed as the necessary actions to control these unruly spirits. In reality, however, the low-status participants in these rituals created what amounted to a cult devoted to these peripheral spirits, a cult that allowed them to continue protesting, up to a point, the oppression they faced from their societies' power structures. The spirit-possessed were in reality connivers in a dissident cult that the dominant forces of society sanctioned without fully recognizing its subversive potential.

Though influential for a generation in anthropological investigation of spirit possession, Lewis's theory is now regarded as a totalizing model that reduces the varieties of possession phenomena across societies to a manifestation of social pathology.[5] Neither the Beelzebul Controversy nor Jesus' exorcistic activity in general fits this model. In Lewis's model, a successful exorcism would further the goals of the elites since it would remove the powerful avenue of protest that spirit possession provided. For Lewis's model to work, the shamans must ensure that spirit possession is a chronic problem so that they and the possessed can repeatedly participate in the ostensibly exorcistic ceremonies that, in fact, constitute the peripheral cult that empowers them. In successfully exorcizing demons, Jesus takes the side of the dominant social forces in Judaism. Further, if the Beelzebul Controversy were to occur along the lines of Lewis's model, the story would have shown how Jesus is in fact aligned with Satan in creating a cult that challenges the officially sanctioned cult of Israel's God. The story as told in Mark and Q does nothing of the sort; rather, it portrays both Jesus and his opponents aligning themselves with the God of Israel.

Jesus and his opponents agree more than they disagree. They all agree that Jesus' exorcisms truly show him wielding supernatural power and not simply fooling the credulous with tricks and artifice. They agree that the spirits that Jesus exorcises are malevolent servants of Satan. They differ only on the point of where Jesus obtains the supernatural power to vanquish Satan's minions. The dispute takes place wholly within the thought world of Second Temple Judaism and centers on Jesus' place in the conflict between God and Satan. That the Beelzebul Controversy takes place wholly within this Jewish worldview indicates that the early tellers and hearers strove to make sense of Jesus' place within the traditions of Judaism, especially in the face of Jews who claimed these traditions but who did not follow Jesus.

Jesus Followers and Non-Jesus Following Jews

Chapter 2 examined why religious groups expend such intellectual energy discussing the groups most similar to themselves and what makes them different from these near-others. The idea that an out-group with a similar worldview would pose a symbolic threat to the in-group's self-identity helps explain why the near-other so engages the thoughts of religious groups: groups need to articulate their distinctiveness vis-à-vis the near-other to maintain their own identity. Early Jesus followers would have confronted a symbolic threat in non-Jesus following Jews. One challenge that early Jesus followers faced would have been explaining to themselves and others how it is that so many Jews would fail to follow Jesus if Jesus were the fulfillment of God's promises to these same Jews. Telling the story of the Beelzebul Controversy allowed early Jesus followers to articulate for themselves what made Jesus distinct from other Jews and why his followers were distinctly correct in following him when so many other Jews did not. Two other examples from early Jesus followers, specifically Paul and Justin Martyr, show how acutely they felt this need to account for themselves and to explain the continued existence of non-Jesus following Jews.

Paul demonstrates this need in Romans. One of Paul's aims in Romans is to explain how both Jews and Gentiles require the redemption that Christ brings. He claims, "Jews and Greeks all are under sin" (Rom 3:9). Being in the same condition of sinfulness, both Jews and Gentiles have the same need of redemption: "for there is no distinction, for all have sinned and fallen short of the glory of God; they are justified in his grace as a gift through the redemption that is in Jesus Christ" (3:22–24). However, at the same time as Paul casts Jews and Gentiles together in sin and in need of Christ's redemption, he views Jesus through the history of the God of Israel, so he affirms the value of the Jewish tradition: "to them [i.e., Jews] belong the adoption, and the glory, and the covenants, and the giving of the law and the worship and the promises, theirs are the patriarchs and from them is Christ according to the flesh" (Rom 9:4–5). Paul is deeply troubled that so many of his fellow Jews have failed to recognize their own Messiah (9:2–3). He then accounts for the situation of the non-Jesus following Jews.

Paul turns to Jewish Scripture to explain why many Jews have not recognized Jesus as the Jewish Messiah. First he observes that Isaac alone of Abraham's sons received the inheritance as an analogy for the fact that even though all Jews are physical descendants of Abraham, only some among them are receiving the fulfillment of God's promises to Abraham, which for Paul occurs in Christ (9:7–9). Next, Paul argues that God's prenatally choosing Jacob and rejecting Esau indicates that God is free to select only a portion of Israel to receive redemption in Christ (9:10–13). Paul also points both to Isaiah's prediction (Isa 10:22) that only a remnant of Israel would be saved (Rom 9:27) and to the persistence of only seven thousand in Israel who did not worship Baal in the time of Elijah (Rom 11:2–5, referring to 1 Kings 19:18) as evidence that sometimes God's plan involves saving only a fraction of Israel. Paul additionally refers to Hosea's promise (Hos 2:23) that God will accept as a people those that were formerly not God's people as evidence that God's plan also involves saving some who were not part of Israel (Rom 9:25–26). For Paul, the receipt of God's redemption by only some Jews along with some Gentiles is explicable in terms of God's promises from Israel's Scripture.[6]

Writing in the second century, Justin Martyr devotes his entire *Dialogue with Trypho* to differentiating Christianity from Judaism and to explaining why Christianity is the true heir to the traditions of Israel. Justin's Jewish dialogue partner, Trypho, personifies the symbolic threat Judaism posed to Christianity. Trypho raises objections to Christian practice and belief, objections that Justin then refutes. Both Trypho and Justin argue on the basis of the Scriptures of Israel. The *Dialogue* represents Justin's attempt to give Christianity legitimacy within the worldview it shares with the symbolically threatening Judaism. For instance, after Justin interprets Daniel's vision of the Ancient of Days and the son of man (Dan 7:9–14) as referring to Jesus,

Trypho objects, "These and such like Scriptures, sir, compel us to wait for him who, as Son of Man, receives from the Ancient of Days the everlasting kingdom. But this so-called Christ of yours was dishonorable and inglorious, so much so that the last curse contained in the law of God fell on him, for he was crucified" (32). Justin then explains that the prophecies of a glorious Messiah refer to Christ's second coming, and he offers scriptural justification for the first, lowly coming of Christ. The *Dialogue* does not present a balanced debate between a Jesus follower and non-Jesus following Jew; rather, it attempts to explain the Jesus movement vis-à-vis non-Jesus following Judaism. Trypho serves as the proximate other against which Justin defines himself. The *Dialogue* is, in essence, an extended controversy that seeks to neutralize the threat that Jews, as proximate others, posed to the self-understanding of early Jesus followers.[7]

Both Justin and Paul need to explain Jesus' importance in terms of Israel's Scriputres and to demonstrate why non-Jesus following Jews are wrong. In their efforts, these non-Jesus following Jews are not true dialogue partners, but rather objects to be thought about and thought with. Paul addresses his letter to the Romans to the Jesus followers in Rome, and there is no attempt here to convince non-Jesus following Jews to change their minds, only hope that they will. Similarly, Trypho's anemic responses to Justin's argument do not bespeak a serious effort to engage with those who do not follow Jesus. The authors' aim is not to convince non-Jesus following Jews about Jesus; rather, it is to convince Jesus followers that Jesus does fulfill the promises of Israel and that non-Jesus following Jews are wrong not to recognize this fulfillment. Although they talk about the out-group (non-Jesus following Jews), both authors show more interest in creating an identity for the in-group (Jesus followers) and perhaps even of fending off rivals within the in-group (Jesus relates to the traditions of Israel in this way, not in that way). Similar dynamics are at work in the Beelzebul Controversy.

The Beelzebul Controversy and Self-Definition

The Beelzebul Controversy serves much the same function as Justin's *Dialogue.* The Jewish opponents exist not to provide Jesus with substantive debate partners but to provide a brief objection that serves as the pretext for Jesus' self-justification. Telling this controversy story shaped early Christian collective memory in terms of conflicts with non-believing Jews from the very beginning of the movement. Jesus' response to his opponents also provides the tellers an opportunity to articulate how he fits into the worldview that early Jesus followers shared with other Jews. Much as Trypho's objection quoted above provides Justin the opportunity to discuss how Jesus fits in the eschatological schema of Hebrew prophecy, the opponents in the Beelzebul Controversy provide Jesus an opportunity to interpret his ministry in light of the eschatological expectations for Satan's defeat. The tellers of this story emphasized that the proper understanding of Jesus' place in the eschatological drama marks the difference between Jesus and his opponents, and, by extension, between Jesus followers and other Jews.

Both Mark and the Double Tradition have Jesus' opponents begin the Controversy with the accusation that Jesus' exorcistic power comes from Beelzebul, the prince of the demons. Chapter 3 introduced Beelzebul the prince of demons among the demons conjured in the *Testament of Solomon,* a work roughly contemporaneous with the Synoptics. Jesus equates this figure with Satan, one of the names or titles of the evil supernatural entity that opposes God. The defeat of Satan had become a common feature in eschatological depictions of God's ultimate victory.

Jesus claims that his exorcisms are eschatological signs of God's impending victory when he responds to his opponents' accusation by claiming that his exorcisms demonstrate the defeat of Satan. The idea that exorcisms somehow manifested this eschatological victory does not occur in much early Jewish literature. A fragmentary Qumran document (11Q11.4) preserves an apotropaic prayer to ward off demons that uses the threat of God's eschatological punishment to deter an attacking demon, but this is as close as most Jewish literature gets to assigning eschatological significance to exorcisms. [8] Jewish literature prior to or contemporary with the New Testament does not interpret exorcisms as prefiguring God's ultimate victory over the ruler of the demons. [9] Jesus' response that his exorcisms demonstrate Satan's defeat interprets the Jewish traditions about Satan's leadership of a hoard of demons and his ultimate defeat in a creative way that asserts Jesus' eschatological significance.

Telling this controversy story would have been one way that early Jesus followers could account for the fact that not all Jews accepted Jesus as their lord or even as a legitimate teacher. Such Jews, like Jesus' opponents, failed to recognize how Jesus' exorcisms manifested God's promised defeat of evil. The story suggests that those who follow Jesus have joined the victorious side in the eschatological battle between God and the forces of Satan. By depicting a dispute that occurs in the context of Jewish traditions about Satan, his cohorts, and their ultimate fate, the authors could bolster the distinctive identity of Jesus followers as those who have recognized God's fulfillment of the promised defeat of evil even as many Jews continued to believe in these promises, but not in Jesus as their fulfillment.

THE BEELZEBUL CONTROVERSY IN MARK

The two versions of the Beelzebul Controversy link Jesus' miracles to the eschatological defeat of Satan, but they construe this eschatological victory by envisioning different roles for Jesus and his followers in the unfolding eschatological drama. Q presents Jesus and his followers participating together in the corporate victory of the kingdom of God. For Mark, the miracles demonstrate that Jesus is the powerful figure who bests Satan in single combat. The role of Jesus' followers in Mark therefore is to recognize that Jesus is this important eschatological figure; Jesus' opponents, by failing to recognize that Jesus is overcoming Satan, place themselves on the wrong side of the eschatological struggle.

The Controversy

Mark opens the Beelzebul Controversy by identifying the opponents as "the scribes who had come down from Jerusalem" (3:22). The scribes have appeared before in the Gospel. In Jesus' inaugural teaching at the Capernaum synagogue, Mark had the people exclaim that Jesus teaches with authority, in contradistinction to the scribes (1:22). By the time the Beelzebul Controversy arises, the scribes have already accused Jesus of blasphemy (2:6–7) and have challenged his table fellowship with tax collectors and sinners (2:16). After the Beelzebul Controversy, scribes from Jerusalem join the Pharisees in challenging Jesus about his disciples' eating with unwashed hands (7:1–5). In both the Beelzebul Controversy and the hand washing pericope, Mark's Jesus uses Jewish traditions (the idea of Satan's eschatological defeat; observance of the Torah) to argue for the legitimacy of his or his disciples' actions against scribes from Jerusalem. The added detail of the scribes' Jerusalem origin highlights the paradox that those most connected to the traditions of Israel fail to see Jesus' identity as the savior those traditions promise.

The reference to Jerusalem also foreshadows the fate that awaits Jesus. As the Gospel progresses towards the cross, the scribes appear alongside the chief priests and the elders as the instigators of Jesus' death. The first passion prediction connects Jesus' rejection by the scribes, along with the chief priests and elders, to his death and rising again (8:31); later Jesus makes the scribes' agency in his death, with Jerusalem as its locale, explicit: "We are going up to Jerusalem and the Son of Man will be handed over to the chief priests and to the scribes, and they will condemn him to death and hand him over to the Gentiles" (10:33). In Jerusalem, the scribes, along with the chief priests, look for a way to kill Jesus (11:18, 14:1). It is the scribes, chief priests, and elders who send the mob with Judas to arrest Jesus (14:43), and the scribes sit with the chief priests and the elders in judgment of Jesus (14:53). Once they have condemned Jesus, the scribes help the chief priests and elders lead Jesus to Pilate (15:1). By specifying Jesus' opponents as "scribes who had come down from Jerusalem," Mark scores the Beelzebul Controversy as an early note in the scribes' crescendo of hostility that will end with Jesus' death in Jerusalem.

These hostile scribes in Mark make two parallel accusations: "He has Beelzebul," and "By the prince of the demons he casts out demons" (3:22). The first accusation implies that Jesus is possessed by the devil, while the second implies that Jesus is in league with him. The Q version provides just one accusation, which parallels Mark's second: that Jesus exorcizes by the power of Beelzebul, the prince of demons (Mt 12:24//Lk 11:15); this one accusation is a sufficient prompt for Jesus' response that his exorcisms demonstrate the downfall of the devil. Mark's added accusation provides an opportunity to make a point about the origin of Jesus' power: it comes from the Holy Spirit. Mark connects the accusation of demonic possession to Jesus' statement about the unforgiveable sin: "'Amen I say to you that all sins will be forgiven to the sons of men and whatever blasphemies they blaspheme, but whoever blasphemes against the Holy Spirit will not have forgiveness eternally, but is guilty of an eternal sin.' Because they said, 'He has an unclean spirit'" (3:28–30). That the logion about the unforgivable sin comes in response to the accusation that Jesus has an unclean spirit implies that Jesus is not possessed by an unclean spirit, but by the spirit of God. Thus, when the scribes accuse Jesus of having Beelzebul, they are committing the unforgivable sin of blaspheming the Holy Spirit by calling it Beelzebul.[10] The accusation that Jesus has Beelzebul allows Mark to show that the scribes are not merely wrong, but guilty of an eternal sin.

The accusation that Jesus has "an unclean spirit (πνεῦμα ἀκάθαρτον)" in 3:30 further situates the dispute in the Jewish worldview by placing it in the context of the antimony between holiness and impurity. The scribes believe Jesus to have an impure spirit, but in actuality Jesus has the Holy Spirit. In his other exorcisms Mark's Jesus expels unclean spirits (1:23, 5:2, 7:25). When Jesus heals the man with leprosy, Mark frames it in terms of cleansing him (1:40–44), and in the dispute over hand-washing, the Markan narrator suggests that Jesus declared all foods clean (7:19). While Jesus and his opponents may disagree over what constitutes proper purity, they both carry on the dispute in the Jewish idiom of ritual purity.[11]

Jesus responds to the scribes' accusation "in parables" (3:23). This authorial description of the upcoming argument is accurate, but hardly necessary. In the course of the narration, the reader will come to see the technique of parable by which Jesus answers the accusation. The explicit mention of parables links the Beelzebul Controversy to Jesus' discussion of parables in the following chapter.[12] There Jesus tells his disciples, "To you has been given the secret of the kingdom of God, but for those outside, everything comes in parables; in order that 'they may indeed look, but not perceive, and may indeed listen, but not understand; so that they may not turn again and be forgiven'" (4:11–12, echoing Isa 6:10). The parables allow Jesus to proclaim his message in a way that guarantees a lack of understanding. They separate outsiders, to whom the message comes only indirectly, from the insiders, who receive the explanation of Jesus' message (see also Mark 4:34; 7:17). The only time Mark presents the hearers understanding a parable without Jesus' interpretation comes in the parable of the Vineyard, which Jesus tells against the chief priests, scribes, and elders (11:27–12:12). Parables in this Gospel delineate insiders, who receive eschatological reward, from the outsiders who will eventually pay for their rejection of Jesus' message.

The parable chapter also ties into the Beelzebul Controversy in the mention of Satan. In his explanation of the parable of the sower, Mark explicates the seed that falls on the path and is eaten by birds as those who, "when they hear, Satan immediately comes and takes away the word that is sown in them" (Mark 4:15). These hearers of the word, like seed, lie passive and helpless as Satan attacks them. Satan is the foe not just of Jesus, but of those who hear his word. However, while Jesus battles with Satan, his auditors are potential victims of Satan's depredation without any role in fighting him.

In the Beelzebul Controversy, Jesus' response to the scribes begins with a rhetorical question, "How is Satan able to cast out Satan?" (3:23), which implies that the scribes' accusation is ridiculous. Jesus illustrates the absurdity of the scribes' accusation by a set of comparisons: "if a kingdom were divided against itself, that kingdom cannot stand, and if a house were divided against itself, that house could not stand, and if Satan rose up against himself and is divided, he cannot stand but has his end" (3:23–25). The momentum of these three parallel sayings moves from large corporate entity (kingdom) to smaller corporate entity (house) to individual (Satan). Jesus does not mention a Satanic kingdom or household, just Satan and his individual end.[13] Mark's interest lies in the victory of Jesus over Satan, not God's kingdom over Satan's.

Jesus proceeds immediately to the saying about the strong man: "No one is able to enter the house of a strong man to steal his property unless he first binds the strong man and then he can plunder his house" (Mark 3:27). Jesus here pictures a thief tying up a householder and then stealing the possessions in the house. Jesus' exorcisms are analogous to plundering the possessions of a strong man, so Jesus' success must mean that Satan's power has been overcome.[14] The analogy construes the combat between Jesus and Satan on a personal, rather than corporate, level—it is a one-on-one conflict between the strong man and the thief, and between Jesus and Satan.[15]

The description of the overcoming of the strong man as "binding" (δήσῃ) further links this metaphor with the eschatological defeat of Satan. Jewish literature often depicts the binding of Satan and his minions as the prelude to their ultimate judgment. In *Jubilees*, when Noah seeks relief from demonic attacks on humanity, he prays that God bind and shut up the demons (10.3–8). Similarly, in *1 Enoch*, God orders Raphael to bind Azazel until the judgment day (10.4). Such binding often becomes the demons' eschatological fate. Isaiah speaks of the day when "the Lord will punish the host of heaven in heaven, and on earth the kings of the earth. They will be gathered together like prisoners (אֲסִיר, from אסר, "to bind") in a pit; they will be shut up in a prison" (Isa 24:21–22). The Septuagint at this point lacks the etymologic connection with binding but keeps the idea of confinement: "God will lay his hand upon the inhabitants of heaven and the kings of the earth; and they will gather them and confine them in a fortress and a prison (ἀποκλείσουσιν εἰς ὀχύρωμα καὶ εἰς δεσμωτήριον)" (Isa 24:21–22 LXX). God will imprison both terrestrial and heavenly foes. In his *Testament*, the patriarch Levi promises the coming of a new priest by whom Beliar will be bound (δεθήσεται) (18.12). New Testament authors also depict God binding Satan and/or the demons to await their eschatological judgment (Jude 6; 2 Pet 2:4) or God binding them as ultimate punishment (Rev 20:1–3). The language of binding locates the metaphor of the strong man in this apocalyptic stream of thinking.

Mark's version of the Beelzebul Controversy makes Jesus, battling personally against Satan and Satan's agents, the key figure in this eschatological struggle. Mark also frames the story to make Jesus' interlocutors guilty of committing the unforgivable sin against the Holy Spirit by defaming Jesus. Recognition of Jesus' singular status as eschatological agent is the crux of the dispute. Such a story would have had maximum relevance among hearers who shared the eschatological schema of conflict between God and Satan that developed in Second Temple Judaism. This conflict story could help maintain group integrity vis-à-vis proximate out-groups (i.e., Jews who did not follow Jesus) by emphasizing the distinctiveness of Jesus' role in this eschatological drama as opposed to those who did not recognize Jesus having such a role. Telling the story the way Mark does shapes collective memory of Jesus as God's special agent battling Satan. It also fosters a memory of Jesus disputing with other Jews who failed to recognize him as such.

Co-text 1: The Surrounding Pericopae

Mark intercalates the Beelzebul Controversy within the story of Jesus' redefining his family.[16] Before the Beelzebul Controversy, Mark relates, "And he came home; and the crowd came together again, so that they could not even eat bread. When his family (οἱ παρ' αὐτοῦ) heard it, they went out to restrain (κρατῆσαι) him, for they were saying, 'He has gone out of his mind (ἐξέστη)'" (Mark 3:19–22). The Beelzebul Controversy then interrupts this brewing family conflict. After Jesus has refuted the scribes and accused them of an unforgivable sin, Mark resumes the story about Jesus' family seeking him, which prompts Jesus to ask and answer his famous question, "Who are my mother and my brothers? . . . Whoever does the will of God is my brother and sister and mother" (3:33, 35).

By placing the Beelzebul Controversy in the midst of the story of Jesus' family, Mark invites the reading of the two stories in light of one another.[17] The family's perception that Jesus has gone out of his mind parallels the scribes' accusation that Beelzebul has possessed him.[18] Like the scribes, Jesus' family does not understand the significance of his actions and interprets them negatively. They seek to restrain him, but he is the one who does the restraining by binding the strong man and plundering his possessions. As they seek to restrain Jesus, the natal family cannot even approach Jesus, so dense does the crowd throng. The crux of the story comes in Jesus' redefinition of his family as those who do the will of God. One's relationship to Jesus is crucial; the reward for doing God's will is being part of Jesus' family, and Jesus' natal family, by misconstruing the agent of God's redemption as a madman, have their closeness to Jesus discounted. The locations reinforce this point. Jesus comes "home (εἰς οἶκον)," which is where the crowds convene and where Jesus is trying to eat, an activity that takes place inside, at home. To talk to him his natal family "went out (ἐξῆλθον)," emphasizing that Jesus is not eating with them and that his home is not with his natal family, who is not Jesus' "real" family at all. While the natal family is making their way out to him, Mark introduces another set of outsiders, the scribes from Jerusalem, who also misunderstand who Jesus is. By embedding the Beelzebul Controversy in this story of Jesus' family, Mark directs attention to the importance of relating to Jesus correctly—recognizing him as the eschatological victor over Satan.

Co-text 2: The Exorcism in the Capernaum Synagogue

The exorcisms in the rest of Mark's narrative also point to Jesus' identity as the one who overcomes Satan. After calling his first disciples, Jesus' initial public action is to teach in the Capernaum synagogue. Just as the Beelzebul Controversy places Jesus' way of thinking and arguing within the thought world of Judaism, so this pericope physically locates Jesus in the practices of Judaism by having him in a synagogue on the Sabbath. Jesus amazes the people with his teaching, and

> Immediately there was in their synagogue a man with an unclean spirit (πνεύματι ἀκαθάρτῳ) that cried out, saying, "What is it to us and to you, Jesus Nazarene? Have you come to destroy us? I know who you are, the Holy One of God (ὁ ἅγιος τοῦ θεοῦ)." And Jesus rebuked (ἐπετίμησεν) him saying, "Be muzzled and come out from him." And the unclean spirit, wrenching him and crying out in a loud voice, came out from him. And all were amazed and asked one another saying, "What is this? A new teaching with authority (κατ' ἐξουσίαν)! He commands even the unclean spirits and they obey him! (Mark 1:23–24)

Like a moth to a flame, the unclean spirit approaches the power that will be its undoing. His question, "What is it to us and to you, Jesus Nazarene? Have you come to destroy us?," might refer to Jesus' coming to Capernaum, but the plural objects ("us" vs. "me") suggests a more programmatic insight into Jesus' mission to overcome all demons, as both the demon and the narrator refer to the demon in the singular throughout the rest of the pericope.[19] The unclean spirit identifies Jesus as "the Holy One of God," with the definite article emphasizing Jesus' special status as premier agent of God's victory over evil spirits.[20] Throughout Mark, the unclean spirits have insight into Jesus' identity and recognize him as the Son of God (Mark 3:11), a recognition that no human character makes until the centurion at the foot of the cross (15:39). Jesus expels the unclean spirit with a rebuke that echoes the rebuke of God in overcoming the powers of chaos in creation: "The pillars of heaven tremble and are astonished by his rebuke (הרגע/ἐπιτιμήσεως)" (Job 26:11). Similarly, God will rout his enemies with a rebuke: "The nations roar like the roaring of many waters, but he will rebuke (וגער) them, and they will flee far way, chased like chaff on the mountains before the wind and whirling dust before the storm" (Isa 17:13).[21] Jesus, like God, overcomes his cosmic opponents by the power of his rebuke.[22] The rebuke includes the command to come out, but also the command to be muzzled, a sort of binding.

Jesus' rebuke overcomes the demon, who departs violently. The violent departure emphasizes the struggle that occurs as Jesus overcomes the demon, and it proves that the demon has really left. The crowd's amazement is a stock feature of many ancient miracle stories, and it emphasizes both just how wonderful the miracle is and that it was witnessed.[23] The episode as a whole demonstrates Jesus' special status as God's agent in the eschatological war against Satan's demons, of which this exorcism is the first sortie.[24]

Co-text 3: The Gerasene Demoniac

Mark's next extended narration of Jesus' encounter with demons comes when Jesus crosses the Sea of Galilee and arrives in Gerasa:

> And when he had exited the boat, immediately a man with an unclean spirit came from the tombs to meet him. He had his dwelling in the tombs and no longer was anyone able to bind (δῆσαι) him with chains because he had been bound (δεδέσθαι) many times with fetters and chains and he had ripped free from his chains and broken the fetters, and no one was strong enough (ἴσχυεν) to subdue him. (Mk 5:2–4)

This demoniac receives a much fuller introduction than the man in the Capernaum synagogue. Mark emphasizes how difficult this man has been to control, which makes all the more remarkable Jesus' curing him and all the more astonishing when the townspeople find him calmly seated at Jesus' feet

(5:15). Mark twice emphasizes the impossibility of binding the man with the same word (δέω) used in the binding of the strong man (3:27). Just as Jesus was able to overcome the strong man (ἰσχυρόν) Satan, so can he also subdue the demoniac when no one else was strong enough (ἴσχυεν) to do so.

Like the demoniac in Capernaum who could not help but confront Jesus, the Gerasene demoniac rushes toward him: "and seeing Jesus from afar, he ran and bowed down (προσεκύνησεν) to him and crying out in a loud voice he said, 'What is it to me and to you, Jesus, Son of the Most High God? I adjure you by God, do not torture me!'" (Mk 5:6–7). The demon recognizes Jesus' power and status and does obeisance to him. Like the demon in Capernaum, this demon recognizes Jesus' special relationship with God and gives him a title connecting him to God. He also recognizes Jesus' mission to fight against demonic powers and therefore begs Jesus not to torture him. The demon knows his opponent when he sees him.

Taking control of the situation, Jesus asks the demon its name, to which it responds, "My name is Legion, for we are many" (5:9). This legion of demons recognizes that Jesus will expel it and therefore requests that he allow it to enter a herd of nearby pigs. Jesus accedes to their foolish request, and the possessed swine promptly rush into the lake and drown (5:12–13). The demons' self-identification as Legion suggests an anti-imperial subtext to this story, especially given the role of Legion X Fretensis, whose sigil was a boar, in fighting the insurgents in the First Jewish Revolt.[25] However plausible this political reading of the story may be, Mark does not develop the theme of opposition to Rome; in its Markan context, the military title of the demon calls to mind the battle between Jesus and Satan rather than between Jesus and Rome.[26] Jesus himself can best a legion of demons, much as he can overcome their prince.

In relating the reaction to this exorcism, Mark effaces the distinction between Jesus and God, which demonstrates how the exorcisms function in Mark to reveal Jesus' divine identity. Jesus' victory over this Legion causes no little uproar amongst the populace, who beseech Jesus to leave their area (5:14–18). Before doing so, Jesus charges the formerly possessed man, "Go home to your friends, and tell them how much the Lord has done for you (ὅσα ὁ κύριός σοι πεποίηκεν), and what mercy he has shown you" (5:19). Jesus does not make clear whether by "the Lord" he means God or himself, but the man clearly takes it to mean Jesus as "he went out and began to proclaim in the Decapolis how much *Jesus* did for him (ὅσα ἐποίησεν αὐτῷ ὁ Ἰησοῦς), and all were amazed" (5:20). This subtle shift in subject assimilates Jesus to God—proclamation about Jesus substitutes for proclamation about God. Elsewhere in the Gospel, Mark uses ὁ κύριός to talk about Jesus. In 11:3, Jesus clearly uses ὁ κύριός as a self-referent. Mark takes the Isaianic prediction of a voice crying in the wilderness to prepare the way of the Lord as representing John the Baptist's preparation for Jesus, which would imply that Jesus is the Lord (1:2–4). Mark's Jesus also proclaims that "the son of man is lord even of the Sabbath" (2:28). The Geresene Demoniac, like the demons themselves, recognizes the lordship (or Lordship) of Jesus. In Mark, Jesus acts as God's agent in conquering Satan and his forces of evil, and Mark blurs the distinction between Jesus and God.[27] This blurring is of a piece with the way Mark talks about Jesus throughout the Gospel: as the divine agent who overcomes Satan and not as one participant alongside others in the larger victory of God's kingdom.

Co-text 4: The Syro-Phoenician Woman and Her Daughter

After demonstrating that he can best the demons face to face, Mark's Jesus next shows that he can exorcize even at a distance. The Syro-Phoenician woman begs Jesus to expel the demon who torments her daughter (7:25–26). Jesus does not encounter the demon; rather, the narrative focuses on his encounter with the mother of the possessed child. In response to her request, Jesus replies, "Let the children be satisfied first, for it is not right to take the children's bread and cast it to the dogs" (7:27). The woman cleverly replies, "Lord, even the dogs under the table eat from the children's crumbs" (7:28), which impresses Jesus enough that he agrees to perform the exorcism. Although he does not recount the exorcism, Mark states that when the woman returns home, she finds her daughter cured of the demon (7:29–30).

Although Jesus' treatment of the woman seems harsh on its face, several ancient parallels show how such a story redounded to Jesus' credit.[28] Dio Cassius tells a story of a woman accosting the emperor Hadrian with a request. Hadrian protests that he is too busy with his duties as emperor to help her, to which the woman responds, "Then stop being emperor." Hadrian then granted her a hearing (69.6.3). Similarly, Macrobius relates a story of a veteran asking Augustus to appear for him in court. Augustus offered to send one of his functionaries to represent him; the veteran showed Augustus his scars and loudly reminded the emperor that at Actium he did not seek a substitute, but fought for the future Augustus in person. Chastened, Augustus appeared in court himself on the veteran's behalf (*Saturnalia* 2.4.27). A similar narrative appears in the Babylonian Talmud where Rabbi Judah the Prince opens his storehouse in a famine only to those with rabbinic learning. When Jonathan ben Amram asks for food, he pretends that he is unlearned so that Judah will rebuff him. After Judah refuses, Jonathan replies, "Give me food, for even a dog and a raven are given food." Abashed, Judah allows all, the learned and the unlearned, to eat from his storehouse (*b. Baba Batra* 8a). The authority figure whom a petitioner chastens into providing aid he initially refused is a trope in ancient literature. These stories demonstrate the virtue of *praotes*, conventionally translated "meekness," which denotes a willingness to forego a prerogative to which one is entitled in order to help someone else.[29] Mark's story of this exorcism furthers the characterization of Jesus: he is a *praos* authority figure. The exorcism again focuses attention on Jesus and his personal excellence.

Co-text 5: The Convulsed Boy

Mark's next exorcism story occurs as Jesus descends the mountain after his Transfiguration with Peter, James, and John. A crowd has gathered and has witnessed the other disciples' failure to exorcize a demon that convulses a boy, and now some scribes argue with the disciples (9:14–18). Jesus responds, "O faithless generation (γενεὰ ἄπιστος), how much longer (ἕως πότε) must I be with you? How much longer (ἕως πότε) must I endure you?" (9:19). Jesus' complaint against his contemporaries echoes Moses' complaint about the Israelites in the wilderness who were "a perverted and twisted generation" (דור עקש ופתלתל/γενεὰ σκολιὰ καὶ διεστραμμένη Deut 32:5). God makes a similar complaint about the wilderness generation, calling them "a generation of perversity (דור תהפכת/γενεὰ ἐξεστραμμένη)" (Deut 32:20). God, like Jesus, also asks rhetorically how long these people will vex him: "How long (עד־אנה/ἕως τίνος) will this people provoke me and how long (עד־אנה/ἕως τίνος) will they not believe (אמינו/πιστεύουσίν) in me, in spite of all the signs that I have done among them?" (Num 14:11). The lack of faith of the wilderness generation vexed God just as the lack of faith on the part of Jesus' contemporaries vexes him. By having Jesus complain about a faithless generation, Mark both echoes the Penteteuchal trope of God's displeasure with the Israelites in the wilderness and also puts Jesus into the role of God in this reply.[30] Even apart from the scriptural echoes, the complaint against his contemporaries as a "faithless generation" makes it seem that Jesus does not belong in the same categories as other people, that he is not part of this generation, that he longs to be done with them and perhaps go to the divine world where he belongs.[31] Again, Mark's exorcism story separates Jesus from the rest of humanity and suggests that he and God are somehow the same.

Mark further portrays Jesus as divine in his depiction of the exorcism itself and Jesus' ensuing discussion of prayer. Unlike the previously encountered demons, who speak with Jesus before he expels them, this demon reacts to Jesus' presence by convulsing the boy (9:20). Instead of talking with the demon, Jesus speaks with the boy's father, which leads to the famous exchange:

> "If you can do anything, have pity on us and help us."
> But Jesus said to him, "'If you can!' All things are possible for the one who believes."
> Immediately the father of the child cried out saying, "I believe, help my unbelief!" (9:22–24)

In response to the father's plea, Jesus expels the demon (9:25). When the disciples ask why they failed, Jesus answers, "This kind can come out in no way except by prayer" (9:29). Mark, however, does not narrate Jesus praying for the demon to come out; Jesus simply commands the demon to do so.[32] Where the disciples require prayer to give them power, Jesus simply possesses the requisite power. The only place in the pericope where anything like a prayer occurs is in the father's request to Jesus.[33] Jesus again functions in the role of God, the one to whom prayers for help are addressed.

The description of the exorcism itself foreshadows Jesus' future suffering. Mark makes some effort to describe the process of the demon's expulsion: "Crying out and convulsing much, it came out. And he [the child] was like a dead person (νεκρός) so that the crowd said that he had died (ἀπέθανεν). But Jesus, grasping his hand, raised (ἤγειρεν) him and he arose (ἀνέστη)" (9:26–27). To advance the plot, all that Mark needed was to show that the exorcism succeeded. Narratively, these details are extraneous and therefore invite consideration as to why Mark included them. Moreover, Mark's description is doubly redundant—the boy seemed so dead that people thought he was dead, but Jesus raised him and he rose. These pleonasms create a density of references to dying and rising, a theme of Mark's Gospel:

> And he began to teach them that it is necessary that the Son of Man suffer many things and be rejected by the elders and the chief priests and the scribes and be killed and after three days rise (ἀναστῆναι). (8:31)

> And when they came down from the mountain, he ordered them not to tell anyone what they saw until the Son of Man had risen from the dead (ἐκ νεκρῶν ἀναστῇ). And they kept the word amongst themselves discussing what rising from the dead (ἐκ νεκρῶν ἀναστῆναι) might be. (9:9–10)

> He was teaching his disciples and was saying to them that the Son of Man would be betrayed into the hands of men and they would kill him and having been killed after three days he would rise (ἀναστήσεται). (9:31)

> And they will mock him and spit on him and scourge him and kill him, and after three days he will rise (ἀναστήσεται). (10:34)

> When they rise from the dead (ἐκ νεκρῶν ἀναστῶσιν) they do not marry nor are they given in marriage, but they are as the angels in heaven. But about the dead that they are raised (τῶν νεκρῶν ὅτι ἐγείρονται), have you not read in the Book of Moses how God said to him, 'I am the God of Abraham and the God of Isaac and the God of Jacob.' He is not the God of the dead (νεκρῶν), but of the living." (12:25–26)

> But after I have been raised (ἐγερθῆναί) I will go ahead of you into Galilee. (14:28)

> He said to them, "Do not be amazed. You seek Jesus of Nazareth who was crucified. He has been raised (ἠγέρθη); he is not here. Behold the place where they laid him." (16:6)

The superfluous references to dying and rising in this pericope parallel the passion predictions that surround the story of this exorcism. The boy suffers, seems to die, and rises, which, *mutatis mutandis,* prefigures Jesus' own passion experience. Another link to Jesus' passion comes at the beginning of the pericope, where Mark has even introduced the scribes as spectators to the disciples' failed exorcism (9:14). Like the description of the boy's apparent dying and rising, the mention of the scribes does not advance the plot of the pericope, but their presence provides another thematic link between the story of this exorcism and the story of Jesus' death and rising. This exorcism maintains a Christocentric focus—it demonstrates Jesus' power relative to that of his disciples and foreshadows the death and resurrection that Jesus will undergo.

Exorcism and Identity in Mark

These co-texts reveal a pattern in Mark's deployment of exorcism stories. Though not displaying a uniform eschatological outlook, these four exorcism stories are consistent in their Christological focus, whether depicting Jesus as the opponent of Satan's host, as the meek ruler, or as the one who overcomes death. The exorcisms reveal different facets of Jesus, but they all point to Jesus' special identity. The Beelzebul Controversy in turn provides an interpretive key for these four stories by showing that exorcisms demonstrate Jesus acting as God's eschatological champion in conquering Satan. This cosmic conflict between Jesus and Satan has an earthly parallel in Jesus' conflict with the scribes and the other human opponents who will bring about Jesus' death. The exorcisms allow Mark to demonstrate Jesus as the powerful, perhaps divine, figure who undergoes death but conquers Satan in the process. The Beelzebul Controversy in its Markan form differentiates Jesus followers from non-Jesus followers on the basis of their ability to see in his exorcisms evidence of Jesus' identity as this powerful figure who conquers Satan.

THE BEELZEBUL CONTROVERSY IN THE DOUBLE TRADITION

In Mark's version of the Beelzebul Controversy, the exorcisms demonstrate Jesus' personal victory over Satan. The Q version of this story focuses not on Jesus' defeat of Satan, but on the kingdom of God's defeat of the kingdom of Satan, a victory of which Jesus' miracles are a part. The Double Tradition uses corporate metaphors for the conflict between good and evil that invite readers to imagine themselves alongside Jesus in this fight. Those who recognize Jesus' exorcisms as signs of the dawning kingdom of God can join the winning side of the decisive eschatological conflict. Whereas in Mark being on the winning side meant recognizing Jesus as the one who overcomes

Satan, the winning side in Q are those who participate with Jesus in the victory of God's kingdom over Satan's. While Mark strives to demonstrate the uniqueness of Jesus, Q depicts Jesus as one combatant among many in the fight against Satan's kingdom.

While Mark narrates a number of exorcisms that serve as co-texts for the Beelzebul Controversy, the Q material contains only one exorcism. The account, which immediately precedes the Beelzebul Controversy, depicts Jesus amazing a crowd by exorcizing a demon that causes deafness (Luke 11:14) or deafness and blindness (Matt 12:22–23). In distinction from the Markan exorcisms, this lone Q exorcism provides no repartee between Jesus and the demon, no opportunity for the demon to recognize Jesus' divine mandate or for Jesus to talk with petitioners and demonstrate his authority. Rather, Q tells the exorcism succinctly; the emphasis in the telling is the effect that the exorcism has on the formerly deaf person (he can now hear and talk) and on the crowd (they are amazed).

The exorcism demonstrates Jesus' power, but the Q version does not expand the story to highlight the specialness of that power the way Mark so often does. Also in contrast to Mark, Q briefly mentions that Jesus could read the thoughts of the hostile accusers (Matt 12:25// Luke 11:17) while Mark makes no such indication. Although the narration in Q does not explore the nature of Jesus' power the way Mark so often does, Q nevertheless portrays Jesus as possessing supernatural ability.

As in Mark, so in both Matthew and Luke, Jesus begins to refute the accusation that he is in league with Beelzebul by comparing the fate of a divided Satan to that of divided human institutions (underlines represent Double Tradition material):

> And if a kingdom were divided against itself, that kingdom cannot stand, and if a house were divided against itself, that house could not stand, and if Satan rose up against himself and is divided, he cannot stand but has his end. (Mark 3:24–26)

> But Jesus, knowing their thoughts, said to them, "Every kingdom divided against itself is laid waste, and every city or house divided against itself does not stand. And if Satan casts out Satan, he is divided against himself. How then will his kingdom stand? (Matt 12:25–26)

> But Jesus, knowing their minds, said to them, "Every kingdom divided against itself is laid waste and house falls upon house. And if Satan is divided against himself, how will his kingdom stand? (Luke 11:17–18)

Rather than the narrowing from kingdom to house to Satan as an individual, Matthew and Luke both begin with the fall of a generic kingdom and then return to the fall of Satan's *kingdom*. As noted in the last chapter, the specific idea of a kingdom of Satan was not widely attested in Jewish literature.

However, the idea that Satan had dominion over the other demons was wide-spread. The Double Tradition has here taken a familiar idea from Second Temple Jewish thought and created a novel term for it. This idea of Satan's kingdom focuses attention on evil as a corporate entity. The Double Tradition also differs from Mark in saying that the fate of a divided kingdom is to be "laid waste (ἐρημοῦται)" rather than simply being unable to stand. The Q version gives a heightened sense of destruction that this kingdom has undergone. The logical force of the argument also differs. In Mark the argument works by analogy: just as a divided kingdom cannot stand, so too could a divided Satan not stand. In the Double Tradition, the argument goes from the general to the specific: any kingdom divided is destroyed, so if Satan's kingdom is divided it must fall. The defeat of evil thus comes in the destruction of this corporate entity rather than in the defeat of an individual spiritual entity.

The Double Tradition does not explicitly connect its presumed readers to God's forces fighting the kingdom of Satan.[34] However, envisioning the ultimate victory over evil as the defeat of an army or kingdom creates a heightened metaphorical level of participation in evil's defeat as compared to the metaphor of Satan's defeat in single combat. If God, or Jesus, or a single angel defeats the devil in one-to-one combat, others can participate only vicariously in the victory. However, if the victory is a war between the forces of good and the forces of evil, then widespread direct participation in this victory is possible. The corporate metaphor shifts focus from the individual victory of God or God's agent to the shared victory of all those on God's side. Compared to Mark, the Double Tradition deemphasizes the unique role of Jesus in order to emphasize the role of those who follow him as participating in the group victory that is the kingdom of God's conquest of the kingdom of Satan.

This more corporate and participatory paradigm, along with its attendant de-emphasis on Jesus' uniqueness, appears in the rest of the Q version of the Beelzebul Controversy. After the analogies of the divided kingdom and houses, the Double Tradition contains a rebuttal to the Beelzebul accusation that has no parallel in Mark:

> And if I cast out demons by Beelzebul, by whom do your sons cast them out? Because of this they will be your judges. But if by the spirit of God I cast out demons, then the kingdom of God has come upon you. (Matt 12:27–28)

> And if I cast out demons by Beelzebul, by whom do your sons cast them out? Because of this, they will be your judges. But if by the finger of God I cast out demons, then the kingdom of God has come upon you. (Luke 11:19–20)

Jesus here puts himself in the company of exorcists of whom his opponents do approve, and by so doing, he shows their inconsistency in opposing him.[35]

This linking of Jesus to the other exorcists implies that the other exorcists are also manifesting the kingdom of God.[36]

Mark provides an example of how an author could imply a difference between Jesus' exorcisms and those of other exorcists. John reports to Jesus, "Teacher, we saw someone casting out demons in your name (ἐν τῷ ὀνόματί σου), and we stopped him, because he did not follow us" (Mark 9:38). An exorcist not attached to Jesus exists and can do what Jesus' disciples failed to do with the convulsed boy (9:14–29), but his exorcisms are clearly derivative of Jesus' power.[37] The Double Tradition makes no such explicit qualification about the exorcisms of the "sons" in Matthew 12:27//Luke 11:19. Indeed the force of the argument relies on the similarity of Jesus and the sons, for Jesus here is telling his opponents that consistency would demand that Satan empowered the sons' exorcisms if Satan empowered his. An accusation against Jesus is an implicit accusation against the sons, and so the sons will be the judges in this dispute. Unlike in Mark, where Jesus is the font of the unknown exorcist's power, here in Q Jesus exists alongside other exorcists who likewise participate in the victory of the kingdom of God.

This note that the sons will be the judges (κριταὶ) of Jesus' opponents is a clever double entendre. Within the scope of the dispute, it can be taken to mean that the sons will judge who is in the right, Jesus or his opponents. However, in a pericope infused with such eschatological overtones, the promise that his opponents will be judged calls to mind also the final judgment. Elsewhere in the Double Tradition Jesus promises that other human beings, namely his disciples, will serve as eschatological judges:

> You will sit upon twelve thrones judging (κρίνοντες) the twelve tribes of Israel (Matt 19:28)

> You will sit on thrones judging (κρίνοντες) the twelve tribes of Israel (Luke 22:30)

In the Double Tradition, it is not only Jesus who is the eschatological judge, but those who side with him also get to be judges. Those who participate in the eschatological battle with the forces of Satan participate in the subsequent judgment. The double entendre thus claims the opponents' sons as coworkers with Jesus. Q does not show much concern here to emphasize the uniqueness of Jesus' power.

Rather than emphasize Jesus' uniqueness, the Q version emphasizes the exorcisms as signals of the coming kingdom of God. The kingdom of God counters the kingdom of Satan mentioned in the prior verse. Thus, whereas the Markan version of the Beelzebul Controversy frames the conflict as an encounter between Jesus and Satan, the Q version maintains a more corporate emphasis and frames the conflict as a clash of two kingdoms, of which Jesus and Satan are the key figures. The last chapter noted that the kingdom of God could symbolize the whole story of God's sovereignty, but that in much turn-of-the-Era literature it had a strong eschatological thrust. The review of the kingdom of God elsewhere in the Double Tradition confirmed its eschatological nature, especially when it is spoken of as coming. Here in the Beelzebul Controversy the kingdom of God is again spoken of as coming, but in this case the coming is not in the future. Jesus says that the kingdom of God "has come (ἔφθασεν)" in his exorcisms. In classical Greek, φθάνω has a range of meanings that includes "anticipate," "precede," "overtake," or "arrive at."[38] In New Testament Greek the word almost exclusively is used to denote arrival.[39] The use of the aorist tense in Matthew 12:28//Luke 11:20 denotes an action that has been completed. Thus, the most natural meaning of Jesus' statement is that his exorcisms demonstrate that the kingdom of God has arrived and is therefore already present.[40]

Whereas Mark's version emphasizes the exorcisms as demonstrations of Jesus' overcoming Satan, the version from the Double Tradition claims that the exorcisms demonstrate the arrival of the kingdom of God, a kingdom that will conquer the kingdom of Satan. Throughout the Q version of the Controversy, the emphasis has been on this battle between the forces of good and the forces of evil in which Jesus is one participant among others. For Q, the exorcism is of little value unless it is part of this larger victory of good over evil.[41] The Double Tradition's Jesus speaks of the unfortunate state of a person who though successfully rid of a single possessing demon finds himself in a worse state when that demon brings his comrades and repossesses the person (Matthew 12:43–45//Luke 24–26). Jesus and many other people can exorcise demons, but for the exorcism to have any lasting significance it must be part of the victory of the kingdom of God over the kingdom of Satan, a victory in which Jesus participates along with those who follow him.

Although Jesus is one participant among others, he still claims a position of importance in the struggle. Even as Q's Jesus emphasizes his own eschatological importance he simultaneously emphasizes his follower's participation in his eschatological task. At the end of the dispute, Q's Jesus makes his importance clear: "Whoever is not with me is against me, and whoever does not gather (συνάγων) with me scatters (σκορπίζει)" (Matt 12:30//Luke 11:23). The saying focuses on allegiance to Jesus as the critical decision and in good apocalyptic fashion gives only two options, for or against.[42] Jesus repeats this binary in two ways: being with Jesus or against Jesus, gathering or scattering. Gathering (συνάγω) language appears elsewhere in Q in the mouth of John the Baptist predicting eschatological judgment:

> His winnowing fork is in his hand and he will clear his threshing floor and will gather (συνάξει) his wheat into the barn, but the chaff he will burn with unquenchable fire. (Matt 3:12)

His winnowing fork is in his hand to clear his threshing floor and to gather (συναγαγεῖν) the wheat into his barn, but the chaff he will burn with unquenchable fire. (Luke 3:17)

The Baptist uses the agricultural metaphor of winnowing and collecting grain to speak of the eschatological gathering of the saved by the one coming after John, which the text implies is Jesus. However, when Jesus uses this same gathering language to speak of separating the good from the wicked, he broadens the participation in this task. Jesus does not speak of those who are gathered *by* him versus those who are scattered, but those who gather *with* him and those who scatter. Where John's language envisions Jesus working alone to separate the saved from the condemned, Jesus' language paints the binary as those working with him and those working against him. Jesus is the key figure about whom a decision is demanded, but the decision in the Beelzebul Controversy is whether to be Jesus' coworker or Jesus' opponent.

Throughout the Q version of the Beelzebul Controversy, Jesus construes his miracle working in the context of the eschatological victory over Satan, just as Mark does. However, in the Double Tradition, Jesus uses metaphors—the kingdoms of God and Satan—that emphasize the corporate nature of the opposing forces of good and evil, and Jesus strongly implies that others, such as the other exorcists and those who gather with him, participate alongside him in the conquest of Satan. The exorcisms show that this conquest is occurring, and these miracles invite others who recognize them as indicators of this conquest to join with Jesus in the victory of the kingdom of God over the kingdom of Satan.

CONCLUSION

Chapter 2 looked at accusations of magic in the ancient world and found that the accusers and respondents were engaged in a double contest both to place the miracle worker in a category of deviance or of social acceptability and also to define these categories. Someone who tells the story of such a dispute gets to determine how these contests play out. Both Mark and the Double Tradition construct their contests so that the disputants do not define their categories in terms of evil magic versus legitimate miracle working or in terms of fraud versus actual supernatural occurrence, categories with widespread currency in turn-of-the-Era literature among both Jews and non-Jews. Rather, the authors have Jesus and his opponents define their categories in terms of alliance with or opposition to Satan, and so they draw on the specifically Jewish story of the arch-fiend who opposes the God of Israel. The authors have Jesus emphasize the eschatological significance of such alliance or opposition. In both versions Jesus turns the accusation back on the accusers by implying that their failure to locate Jesus in the proper category shows that they are the deviant ones: in Mark the accusers are guilty of the eternal sin, while in Q they will be judged by their sons.

Jesus and his opponents share belief in the existence of a chief demon who opposes Israel's God and will meet his doom in the eschaton. Within their shared worldview the difference between Jesus and his opponents is slight: they locate Jesus differently in the combat between God and the devil. Just because this distinction is slight, does not mean it is unimportant. This distinction in where Jesus fits into the grand eschatological drama makes the difference between those who are right and those who are wrong. The narrative serves the narcissism of minor differences in magnifying this distinction into the crucial boundary between right and wrong. In repudiating his opponents in the Beelzebul Controversy, Jesus symbolically repudiates those who share the belief in the victory of Israel's God over the forces of evil but who fail to see that this victory is occurring in Jesus' ministry, such as non-Jesus following Jews. The Controversy also implies that recognition of Jesus' eschatological role is one aspect of the identity of Jesus followers, so this story could also marginalize fellow followers who did not recognize an eschatological role for Jesus. Telling the story would have been one way for early Jesus followers to create identity for themselves by explaining why the difference between following Jesus and not following Jesus was so important: because to follow Jesus meant to be on the right side of the coming eschatological victory over evil.

Claiming a singular eschatological role for Jesus is a way to create a group identity for Jesus followers, but this singularity comes at a price. The more singular Jesus' role becomes, the less and less do his followers participate directly in this victory. Mark, by framing the exorcisms as evidence of Jesus' conquest of Satan, makes Jesus central to God's eschatological victory. The early Jesus followers that told this version of the story could see themselves as the beneficiaries of the eschatological victory. Their recognition of Jesus as the eschatological victor clearly marked them off against those who did not share this recognition. The Double Tradition, by framing the exorcisms as evidence of the victory of the kingdom of God over the kingdom of Satan, makes Jesus the key participant in the battle between God's forces and Satan's. The early Jesus followers who told this version of the story could envision themselves as Jesus' co-workers in this victory and see that allegiance to Jesus marked which side one took in this battle. The major distinction is between viewing Jesus as winning the eschatological victory, from which his followers benefit, and viewing Jesus working together with his followers in this victory.

NOTES

1. The MT does not name the Egyptian magicians, although the names do appear in Targum Pseudo-Jonathan to Exod 7:11. 2 Tim 3:8 mentions that "Jannes and Jambres opposed Moses."

2. I. M. Lewis, *Ecstatic Religion: A Study of Shamanism and Spirit Posession* (London: Routledge, 2003). This model is frequently employed by New Testament scholars to understand the Beelzebul Controversy as evidence of Jesus' solidarity with the excluded and downtrodden in their struggle against their society's elites. See Paul W. Hollenbach, "Jesus, Demoniacs, and Public Authorities: A Socio-Historical Study," *JAAR* 49.3 (1981): 567–88; Ched Myers, *Binding the Strong Man: A Political Reading of Mark's Story of Jesus* (Maryknoll, NY: Orbis, 1988), 164–65; Santiago Guijarro, "The Politics of Exorcism: Jesus' Reaction to Negative Labels in the Beelzebul Controversy," *BTB* 29.3 (1999): 118–29; Amanda Witmer, *Jesus the Galilean Exorcist: His Exorcisms in Social and Political Context* (London: T&T Clark, 2012), 27, 116–17; Cheryl S. Pero, *Liberation from Empire: Demonic Possession and Exorcism in the Gospel of Mark* (New York: Peter Lang, 2013), 25.

3. Lewis, *Ecstatic Religion,* 59–89, 90–113.

4. Ibid., 27.

5. Janice Boddy, "Spirit Posession Revisited: Beyond Instrumentality," *Annual Review of Anthropology* 23 (1994): 410–14.

6. Paula Fredriksen, "The Question of Worship: Gods, Pagans, and the Redemption of Israel," in *Paul Within Judaism: Restoring the First-Century Context to the Apostle,* eds. Mark D. Nanos and Magnus Zetterholm (Minneapolis: Fortress, 2015), 195–98; James M. Scott, *Paul and the Nations: The Old Testament and Jewish Background of Paul's Mission to the Nations with Special Reference to the Destination of Galatians* (Tübingen: Mohr Siebeck, 1995), 73, 133–35; Terence L. Donaldson, *Judaism and the Gentiles: Jewish Patterns of Universalism* (Waco, TX: Baylor University Press, 2007), 505, 509.

7. Tess Rajak, "Talking at Trypho: Christian Apologetic as Anti-Judaism in Justin's *Dialogue with Trypho the Jew,*" in *Apologetics in the Roman Empire: Pagans, Jews, and Christians,* eds. Mark Edwards, Martin Goodman, and Simon Price (Oxford: Oxford University Press, 1999), 61–62; Jennifer Wright Knust, "Roasting the Lamb: Sacrifice and Sacred Text in Justin's Dialogue with Trypho," in *Religion and Violence: The Biblical Heritage,* eds. David A. Bernat and Jonathan Klawans (Sheffield: Sheffield Phoenix, 2007), 100–103.

8. Collins, *Mark,* 271.

9. Hüneburg, *Jesus,* 212.

10. Marcus, *Mark 1–8,* 284; Collins, *Mark,* 234–35. For more on Mark's interpretation of the unforgivable sin logion, see James G. Williams, "Note on the Unforgivable Sin Logion," *New Testament Studies* 12.1 (1965): 75–77; John Cochrane O'Neill, "The Unforgivable Sin,' *Journal for the Study of the New Testament* 19 (1983): 37–42.

11. Klutz, *Exorcism,* 125–33.

12. Humphries, *Christian Origins,* 51.

13. Humphries, *Christian Origins,* 52.

14. Marcus, *Mark 1–8,* 282.

15. Humphries, *Christian Origins,* 53.

16. Elizabeth Struthers Malbon, "Narrative Criticism: How Does the Story Mean," in *Mark and Method,* eds. Janice Capel Anderson and Stephen D. Moore (Minneapolis: Fortress, 2008), 39.

17. David Rhoads and Donald Michie, *Mark as Story: An Introduction to the Narrative of a Gospel* (Philadelphia: Fortress, 1983), 51. Also see Robert M. Fowler, *Let the Reader Understand: Reader-Response Criticism and the Gospel of Mark* (Philadelphia: Fortress, 1991), 143, and Scott G. Brown, "Mark11:1–12:12: A Triple Intercalation?" *CBQ* 64.1 (2002): 78–79.

18. The NRSV seeks to soften the attitude of Jesus' family by translating 3:21, "When his family heard it, they went out to restrain him, for *people* were saying, 'He has gone out of his mind'" (emphasis mine). The Greek does not provide an explicit subject for the last independent clause (ἔλεγον γὰρ ὅτι ἐξέστη). The nearest plural antecedent is Jesus' family (οἱ παρ' αὐτοῦ), and they are the most natural referents as the ones saying this about Jesus.

19. Marcus, *Mark 1–8,* 188.

20. Collins, *Mark,* 173.

21. LXX lacks rebuking: "many nations as so much water, as so much water falling violently, he will condemn them and pursue them as the dust of chaff when men winnow in the wind and as a storm carries dust in a circle."

22. Howard Clark Kee, "The Terminology of Mark's Exorcism Stories," *NTS* 14.2 (1968): 242–45.

23. Gerd Theissen, *The Miracle Stories of the Early Christian Tradition,* tr. John Kenneth Riches (Edinburgh: T&T Clark, 1983), 70.

24. Marcus, *Mark 1–8,* 190–92; Collins, *Mark,* 173.

25. Markus Lau, "Die Legio X Fretensis und der Besessene von Gerasa. Ammerkungen zur Zahlenangabe 'ungefähr Zweitausend' (Mk 5,13)," *Biblica* 88.3 (2013): 351–64.

26. Collins, *Mark,* 270.

27. Macrus, *Mark 1–8,* 354.

28. Amy-Jill Levine, "Matthew's Advice to a Divided Readership," in *The Gospel of Matthew in Current Study,* ed. David E. Aune (Grand Rapids, MI: Eerdmans, 2001), 37–38.

29. Wendy J. Cotter, *The Christ of the Miracle Stories: Portrait Through Encounter* (Grand Rapids: Baker Academic, 2010), 10–12.

30. Marcus, *Mark,* 2:653.

31. Collins, *Mark,* 437.

32. Ibid., 439.

33. Marcus, *Mark 8–16,* 665.

34. In contrast to the Qumran *War Scroll,* which explicitly depicts the Qumran sectarians fighting battles against the Dominion of Belial (1QM 1.13–15, 18.1). See Collins, *Mark,* 232–33.

35. Fledderman, *Q,* 506.

36. Humphries, *Christian Origins,* 33; Fledderman, *Q,* 506; Huneburg, *Jesus,* 212. For an argument against, see Twelftree, *Jesus the Exorcist,* 109. Twelftree's arguments ultimately are not persuasive because if the authors of the Double Tradition had meant to qualify the relationship of other exorcists to Jesus, they could have done so.

37. Joseph Vlcek Kozar, "Meeting the Perfect Stranger: The Literary Role and Social Location of the Encounter Between Jesus and the Strange Exorcist in Mark 9:38–41," *Proceedings of the Eastern Great Lakes and Midwestern Biblical Society* 24 (2004): 103–23; Harry Fleddermann, "The Discipleship Discourses (Mark 9:33–50)," *CBQ* 43.1 (1981): 64–66; Robert H. Gundry, *Mark: A Commentary on His Apology for the Cross* (Grand Rapids: Eerdmans, 1993), 510; Richard A. Horsley, *Hearing the Whole Story: The Politics of Plot in Mark's Gospel* (Louisville, KY: Westminster John Knox, 2001), 96.

38. BDAG 856–57, φθάνω. Also, Meier, *Marginal Jew,* 2:412; Beasley-Murray, *Kingdom,* 78.

39. e.g. Rom 9:31, 2 Cor 10:14, Phil 3:16, 1 Thess 2:16. Only in 1 Thess 4:15 does it carry the meaning "to precede."

40. Meier, *Marginal Jew,* 2:412; Twelftree, *Jesus the Exorcist,* 92.

41. Klutz, *Exorcism,* 131–33.

42. Jacques Schlosser, "Q et la christologie implicite," in *The Sayings Source Q and the Historical Jesus,* ed. Andreas Lindermann (Leuven: Leuven University Press, 2001), 314.

Chapter Five

The Commissioning of the Disciples

According to the Grand Inquisitor, the Church claims to act as Jesus' successor while it wields the power of miracle that Jesus actually rejected. The relationship among Jesus, his successors, and the power of miracles features also in Mark and the Double Tradition; both describe Jesus delivering the power to heal in his Commissioning of the Disciples. Telling such a story generated a positive group identity for Jesus followers by affirming that Jesus' healing power persisted among them even when Jesus was physically gone. Mark and Q, however, differently construe how healings demonstrate the continuity between Jesus and his followers. For the Double Tradition, the healings manifest the presence of eschatological blessings; in their healings the disciples make present the Kingdom of God as Jesus did. In Mark, however, the healings demonstrate the power of Jesus, and the disciples' healings show that they derive their power from him.

To make this argument, this chapter begins by laying out the Mark and Double Tradition versions and then moves on to examine them using Max Weber's concept of charisma in the context of religious groups handling successions. Weber's framework demonstrates how the story of Jesus handing over healing power allowed the tellers to inculcate a positive identity for the group of early Jesus followers. The chapter then turns to the Mark and Q versions of the Commissioning along with their relevant co-texts to demonstrate the distinct ways these two versions depict the relationship between the disciples' healings and those of Jesus.

Mark's Commissioning comes in the sixth chapter:

> And he called the twelve and he began to send them two by two and gave them authority over unclean spirits. And he ordered them to take nothing on the road except only a staff, neither bread, nor a bag, nor copper in their belts, but to bind their sandals and not wear two tunics. And he said to them, "Whenever

you enter into a house, stay there until you leave from that place. And whatever place does not receive you or does not hear you, when you leave from there
shake off the dust from under your feet as a testimony against them." And
going out they proclaimed that people should repent, and they cast out many
demons, and they anointed many sick people with oil and healed them. (Mark
6:7–13)

In Luke Jesus sends out his disciples twice. First Jesus sends out the Twelve:

And calling the twelve together he gave them power and authority over all the
demons and to cure diseases, and he sent them to proclaim the kingdom of God
and to heal the sick. And he said to them, "Do not take anything on the road,
neither a staff, nor a sack, nor bread, nor silver nor two tunics to have at hand.
And into whatever house you enter, stay there and go out from there. And
whoever does not receive you, when you go out from that city, shake off the
dust from your feet as testimony against them." And going out, they passed
through the villages, proclaiming the good news and healing everywhere."
(Luke 9:1–6)

A little later, Jesus sends a group of seventy-two with similar instructions:

And after these things the Lord appointed another seventy-two and sent them
two by two before him into all the cities and places where he was about to go.
He said to them, "The harvest is plentiful, but the workers are few. Pray then
that the Lord of the harvest send out workers into his harvest. Go. Behold I
send you as sheep in the midst of wolves. Do not carry a purse, nor a sack, nor
sandals, and do not greet anyone along the road. Into whatever house you
enter, say first, 'Peace to this house.' And if there is a son of peace is there, let
your peace rest on him, but if not, let your peace turn back to yourselves.
Remain in that house eating and drinking whatever is from it, for the worker is
worthy of his wages. Do not go about from house to house. And into whatever
city you enter and they receive you, eat what is set before you and heal the sick
in it and say to them, 'The kingdom of God has come near to you.' But into
whatever city you enter and they do not receive you, go out into its main street
and say, 'Even the dust of your city that clings to our feet, we wipe off in
protest against you. Yet know this, that the kingdom of God has come near.' I
tell you, on that day it will be more tolerable for Sodom than for that city."
(Luke 10:1–12)

Matthew presents a single set of mission instructions that combines elements
found in both Lukan versions:

Then he said to his disciples, "The harvest is plentiful, but the workers are few.
Pray then that the Lord of the harvest send out workers into his harvest." And
calling his twelve disciples, he gave to them authority over unclean spirits to
cast them out and to heal all illness and every malady. . . . These twelve Jesus
sent, ordering them, saying "Do not go into the way of Gentiles nor enter a city
of Samaritans, but go rather to the lost sheep of the house of Israel. And as you

go, proclaim saying that the kingdom of heaven has come near. The sick heal, the dead raise, those with leprosy cleanse, demons cast out. Freely you received, freely give. Do not put gold or silver or copper into your belts, nor a sack for the road nor two tunics nor sandals nor a staff, for the worker is worthy of his food. Into whatever city or town you enter, inquire who in it is worthy. Stay there until you leave. When you enter into the house, greet it and, if the house is worthy, let your peace come upon it, but if it is not worthy, let your peace return to you. And whoever does not receive you or hear your words, when you go out from that house or that city, shake off the dust from your feet. Amen I say to you, it will be more tolerable for Sodom and Gomorrah on the day of judgment than for that city. Behold I send you as sheep in the midst of wolves. Become then as wise as serpents but as innocent as doves." (Matt 9:38–10:16)

These passages present another example of overlap between Mark and the Double Tradition. Among supporters of the Q hypothesis, the consensus has been that Luke 9:1–6 (the sending of the Twelve) represents Luke's rendering of the Markan version, while Luke 10:1–11 represents a rendering of the Q version; Matthew has combined elements of the Markan and Q versions in one discourse.[1]

The features found in Matthew and Luke, but absent from Mark, include:

1. The link between the disciples' healing the sick and proclaiming the kingdom of God (Matt 10:7//Luke 9:2, 10:9)
2. Jesus' saying about the harvest and the laborers (Matt 9:37–38//Luke 10:2)
3. Jesus forbidding the disciples from taking silver, sandals, or a staff on their journey (Matt 10:9–10//Luke 9:3, 10:4)
4. The disciples' peace resting on a house or returning to them (Matt 10:12//Luke 10:5)
5. The saying that it will be more tolerable for Sodom than for a town that rejects the disciples (Matt 10:15//Luke 10:12)
6. Jesus' saying about sheep in the midst of wolves (Matt 10:16//Luke 10:3)
7. Jesus' saying about laborers being worthy of their wages or food (Matt 10:10//Luke 10:7)

For the purposes of this book, the linking of the disciples' healing miracles and the kingdom of God in the Double Tradition is the most salient:

And as you go, proclaim saying that the kingdom of heaven has come near (ἤγγικεν). The sick heal, the dead raise, those with leprosy cleanse, demons cast out. Freely you received, freely give. (Matt 10:7–8)

And heal the sick in it [i.e., the city the disciple has entered] and say to them:
the kingdom of God has come near (ἤγγικεν) to you. (Luke 10:9)

Both Matthew and Luke have Jesus command the disciples to heal the sick combined with the command to proclaim that the kingdom of God/heaven has come near. In Mark Jesus empowers the disciples to perform miracles: "[He] gave them authority (ἐξουσίαν) over the unclean spirits" (Mark 6:7). Mark's brief résumé of the disciples' subsequent activities also mentions miracle working: "And going out they proclaimed that people should repent, and they cast out many demons, and they anointed many sick people with oil and healed them" (Mark 6:12–13). The investigation of the Commissioning in Mark and Q will begin with what they share: Jesus empowering the disciples to perform miracles.

CHARISMA AND SUCCESSION

The Commissioning depicts Jesus passing on the ability to perform miracles to the people who would lead his movement after his death. Telling this story generated a sense of continuity among Jesus followers by portraying their lord's charismatic authority persisting beyond his death.

The succession of charismatic authority frequently becomes contentious for New Religious Movements (NRMs) when the founder dies and the group must create an identity that persists in the founder's absence. Examples from modern NRMs show that claims regarding a second-generation leader's access to the charismatic authority of the founder run on a spectrum. On one end, followers depict the second-generation leaders with nearly equal charisma as the founder. On the other end, the group restricts second-generation leadership to sharing only a small portion of the founder's charisma. Biblical examples demonstrate that concerns about succession exist not only in modern NRMs, and these biblical examples also show that the stories of succession of charismatic authority boost communal self-identity even after any conflict over proper succession have been settled. The Mark and Q versions of the Commissioning similarly attempt to demonstrate the continuity of charismatic authority, but they differ in how charisma is shared between Jesus and the disciples.

Charismatic leadership is a common, but by no means universal, feature of NRMs, and the concept of charisma has proven useful for the study of succession in NRMs. Max Weber first developed the concept of charismatic leadership to analyze political power, and sociologists and historians used the concept to study twentieth-century political movements that relied on the personality of their leaders, such as National Socialism.[2] Although Weber developed the concept of charismatic leadership to describe a certain kind of political leadership in the modern West, investigators of NRMs have found charismatic leadership to be a useful concept in their field as well.[3]

Weber studied how groups legitimize the authority of leaders. He developed a three-part typology of legitimating authority. (1) *Legal authority* bases its legitimacy on a set of laws that grant the right to command to those empowered under the laws. (2) *Traditional authority* bases its legitimacy on the traditions of a community that grant power to certain members of that community. Finally, (3) *charismatic authority* legitimizes itself by "devotion to the exceptional sanctity, heroism or exemplary character of an individual person, and of the normative patterns or order revealed or ordained by him."[4] Weber points out both that this typology is a conceptual tool and that any existing authority will not strictly conform to only one type.[5] For instance, Jesus' leadership is based on his extraordinary personal qualities, but he also connects his authority with the traditions of Israel; thereby he mixes charismatic and traditional modes of legitimation.

Succession of charismatic leadership will inevitably cause problems. Weber noted that charismatic leadership is fundamentally unstable because it is based on the force of the leader's personality. The charismatic leader must constantly give evidence of his charisma. If the group is to outlive its original leader, the charismatic authority must somehow transfer to successors in ways that the group perceives as valid. Weber believed charismatic authority to be so unstable that to persist it must be transformed into either traditional or legal authority, a process that Weber called the "routinization of charisma."[6] NRMs that survive the death of their charismatic leaders have to find some way to routinize charisma so that the charismatic authority can persist in the absence of the original leader's compelling personality.

The history of modern American NRM's is littered with groups who failed to routinize charisma successfully. The Oneida Community of New York collapsed as a religious community when it refused to recognize a successor with the charismatic authority of its founder.[7] The Theosophical Society splintered and dissolved after multiple claimants to charismatic authority arose after the founder's death.[8] To transfer charismatic authority successfully, NRM's walk a fine line of viewing the second generation leadership as sharing the founder's charisma while at the same time restricting this charisma in some way so that the group does not collapse under the weight of multiple conflicting claims to authority.[9] NRM's adopt various strategies in sharing or restricting charisma in the second-generation leadership. The several offshoots of the Latter Day Saints (LDS) movement that arose after Joseph Smith's death in 1844 illustrate the ways NRMs can transfer charismatic authority. Although many of these offshoots were relatively short-lived, several managed to persist as distinct communities for some time after Smith's death. These successor movements illustrate the spectrum of strategies available to connect second-generation leadership to the charismatic power of the founder.

Brigham Young led what would become the Church of Jesus Christ of Latter Day Saints based on claims of procedural legitimacy according to the rules laid down by Smith. Charismatic authority in this branch of Mormonism remained highly restricted to Smith, with subsequent leaders claiming a legal authority according to the norms that Smith promulgated. In this branch of the Mormon movement, although leaders retained the status of prophet, there was a great reluctance to add much authoritative teaching to that promulgated by Smith.[10]

The nascent leadership of another branch of the LDS movement, the Reorganized Church of Jesus Christ of Latter Day Saints (RLDS), kept a more charismatic form of leadership. In 1851, Jason Biggs received a revelation from God that Joseph Smith's son, Joseph Smith III, was the prophetic successor, a role the younger Smith ultimately accepted when he became leader of the RLDS Church. In the RLDS Church, succession was determined by the current prophet naming his successor, and the successor prophets were much more willing to add authoritative teaching than the prophets among the Utah Mormons under Young.[11] Charisma was routinized in that a well-established rule determined succession, but the current holder of the charismatic authority, rather than a set of rules, determined who would assume authority. Moreover, charisma was shared among the successor prophets, rather than restricted to Joseph Smith.

James J. Strang spearheaded yet another LDS successor movement after Smith's death. Strang bolstered his claims to authority by producing a document, allegedly written by Smith, that named Strang as Smith's successor. Strang also claimed to have direct revelation from angelic messengers, and he produced a translation of a set of ancient metal plates given him by an angel. Strang claimed charismatic authority by recapitulating Smith's prophetic actions and set himself up almost as a second Smith.[12]

A fourth branch followed another successor who claimed direct divine warrant. William Bickerton organized his Mormon Church by claiming charismatic authority for himself even though he had not known Joseph Smith. Bickerton was baptized in 1845, the year after Smith died. Bickerton claimed that he received visions from God validating him as the restorer of true Mormon teaching that Smith had originally proclaimed, but that had become corrupted. In 1862, Bickerton organized a branch of Mormonism that recognized his teachings as the reestablishment of the pure Church. His followers recognized Bickerton as God's chosen heir to Joseph Smith even though neither he nor his followers had been part of Smith's original movement.[13]

These successors to Joseph Smith demonstrate the spectrum of strategies available for NRMs to maintain continuity in their second generation. On one end of the spectrum, charismatic authority is almost entirely restricted to the founder, and succession is therefore not based on sharing this charisma, as in the case of Brigham Young. On the other end of the spectrum, the second-generation leadership shares the charisma of the founder and recapitulates his striking deeds, as Strang did. The RLDS represents a middle point, with successor prophets claiming charismatic authority in continuity with Smith, but not claiming the sort of direct angelic revelation that Smith and Strang claimed for themselves. Bickerton's success reveals that charismatic succession can occur even when the second-generation leader never met the living founder. Succession can succeed if the successor can convince followers that he or she shares the same source of charismatic authority, which in the LDS case was visionary access to God.

After Jesus' death his early followers faced a dilemma analogous to that of modern NRMs on the deaths of their founders. Jesus' followers needed a way to transfer his charismatic authority to the nascent movement's leadership. In achieving this transfer, they faced the same tension of whether to restrict charisma to Jesus or to impute the same charisma to subsequent leaders. One way that these modern NRMs imputed charismatic authority to the second generation was to represent second-generation leaders sharing the same manifestations of charisma as the founder, as when Strang received ancient texts from angels just as had Smith. Many of these second-generation leaders claimed their charismatic authority on the basis of a commissioning either by the original leader, as in James Strang's claim, or by a divine decree, as with Joseph Smith III and William Bickerton.

The Pauline epistles reveal similar dynamics in claiming charismatic authority. Like William Bickerton, Paul had to convince others of his authority even though he was not part of the movement during the founder's lifetime. Throughout his letters, Paul burnishes his own authority vis-à-vis his opponents, and nowhere does he do so more clearly than in the narration of his calling in the beginning of Galatians:

> For I make known to you, brothers, that the good news that is proclaimed by me is not of human origin, for I did not receive it from a human being nor was I taught it, but I received it through a revelation of Jesus Christ . . . when God, who had set me apart from my mother's womb and called me through his grace, was pleased to reveal his Son to me, so that I might proclaim his good news among the nations, immediately I did not consult with flesh and blood nor did I go up into Jerusalem to those who were apostles before me, but I went into Arabia and again returned to Damascus. Then after three years I went up into Jerusalem to visit Cephas and stayed with him fifteen days. I did not see other apostles except James the brother of the Lord. (Gal 1:11–12, 15–19)

Paul here makes clear that his authority comes from God, not from Peter, James, or any other of the Jerusalem apostles. The series of negatives ("not of human origin," "not . . . from a human being," "not . . . with flesh and blood," "nor . . . up to Jerusalem," "not . . . other apostles") emphasizes that his message, and hence his authority, has a divine, not human, source.[14] Paul claims for himself a charismatic authority that sets him as an equal to the other apostles and not as an inheritor of a traditional authority handed down to him.[15]

Elsewhere in his letters, Paul appeals to his miracle-working powers to substantiate his charismatic authority. Regarding his dispute with the super-apostles in Corinth, Paul assures the Corinthians, "I am in no way inferior to the super-apostles . . . the signs of an apostle were performed among you in all endurance, signs and wonders and deeds of power" (2 Cor 12:11–12). Miracles here function to verify apostolic authority. Similarly, Paul tells the Romans of "what Christ has accomplished through me toward the obedience of the Gentiles," which includes "signs and wonders" (Rom 15:18–19). Paul reminds the Romans that he has led Gentiles by the power of his miraculous deeds. Paul defends his legitimacy as a leader with reference to the miracles that manifest his charismatic authority.[16]

Paul's claims to charismatic authority are certainly self-serving, but such claims also serve the interests of his hearers. Recognizing a charismatic leader legitimizes the group that follows that leader, and the divine warrant of the leader generates a positive social identity for the group that follows him.[17] Thus, although a story of a second-generation leader receiving the charisma of the group's founder may bolster that leader's claim to authority against rival claimants, as in the case of Paul's call narration from Galatians, the story continues to enhance in-group positivity even without an active conflict over leadership. In other words, the *Sitz im Leben* of such stories can be a situation of rival leaders, but it does not have to be.

The Tanakh provides several examples of such commissioning stories without the polemical edge of Paul's autobiographical narration. Moses serves as a charismatic leader of the Israelites during the Exodus in that he receives his call to leadership from God and performs signs and wonders to liberate God's people. Upon his death, Moses, with God's prompting, com-missions Joshua as his successor to lead the Israelites into the Promised Land (Num 27:18–23, Deut 31:7–23). God chooses Joshua as Moses' successor, and Moses duly recognizes Joshua's legitimacy and makes it known to the Israelites. While the Pentateuch connects Moses and Joshua via the commis-sioning story, the author of the Book of Joshua does so by means of parallel miracles: just as Moses led the Israelites through the parted Red Sea (Exodus 14), so does Joshua lead them through the parted waters of the Jordan River (Joshua 3). The author makes this connection explicit in depicting God tell-ing Joshua, "This day I will begin to exalt you in the sight of all Israel, so that they may know that I will be with you as I was with Moses" (Josh 3:7). The miracle evidences God's continuing presence both with Joshua as Moses's heir and with the whole community of Israel.

This motif of charismatic power to part the Jordan reappears in the Dueteronomistic History. As Elijah is about to be taken up by the Lord, he with his successor Elisha comes to the Jordan River: "Then Elijah took his mantle and rolled it up, and struck the water; the water was parted to the one side and to the other, until the two of them crossed on dry ground" (2 Kings 2:8). Elisha then asks and receives a double share of Elijah's spirit as the latter goes up to heaven in a fiery chariot; Elisha picks up the mantle that Elijah dropped and uses it to part the Jordan on his way back (2 Kings 2:14). Elisha then performs several miracles that replicate those of Elijah, such as the raising of a dead child (1 Kings 17:22–23, 2 Kings 4:32–37) and multiplying insufficient foodstuffs (1 Kings 17:14–16, 2 Kings 4:42–44). Such parallel miracles form part of a dense intercalation of words, motifs, and stories that relate Elisha to Elijah.[18] The parting of the Jordan in particular links Elisha and Elijah not just to each other, but also to Joshua and Moses, and it creates a sense of continuity, of God's ongoing presence with Israel, throughout the careers of these charismatic leaders.

Such stories of charismatic succession serve both the leader and the community. Modern and ancient NRM's face a crisis of continuity when the original charismatic leader dies. In such environments, stories that show the second-generation leadership receiving charismatic gifts like the founder's help the groups maintain identity and cohesion. The stories of Moses, Joshua, Elijah, and Elisha attribute miraculous powers to the successors of miracle workers to illustrate the continuance of the predecessor's charismatic power. Similarly, the evangelists portray Jesus' power at work in his disciples and so in the group that follows his successors. Such a portrayal would have had maximum relevance for people that were forming their group identity by envisioning themselves as the heirs of Jesus' charisma. However, as noted above, such a group must strike a delicate balance in the extent to which its founder's charisma is shared or restricted. The Mark and Q versions of the commissioning of the disciples present slightly different strategies in this balancing act, and it is to the specifics of each variant that this chapter now turns.

THE COMMISSIONING IN MARK

In the Commissioning, Mark restricts Jesus' charisma so that the disciples share only a derivative form of it. Mark describes the disciples engaging in three primary activities in their mission: exorcising demons, healing the sick, and proclaiming repentance. All three activities replicate an aspect of Jesus' ministry, but in each case the disciples' work emphasizes Jesus' preeminence. Only a portion of Jesus' charisma is evident in his followers' activities.

Although Jesus has many disciples, Mark restricts the commissioning to the inner circle of the Twelve (3:14–19). Twelve, the number of the tribes of Israel, was pregnant with meaning in Second Temple Judaism where the restoration of all twelve tribes of Israel was an eschatological hope; thus by choosing twelve followers, Jesus symbolizes the restoration of the twelve tribes that would take place soon.[19] Displaying similar symbolism, the eschatological king of the Qumran Temple Scroll has as his advisors twelve princes, twelve priests, and twelve Levites (11QT 57:2–15). The twelve disciples prefigure the eschatological community of which Jesus' followers saw themselves a part; these followers can regard themselves as the new or true Israel, an identity that even Mark's Gentile readers can adopt. Telling the story of these Twelve receiving power from Jesus reinforces the idea that Jesus' power remains at work in the community he founds.

At the same time, these Twelve in Mark are far from perfect. James and John seek their own aggrandizement (10:35–37), Peter tries to dissuade Jesus from his divinely appointed suffering (8:32–33), Judas betrays him (14:10), and the remaining eleven desert him at his arrest (14:50). Mark's lack of resurrection appearances leaves no opportunity for rehabilitation of the disciples, as the reader last sees them abandoning Jesus. The disciples fall well short of the example set by Jesus. Despite their imperfection elsewhere in the Gospel, in their mission the disciples demonstrate their connection with their leader. The disciples' activities mirror those of Jesus and demonstrate the continuity between Jesus and the community that he founds, as epitomized by the Twelve.[20] The way Mark links and differentiates the activity of the disciples and the activity of Jesus reveals how the evangelist interprets Jesus' power at work among his followers.

Exorcising Demons

Mark reports that Jesus gave his disciples "authority (ἐξουσία) over unclean spirits" (6:7). Mark could have told of Jesus' transferring power (δύναμις) to his disciples, but he instead uses ἐξουσία. Although these words have similar connotations, there is a subtle difference between them that is most apparent in the verbal forms to which they are both related: ἐξουσία is related to ἔξεστιν (it is allowed) while δύναμις is related to δύναμαι (I am able). At root, to have ἐξουσία indicates that one can do something because a higher entity (laws, society, a deity) allows it, or because no higher entity forbids it, whereas to have δύναμις indicates that one can do something because he or she possesses the ability to do so.[21]

In both its classical and Septuagintal uses, ἐξουσία has a distinctly hierarchical character.[22] One exercises ἐξουσία to the extent that it is vested by a higher power, either God, a god, or the laws of a land. This ἐξουσία denotes an authority over some entity or set of entities, be they inanimate, human, or supernatural. The wielders of ἐξουσία thus occupy a middle position in a hierarchy—they have received this ἐξουσία from a superior to exercise over a set of subordinates. Such a tripartite schema does not hold universally; God does not receive ἐξουσία from some higher power. In the Commissioning, however, the disciples fit this hierarchical scheme: they receive ἐξουσία from Jesus to exercise over unclean spirits.

New Testament writers used the word δύναμις similarly to denote an ability granted, as when the author of Hebrews notes how Abraham in his old age "received the power (δύναμιν) for the creation of offspring" (Heb 11:11). However, δύναμις more frequently refers to the power to do something rather than indicating from whom this power derived or over whom this power was exercised.[23] The word could refer to the abstract quality of power without specific reference to what the possessor was empowered to do, as when Paul speaks about the "power (δύναμις) of Christ" that dwells within him (2 Cor 12:9) or about God's "eternal power (δύναμις)" manifest in creation (Rom 1:20). The word can also refer to miracles, which are concrete manifestations of power (e.g., Acts 2:22; 8:13; 19:11; 1 Cor 12:10, 28–29; 2 Cor 12:12).[24] Mark similarly uses δύναμις to refer to miracles (6:2,5; 9:39) and to the power that either Jesus (5:30; 6:14; 13:26) or God possesses (9:1; 12:24; 14:62). Mark does not use δύναμις in the context of the hierarchical relationship of granter-wielder-subordinate that ἐξουσία denotes. Instead of showing the disciples as possessing δύναμις within themselves, Mark chooses to locate them within the granter-wielder-subordinate hierarchy of ἐξουσία.

Mark places the disciples in the middle of this hierarchy and so emphasizes their subordination to Jesus. The disciples receive their ἐξουσία from Jesus. This ἐξουσία resides within Jesus, and it is his to grant, although Mark's Jesus does not make clear whether this ἐξουσία is innately his or whether God granted it to him. This ἐξουσία subjects the unclean spirits to those who wield it. The previous chapter discussed how Jesus' exorcisms demonstrate his victory over Satan and his demons. In the commissioning of the disciples, Mark describes Jesus' victory over the demons as ἐξουσία that Jesus is able to dispense to his followers. The disciples recapitulate the actions of Jesus in casting out demons, but they do so through the authority Jesus granted them.

The Markan co-texts further illustrate the nature of this authority that Jesus gives to his disciples. In the naming of the Twelve, Mark states that Jesus called them "to be with him and to send them out to proclaim and to have authority (ἐξουσίαν) to cast out demons" (3:14–15). The sending of the Twelve on mission in Mark 6 clearly echoes their initial naming in Mark 3; the sending fulfills the function for which Jesus called them. In Mark 3, the authority is again Jesus' to grant to the disciples whom he chooses. The authority of the Twelve is fundamentally the authority of Jesus.[25]

The word ἐξουσία also appears in the apocalyptic discourse after Jesus predicts his future coming as the Son of Man. He tells his disciples, "Beware, keep alert, for you do not know when the time is. It is as when a man on a journey leaves his house and gives authority (ἐξουσία) to his slaves, to each his work, and the doorman he orders to keep watch" (Mark 13:33–34). In the context of Mark 13, this short parable illustrates the situation that Jesus' followers face as they await the parousia. In the absence of the charismatic leader, the disciple exercises ἐξουσία given by him, but the disciple will also be accountable to that leader upon his return. Just as in the naming and sending of the Twelve, in this parable ἐξουσία again indicates the authority that the disciple exercises in Jesus' name.

Mark elsewhere uses ἐξουσία to refer to the authority that Jesus himself exercises. The word occurs twice in the pericope of Jesus' teaching and exorcism in the Capernaum synagogue as the crowds marvel at the authority evident in Jesus' teaching and exorcism (Mark 1:21–27). When the scribes scoff at Jesus forgiving the sins of the paralytic, Jesus tells them that he will make the paralytic walk so that they know "that the son of man has authority (ἐξουσία) to forgive sins on earth." (Mark 2:10). This issue of authority again becomes a point of contention between Jesus and his opponents in Jerusalem. The chief priests, scribes, and elders approach Jesus and ask, "By what authority (ἐξουσία) do you do these things? Who gave you this authority (ἐξουσία) to do these things?" (Mark 11:28). Jesus counters this question by asking the opponents whence came John's baptism, from heaven or from humans. The opponents refuse to answer Jesus' question, so he refuses to answer theirs. Having seen Jesus' authority in action throughout the Gospel, the reader can answer the question even if Jesus refuses: Jesus' authority comes from God, not from human beings.

In Mark, authority centers on Jesus: Mark uses ἐξουσία to refer only to the authority wielded by Jesus or granted by Jesus.[26] The commissioning of the disciples shows that the disciples share in Jesus' power over demonic forces and thus have a share in Jesus' eschatological victory over the demons. Yet the disciples' power is decidedly qualified: they receive their authority from Jesus, while Jesus, as the Son of Man, exercises his authority directly from God.

The inferiority of the disciples' authority compared to Jesus' comes to expression also in their failures in the rest of the Gospel. Although Mark presents the success of the exorcisms of the Twelve on their mission (6:13), he qualifies the disciples' exorcistic prowess by showing their inability to exorcise the demon from the convulsed boy (9:14–29). Shortly after this account, Mark also qualifies the exclusivity of the disciples' claim to Jesus' exorcistic power:

John said to him, "Teacher, we saw someone casting out demons in your name and we forbade him, because he was not following us." But Jesus said, "Do not forbid him, for there is no one who does a work of power (δύναμις) in my name and who will soon be able to malign me, for whoever is not against us is with us." (Mark 9:38–40)

Here, Jesus' name has so much potency that it can be used as a powerful incantation, much as the name of a deity is invoked in the *Greek Magical Papyri*.[27] This power is effective even in the hands of someone who is not part of Jesus' group. John's complaint against the man is that "he was not following *us*," but Jesus reframes the issue in terms of himself—"one who does a work of power in *my* name and who will soon be able to malign *me*." This alternation of pronouns emphasizes that it is the relationship to Jesus, not to the disciples, that determines whether one is "with us" or "against us."[28] The power to exorcise comes not from membership in the group, but from Jesus himself. The disciples' authority to exorcise demons derives from Jesus, is not as great as that of Jesus, and is paralleled by that of others who also have access to Jesus' power. The exorcisms show that the disciples share in Jesus' charismatic authority, but only in a derivative and partial way.

Healing the Sick

Mark does not narrate Jesus investing the disciples with the power to heal the sick. Nevertheless, Mark reports that "they anointed with oil many sick people and healed them" (Mark 6:13). The reference to anointing differentiates the disciples' healings from those of Jesus, who never heals by this method in Mark's Gospel. Healing by anointing implies the inferiority of the disciples' healings to those of Jesus.

Anointing the sick with oil appears only one other time in the New Testament, near the close of the Epistle of James:

Is someone among you sick? Let him call upon the elders of the church and let them pray over him, anointing him with oil in the name of the Lord. And the prayer of the faithful will save the sick person and the Lord will raise him. (James 5:14)

Both Mark and James assume that the practice of anointing with oil for healing requires no explanation for their audiences.[29] In the ancient Mediterranean world, oil was renowned for medicinal efficacy in addition to having magical and apotropaic properties.[30] Hearers of Mark and James familiar with these uses of oil, would have seen the role of the oil in the healing as mediating divine power.[31]

The use of oil and reliance on prayer to save the sick, without clarification about whether this salvation involves physical healing, differentiates the Jacobean elders from the kind of charismatic healer to which Paul alludes in 1 Corinthians 12:9 in his catalog of the various gifts of the spirit.[32] James frames the aim of the ritual as saving (σῴζω) and raising (ἐγείρω), terms that could just as well apply to ultimate salvation as immediate physical healing. Moreover, the elders in James appear to derive their role in the ritual from their station as elders in the assembly rather than from their idiosyncratic and individualized charisma.[33] Thus, the Jacobean ritual may reflect the institutionalization of the power to heal and the routinization of charisma into legal authority—the physical healings of charismatic wonder workers become a ritual framed in terms of metaphorical healing with officiants chosen based on office.[34] The Markan story of the disciples' healing by anointing likely reflects this practice in the early church, so the story depicts the same routinization of charisma.

The disciples' use of oil differentiates their healings from those of Jesus in Mark. Mark narrates Jesus healing nine individuals.[35] In two of these stories (the paralytic [2:1–12] and the man with the withered hand [3:1–6]) Jesus heals by his word, just as he commands demons with his powerful word. In the other seven stories, Jesus heals by touch with or without words. The power to heal resides in Jesus, in his words and in his body.[36] In two of these instances Jesus uses material besides his touch and word to effect the healing. To heal a deaf man with a speech impediment, Jesus "put his fingers into his [i.e. the man's] ears and spitting, touched his tongue, and looking up to heaven he groaned and said, 'Ephphatha,' that is 'Be opened'" (7:33–34). He similarly uses his spittle in the healing of the blind man (8:22–26). In addition to Jesus' word and touch, his spittle activates the healing. The power of his saliva reflects the power resident in him, a power that pours out from his body.[37]

The disciples' bodies, on the other hand, possess no such intrinsic healing power. Rather, Mark presents them using the symbolically charged medium of oil to effect their cures in a way that likely reflects a nascent ritual in Christian communities as they routinized the charismatic authority enacted by healing. The disciples' healing ministry mirrors that of Jesus, which links the disciples to the power of Jesus. At the same time their ministry reveals their inferior and derivative power. Jesus' healings show Jesus' power, while his disciples' healings demonstrate that Jesus' healing power is greater than theirs.

Proclaiming Repentance

In addition to casting out demons and curing the sick, the disciples "proclaimed (ἐκήρυξαν) that people should repent (μετανοῶσιν)" (Mark 6:12). This report echoes Mark's programmatic description of Jesus' ministry: "Jesus came into Galilee proclaiming (κηρύσσων) the good news of God and saying, "The time has been fulfilled and the kingdom of God has come near. Repent (μετανοεῖτε) and believe in the good news" (1:14–15). The disciples repeat Jesus' proclamation of repentance, but not the good news of the imminent kingdom of God. Chapter 3 discussed how the "kingdom of God" in Mark refers to Jesus' exercise of divine authority, incipiently present in Jesus' earthly ministry and to be realized fully when he comes as the Son of Man. Where Jesus is, there the kingdom of God is. When the disciples go out on their mission, the kingdom of God has not arrived with them.

The disciples share with John the Baptist a proclamation of repentance without mention of the good news of the kingdom of God, and this shared proclamation speaks to the disciples' role as preparers of Jesus' way. John the Baptist appears "proclaiming (κηρύσσων) a baptism of repentance (μετανοίας) for the forgiveness of sins" (1:4). John's message of repentance prepares the way for Jesus (Mark 1:2). Jesus in turn adds a proclamation of the presence of God's kingdom to the proclamation of repentance. Rather than proclaiming the fullness of this message as Jesus does, John instead proclaims only repentance to prepare for Jesus. Since the disciples proclaim the same limited message of repentance, they are preparing the way for Jesus as well. The disciples are not co-heralds of the kingdom of God along with Jesus; they are co-heralds of Jesus along with John.

Miracles and Succession in Mark

By telling the story of the mission of the Twelve, Mark shows that the ministry of Jesus lives on in his followers, though in an attenuated form. Jesus possesses his charisma uniquely, but he can transmit it to his followers. Mark's telling combines the restriction of charisma with the sharing of charisma in a way that allows Jesus' authority to remain distinct from that of the disciples even if they share some aspects of it. Jesus intrinsically possesses the power to heal and exorcise demons, while the disciples merely receive this authority from Jesus. Moreover, it is not membership in the group of disciples that grants one authority, but rather it is one's relationship to Jesus, as the story of the other exorcist (9:38–40) demonstrates. Mark also presents several characters outside the group of disciples as developing the correct attitude toward Jesus in contrast to the disciples. The disciples scorn the woman who anoints Jesus in Jerusalem for an action that Jesus lauds (14:3–9). While the disciples have deserted him, it is the centurion at the cross who is the first human in the narrative to recognize that Jesus is the Son of God (15:39). The evangelist sharply distinguishes the fallible and often blameworthy disciples from Jesus even though the disciples have some small share of Jesus' charismatic authority. Such a mix of restricting charisma to the founder and sharing some aspects of this charisma with successors is one strategy whereby groups maintain cohesion in the wake of their founders' deaths.

THE COMMISSIONING IN THE DOUBLE TRADITION

Mark's version of the Commissioning depicts the continuity between Jesus and his followers but nevertheless restricts much of the charisma to Jesus alone. The Q version, on the other hand, portrays the disciples sharing much more equally with Jesus in charismatic authority. When the disciples are charged to heal, their healings parallel those of Jesus in making present God's eschatological fulfillment. In Q, healing miracles manifest the presence of the kingdom of God even if Jesus is not the one doing the healing.

The Commissioning

In the Double Tradition, Jesus opens the Commissioning by saying, "The harvest is plentiful, but the workers (ἐργάται) are few. Pray then that the Lord of the harvest send out workers (ἐργάτας) into his harvest" (Matt 9:37–38// Luke 10:2). The harvest is a well-attested metaphor for the eschaton.[38] A similar agricultural metaphor appears in the Double Tradition when John the Baptist predicts the coming of the stronger one who will clear the threshing floor and gather wheat into barns (Matt 3:12//Luke 3:17). The previous chapter showed that in the Beelzebul Controversy, Q's Jesus includes others in the work of this eschatological gathering (Matt 12:30//Luke 11:23). Similarly, in the Commissioning Jesus conceptualizes the subsequent mission of the disciples in an eschatological framework, with the disciples laboring in the eschatological harvest.[39] The Double Tradition emphasizes the identity of the disciples as workers (ἐργάται) by repeating this identity in the justification of their receiving hospitality on their mission: "for the worker (ἐργάτης) is worthy of his food/wages" (Matt 10:10//Luke 10:7). While the disciples thus participate as workers in the eschatological harvest, Q's Jesus does not make clear how he fits into this eschatological metaphor. The Double Tradition declines to make explicit whether Jesus is the Lord of the harvest, or whether he is acting on behalf of the Lord of the harvest—i.e., God— in sending out the disciples. Unlike Mark, who sharply differentiates Jesus from the disciples, the Double Tradition presents them as working together in their eschatological task.

The eschatological import of the disciples' mission in Q receives further expression in Jesus' warning about what will happen to a city that does not receive their message:

> It will be more tolerable for Sodom and Gomorrah on the day of judgment than for that city. (Matt 10:15)

On that day it will be more tolerable for Sodom than for that city. (Luke 10:12)

The failure to receive the disciples and accept their message exposes a city to eschatological judgment. For the Double Tradition, the disciples are to proclaim that the kingdom of God/heaven "has come near (ἤγγικεν)," which they are to announce alongside their ministry of healing (Matt 10:7//Luke 10:9). The Double Tradition here uses the same verb in the same perfect tense, ἤγγικεν, as Mark does in describing Jesus' proclamation (Mk 1:15). The examination of Mark 1:15 in the previous chapter reviewed the scholarly debate as to whether the perfect tense of ἤγγικεν in Mark 1:15 reflected the nearness or the presence of God's kingdom. A similar debate exists about the nuance of this verbal form in the Q context.[40] As in the case with Mark, it seems wiser to view the word's nuance in Q as vague and allowing either interpretation. [41] Indeed, chapter 3 showed that Q material presents the kingdom of God both as incipiently present and also as coming in the near future.

The preceding chapter showed that in the Q version of the Beelzebul Controversy Jesus' exorcisms evince the dawning kingdom of God. By linking Jesus' command to proclaim the kingdom to his command to heal, the Q version of the Commissioning similarly links healing and the presence of the kingdom.[42] Unlike the Beelzebul Controversy, however, the Commissioning does not make this connection explicit. The parataxis leaves it up to the reader to draw the connection between the proclamation and the healing. The importance of healing in other Q cotexts provides clues to the connection between healing and the kingdom of God by showing that healings manifest the eschatological blessing that Jesus' ministry makes present.

Co-text 1: The Baptist's Question (Matt 11:2–6//Luke 7:18–23)

The episode of John the Baptist's questioning Jesus' identity gives the clearest indication of the eschatological significance of healing in Q. Via his disciples, John asks Jesus who he is, to which Jesus responds by pointing to his healings.

And while he was in prison, John heard of the works of the Christ and sent his disciples to say to him,	And his disciples told John about all these things and John called two of his disciples and sent them to the Lord saying,
"Are you the one who is to come or should we look for another?"	"Are you the one who is to come or should we look for another?"
	And when the men came to him they said, "John the Baptist sent us to you saying, 'Are you the one who is to

come or should we look for another?'" In that hour Jesus healed many from illnesses and scourges and evil spirts and to many blind people he gave sight.

And answering them Jesus said, "Go, tell John what you have heard and seen: blind people receive sight (τυφλοὶ ἀναβλέπουσιν) and lame people walk (χωλοὶ περιπατοῦσιν), those with leprosy are cleansed (λεπροὶ καθαρίζονται), and deaf people hear (κωφοὶ ἀκούουσιν), and dead people are raised (νεκροὶ ἐγείρονται) and poor people have good news preached to them (πτωχοὶ εὐαγγελίζονται). And blessed is whoever is not scandalized by me." (Matt 11:2–6)

And answering them Jesus said, "Go, tell John what you have seen and heard: blind people receive sight (τυφλοὶ ἀναβλέπουσιν), lame people walk (χωλοὶ περιπατοῦσιν), those with leprosy are cleansed (λεπροὶ καθαρίζονται) and deaf people hear (κωφοὶ ἀκούουσιν), and dead people are raised (νεκροὶ ἐγείρονται), poor people have good news preached to them (πτωχοὶ εὐαγγελίζονται). And blessed is whoever is not scandalized by me." (Luke 7:18–23)

The shared material consists of John's question to Jesus, delivered by John's disciples, about whether Jesus is "the one who is to come," followed by Jesus' response. John's question might more expansively be paraphrased, "Are you the eschatological judge whom I have been predicting?" Jesus answers only indirectly, by giving a list of occurrences in his ministry: 1) blind receiving sight; 2) lame walking; 3) people with leprosy being cleansed; 4) deaf receiving hearing; 5) dead being raised; and 6) poor having good news proclaimed to them. John asks who Jesus is, and Jesus responds with a list of (primarily) miraculous accomplishments in his ministry.

This list of accomplishments draws heavily on Isaiah's predictions of God's glorious blessings to come:

Isaiah 26:19 (LXX): The dead (νεκροί) will rise and those in the tombs shall be raised (ἐγερθήσονται) and those in the earth shall rejoice for the dew from you is healing for them but the land of the godless will fall.

Isaiah 29:18 (LXX): And on that day the deaf (κωφοί) will hear (ἀκούσονται) the words of a book and those who are in darkness, even the eyes of the blind (τυφλῶν) which are in fog, shall see (βλέψονται).

Isaiah 35:5–6 (LXX) Then the eyes of the blind (τυφλῶν) will be opened and the ears of the deaf (κωφῶν) will hear (ἀκούσονται), then the lame person (χωλός) will leap like a deer and the tongue of those with speech impediments will be clear because water has broken forth in the desert and a channel in the thirsty land.

Isaiah 42:7 (LXX): "To open the eyes of blind people (τυφλῶν), to lead prisoners out of chains and those living in darkness out of the prison house"

Isaiah 61:1 (LXX): "The spirit of the Lord is upon me on account of which he has anointed me to proclaim good news to the poor (εὐαγγελίσασθαι πτωχοῖς), he has sent me to heal the broken-hearted, to proclaim release to captives and recovery of sight to the blind (τυφλοῖς ἀνάβλεψιν)."

In this confluence of allusions to eschatological fulfillment in Jesus' answer it is tempting to see Jesus' answer as an indirect assertion of his messianic identity.[43] In this way of thinking, Jesus answers John the Baptist's question about his identity with a checklist of messianic expectations he has accomplished.

However, looking for a specific pre-Christian tradition of messianic expectation that Jesus fulfilled has not proven very fruitful.[44] There were many images of eschatological fulfillment for which Second Temple Jews could hope, including liberation from foreign powers, return of the lost tribes, conquest of enemies, the world-wide acceptance of Israel's God, the end of war, preternatural fecundity of the land, the cessation of human suffering, and the raising of the dead. Eschatological hopes could attach themselves to God's accomplishment of such fulfillment or upon a human intermediary, envisioned in many possible terms: as conquering warrior, as royal descendant of David, as righteous priest, as a prophet like Moses, as Elijah *redivivus*, as anointed one of God (Messiah), or as Son of Man. Those who expected God's decisive action in the world could draw on these traditional images and combine them in distinct ways to express their hopes.[45] Jesus' answer to John is one such combination of these eschatological themes. The list of actions in Jesus' response to the Baptist is not a messianic résumé; rather, it is a catalogue of the blessings God has promised for the eschaton.

Jesus' answer conforms most closely in form and content to the list of healings from Isaiah 35:5–6. Both lists consist of short clauses relating the benefits various groups receive. The subjects of the clauses are the beneficiaries, and the verbs either describe the newly acquired abilities of the subjects in the active voice or the healing of the subjects in the passive voice. The agent of these deeds remains unnamed. In Isaiah 35:5–6, the agent is clearly God. The imitation of this divine passive style in Jesus' reply similarly points attention toward God as the agent of these deeds.

Though Isaiah 35:5–6 provides the framework for Jesus' answer, the wording and content differ conspicuously. The Isaiah passage presents the healing of four groups: the blind, the deaf, the lame, and those with speech impediments. Jesus' reply includes the first three of these and adds three more types of occurrences: people with leprosy being cleansed, dead being raised, and the poor having good news announced to them. The raising of the dead, though not present in Isaiah 35:5–6, has Isaianic background in 26:19:

"the dead (νεκροί) will rise and those in the tombs shall be raised (ἐγερθήσονται)." This verse has a similar style of narration as Isaiah 35:5–6, and the agent of this miracle, though unnamed, is clearly God. The incorporation of the other two elements, cleansing of people with leprosy and evangelization of the poor, however, involves more extensive modification of Isaiah's models.

Jesus' announcement of good news to the poor clearly alludes to Isaiah 61:1, in which the prophet claims this announcement as part of his mission. Here a human agent accomplishes the divine work. This prophetic agent also will give sight to the blind, and this connection to healing the blind explains why the announcement of good news to the poor lends itself to inclusion in a list in the style of Isaiah 35:5–6. Merging the themes of Isaiah 61:1 and 35:5–6 into a stylistically unified list involves a choice: the elements of 35:5–6 could be added to the mission of the one anointed by God in 61:1, or the elements of 61:1 could be added to the list of deeds God accomplishes without mention of a human agent in 35:5–6. That Jesus' response to John uses the latter strategy diminishes the emphasis on the human agent. Jesus takes the well-known action of the prophet from Isaiah 61:1 and changes it into a deed accomplished in the divine passive; thereby, he distances it from its original context as the act of God's human agent.[46]

Unlike the other five elements in Jesus' reply, the cleansing of people with leprosy has no obvious antecedent in Isaiah. Although several possible explanations for its inclusion exist, the simplest is that healing of people with leprosy was included simply because it was a part of Jesus' ministry.[47] This may be true, but setting this particular cure in the midst of such allusions to Isaiah begs closer scrutiny to determine its significance. In the broader OT context beyond Isaiah, the infliction and cure of leprosy appear frequently as divine prerogatives.[48] Cleansing people with leprosy thus fits very well within Jesus' list of God's redemptive accomplishments, even if it does not find expression in the Isiaianic materials that form the background of the rest of Jesus' response.

Jesus' answer modifies the model from Isaiah 35:5–6 not just by adding the three elements of raising of the dead, cleansing people with leprosy, and evangelizing the poor. Jesus' response also changes Isaiah's verb tenses.[49] Whereas Isaiah's list has all the verbs in the future, Jesus' verbs are all in the present. What exists as a prediction for Isaiah becomes for Jesus a present reality. In Jesus' miracles, Isaiah's hopes for God's redemption come true. How exactly this fact answers the Baptist's question, "Are you the one who is to come or should we look for another?" is left to the reader to determine.

Jesus' answer is not so much evasive as indirect, because his response does presume a connection between the person in the question and the time in the answer. After describing this time of salvation, Jesus does not say, "Blessed is whoever is not scandalized by *this*," but rather, "Blessed is whoever is not scandalized by *me.*" Jesus is the one who has been doing these miracles, and they point to his role in bringing about the eschatological blessings promised by Isaiah.

The indirectness of Jesus' answer qualifies the Baptist's question.[50] John has predicted the imminence of eschatological judgment in the person of one who is to come. When John asks if Jesus is that figure, Jesus uses his miracles to point out the arrival of eschatological blessing. Care must be taken in seeing too strong an opposition between eschatological judgment and blessing in Jesus' response, as these are closely linked in the traditions upon which Jesus draws.[51] Just before predicting the blooming of the desert and the healing of the blind, deaf, and lame, Isaiah predicted God's wrathful judgment against the nations (Isa 34:1–17). The one the Lord anointed to announce good news to the poor will proclaim "the year of the Lord's favor, and the day of vengeance of our God" (Isa 61:2). Stories of leprosy can reveal God's punishment in its infliction as well as God's blessing in its cure. Blessing of the righteous and punishment of the wicked are two sides of the eschatological coin.

Jesus' response to John the Baptist's question consists of a three-part argument, of which Jesus gives only the first part explicitly. When the Baptist (through his disciples) asks if Jesus is the eschatological judge John has been predicting, the answer is that (1) God's eschatological promises of blessing are fulfilled in the miracles they have seen, and because (2) Jesus has been performing these miracles, one should conclude that (3) Jesus is God's eschatological agent ushering in both the promised blessings and the promised judgment. The miracles here are used to demonstrate Jesus' identity, but that identity is premised on the miracles illustrating the eschatological fulfillment that Jesus elsewhere calls the kingdom of God.[52] The miracles demonstrate Jesus' special identity only insofar as they instantiate the kingdom he is proclaiming. It therefore makes sense that as the disciples' perform healing miracles in the Double Tradition they are to proclaim the incipient presence of the kingdom of God, for the disciples' healings also manifest the kingdom's presence. Though their healings, the disciples participate with Jesus in demonstrating the present eschatological blessings.

Co-text 2: The Healing of the Centurion's Servant (Matt 8:5–13// Luke 7:1–10)

The other healing narrative in Q concerns the centurion and his dependent, an account that does not emphasize the eschatological import of Jesus' healing. However, the exchange between Jesus and the centurion reflects the Double Tradition's positioning of Jesus as an agent of God. Luke and Matthew differ on quite a few of the narrative details, but they share a narrative framework in which a Centurion with a sick dependent asks Jesus to heal him. Before Jesus can come to his house, the centurion stops him and says:

"Lord (κύριε),	"Lord (κύριε), do not trouble yourself. For
I am not worthy that you should enter under my roof,	I am not worthy that you should enter under my roof. Therefore, I did not consider myself worthy to approach you,
but only speak a word, and my servant will be healed. For I too am a man under authority (ὑπὸ ἐξουσίαν), having under myself soldiers, and I say to one, 'Go,' and he goes, and to another, 'Come,' and he comes, and to my slave, 'Do this,' and he does it." (Matthew 5:8–9)	but speak a word, and my servant will be healed. For I too am a man placed under authority (ὑπὸ ἐξουσίαν), having under myself soldiers, and I say to one, 'Go,' and he goes, and to another, 'Come,' and he comes, and to my slave, 'Do this,' and he does it." (Luke 7:6–8)

Jesus, amazed at the faith of the centurion, promises that the servant will be healed, and those who came to Jesus return to the house to find the servant well.

In this narrative, the actual performance of the miracle is almost an afterthought. The story focuses instead on Jesus' interaction with the centurion (in Matthew) or his proxies (in Luke) and Jesus' amazement at the centurion's faith. The healing itself is never described. The narrative weight thus lies on the interaction between Jesus and the centurion/proxies. The interaction between these characters foregrounds the faith of the centurion, but it does not give a clear description of the content of this faith beyond the belief that Jesus can perform a healing.

Whereas the centurion clearly believes that Jesus can heal from afar with a mere word, what this power implies about Jesus' identity remains unclear. The centurion makes no explicit confession about who he believes Jesus to be. He does address Jesus as "Lord" (κύριε), which could carry implications of divinity from its LXX use as a translation of the Tetragrammaton, but it could also simply represent a polite form of address, equivalent to "sir."[53] Similarly, the centurion's confession that he is not worthy to receive Jesus could imply a status for Jesus ranging from honored person to divine avatar.[54] Jesus' ability to perform miracles make him a person of importance, to whom the centurion shows respect and even faith, but the Q passage does not go further in addressing Jesus' identity.

The centurion does express a belief in Jesus' authority (ἐξουσία), a theme familiar from Mark. The last section showed that ἐξουσία often involves a three-level hierarchy of granter-wielder-subordinate and that Mark places Jesus in the position of granter. The centurion's response in the Double Tradition depicts this same three-level hierarchy, but with Jesus in the position of wielder rather than granter. The centurion expresses his belief in Jesus' authority by his own experience of commanding his soldiers and slaves. This analogy implies that Jesus also has authority to command with a word. However, the centurion introduces this analogy not by saying, "I too am a man *with* authority," but by saying, "I too am a man (placed) *under* authority" (Matt 8:9//Luke 7:8). The centurion sets his authority as analogous to that of Jesus, and the centurion conceptualizes his own authority as having been granted to him.[55] Jesus is like the centurion in that he is "under authority," i.e., in a chain of command such that he can issue orders and have them obeyed. Just as the centurion is an agent of a higher authority, so is Jesus.[56] The centurion acts on the emperor's behalf, and Jesus acts on God's. Even as the centurion likens the authority granted him by the emperor to the authority granted Jesus by God, the superiority of God's authority to Caesar's is apparent: the agent of Caesar must seek help from the agent of God. The Q story only indirectly makes this evaluation of Jesus' identity. The centurion's statement primarily demonstrates his faith in the authority that Jesus wields as God's agent, and the narrative climaxes in Jesus' wonder at this faith.

The narrative subverts the typical pattern of a miracle story in which the audience wonders at the power of the miracle worker; the pattern is well demonstrated in Mark when the congregants in the Capernaum synagogue are amazed at Jesus' exorcism (1:27) or when those gathered around Jesus' house are amazed at the healing of the paralytic (2:12). Here in the Double Tradition, instead, the miracle worker wonders at the faith of the petitioner.[57] This breaking of the miracle-story paradigm arrests the reader's attention and makes Jesus' reaction the climax of the story. The centurion's profession of faith in the authority God has granted Jesus stands in the position that the performance of the miracle would stand in a typical miracle story, for it is the centurion's speech that inspires the wonder that closes the story. Jesus expresses his amazement at the centurion's faith by exclaiming that he has not seen such faith in Israel. The centurion reacts appropriately by showing deference to Jesus as the bearer of authority granted by God, whereas Israel does not.

Co-text 3: The Woes on Chorazin and Bethsaida

In the Commissioning, Jesus warns that the cities who do not welcome the disciples as they make the kingdom of God present in their healing miracles will face eschatological judgment (Matt 10:15//Luke 10:12). This condemnation of cities who do not react appropriately to the miracles appears also in the woes against Chorazin and Bethsaida, which again demonstrates that in the Double Tradition the miracles indicate the dawning of the eschaton. Channeling the biblical prophets, Jesus puts his miracles in the place of the prophetic oracle of salvation that should lead to repentance.

> Woe to you, Chorazin; woe to you, Bethsaida, because if the deeds of power (αἱ δυνάμεις) which happened in you had happened in Tyre and Sidon, long ago would they have repented (μετενόησαν) in sackcloth and ashes. But I say to you, in the day of judgment it will be more tolerable for Tyre and Sidon than for you. (Matt 11:21–22)

> Woe to you, Chorazin; woe to you, Bethsaida, because if the deeds of power (αἱ δυνάμεις) which happened in you had happened in Tyre and Sidon, long ago would they have repented (μετενόησαν), sitting in sackcloth and ashes. But in the judgment it will be more tolerable for Tyre and Sidon than for you. (Luke 10:13–14)

Here Jesus blasts cities in Galilee for not responding to the δυνάμεις, i.e., the miracles, that have been performed among them. As in his response to the Baptist, Jesus is coy about the agency of these miracles. He does not refer to them as "*my* deeds of power "or "the deeds of power *that I did*," but rather as "the deeds of power that happened (αἱ δυνάμεις αἱ γενόμεναι) in you." The reader/hearer is left to infer that Jesus is speaking of the miracles he has performed in these Galilean cities, miracles that the Double Tradition does not recount. Again, Jesus draws attention not to the significance of his performing the miracles, but to the occurrence of the miracles themselves.

Jesus' pronouncement against the cities functions as a prophetic oracle of doom. The occurrence of these miracles should have led to repentance; the miracles are part of Jesus' message to these cities, a message the cities do not heed. The theme of the rejection of a prophet's message and the ensuing punishment is a commonplace in the traditions of Israel.[58] The woe oracle is a familiar prophetic trope, as is the theme of repentance. [59] Especially in the Exilic and post-Exilic prophets, the call to repentance was grounded in the promise of salvation.[60] For instance, in the LXX of Second Isaiah God tells the Israelites, "Remember these things and groan, repent (μετανοήσατε), you that have been deceived, and return in your hearts. . . . I have brought near (ἤγγισα) my righteousness and I will not delay the salvation (σωτηρίαν) that is from me. I have given salvation (σωτηρίαν) to Israel in Zion for glory" (Isa 46:8, 12). The potential for salvation motivates the repentance: if the people turn away from their wickedness and toward God, they will reap God's rewards. Jesus' miracles function similarly to the prophetic oracle of salvation which should prompt the people to repent.[61]

Even Tyre and Sidon, those prophetic paragons of Gentile godlessness, would have turned from their wicked ways had they witnessed Jesus' miracles. The image of pagan cities repenting in sackcloth and ashes calls to mind Nineveh's response to Jonah (Jon 3:5–6). Jesus' miracle-working activity functions as the proclamation of a prophet—those who respond rightly to these miracles can be saved from God's punishment for their previous wickedness.

The prophetic message, however, did not always instill hope for salvation through repentance; the prophets also announced that continued intransigence foreclosed the possibility of salvation. The pre-Exilic prophets frequently mentioned repentance as a missed opportunity, as when Amos predicts punishment for Israel's failure to turn back to God (Amos 4:6–12) or when Isaiah points out that turning back to God would have saved the people of Judah if they had not refused to do so (Isa 30:15).[62] The people could have repented, but now their doom is sealed. Thus, Amos recounts the wickedness of the people of Judah (5:1–13), then exhorts them to desist from evil and do good (5:14–17), but his pessimism about their ability to change their ways comes through in his woe oracle that immediately follows: "Woe to you who desire the day of the Lord! Why do you want the day of the Lord? It is darkness, not light" (5:18). For a people who will not repent, God's visitation brings condemnation, not blessing.

The oracles of woe in the Hebrew prophets imply that the judgment they announce is inescapable.[63] As in the case of Amos, these woe oracles frequently attach to the threatened day of the Lord, when God will save God's people and punish God's enemies.[64] Jesus' proclamation against Chorazin and Bethsaida carries this same finality. Chorazin and Bethsaida's culpability lies not in their intrinsic wickedness, but in their failure to respond to the message of God's salvation enacted in Jesus' miracles.[65] The miracles present an opportunity to turn to God, but this opportunity carries with it the obligation to respond appropriately. Thus, for both Jesus and his disciples, miracles announce the presence of God's eschatological blessing and judgment, which makes those who witness them liable to condemnation if they do not respond with the appropriate repentance.

Miracles and Succession in Q

The Double Tradition frequently interprets Jesus' miracles as eschatological signs. In the Beelzebul Controversy, exorcisms instantiate the kingdom of God. In the woes on the Galilean cities, the miracles demonstrate that the time of judgment is at hand. The response to the Baptist shows that Jesus' healings make eschatological blessings present. When the Double Tradition's mission instruction juxtaposes a command to heal with a command to proclaim the kingdom, the implication is clear: the healings signify the presence of the kingdom.

Although the disciples and Jesus share a ministry of announcing and making present the kingdom through healing, their ministries are not equivalent. It is Jesus who orders the disciples to undertake their ministry, and their ministry follows his pattern.[66] The pericope of the centurion's servant also focuses attention on the specific role of Jesus in effecting God's plan through healing as it is the centurion's faith in Jesus' divinely appointed authority that sets him apart from Israel. The closing macarism of Jesus' response to the Baptist also emphasizes that it is the correct attitude toward Jesus himself that makes one blessed.

The Double Tradition gives Jesus an elevated role as the bearer of God's healing authority, but a comparison of the disciples' mission in Q with that in Mark demonstrates that there is greater correspondence between Jesus and the disciples in Q than in Mark. In Q the disciples are to heal, and the Q commissioning does little to differentiate the disciples' healings from those of Jesus. Q's disciples proclaim the nearly present kingdom of God just as Jesus does; they do not proclaim simply the repentance that prepares for the coming kingdom. In Q, the charisma of healing and preaching the kingdom are shared more evenly between Jesus and his successors. However, Jesus remains the source of whatever charisma the disciples possess: they minister according to Jesus' commands and they follow the pattern his ministry established.

CONCLUSION

Jesus' miracles demonstrate his authority as the bringer of God's eschatological blessing and judgment, and so they define the community of his followers as those on the right side of the coming judgment. By telling about the disciples performing similar miracles, early Jesus followers emphasized that as a group they shared in the eschatological power present in Jesus. In telling the Beelzebul Controversy, these Jesus followers make Jesus' eschatological role the reason why following him is so crucial. In so doing, they define their identity as Jesus followers against any Jesus followers who might not recognize their Lord's eschatological role. By demonstrating an eschatological role for Jesus, the miracle overlaps define the identity of Jesus followers as those who recognize Jesus' eschatological importance and who therefore follow him. Early Jesus followers did not make these assertions about Jesus' identity as they contemplated this identity in the abstract; they did so rather as they forged their own identity as a group in contrast and competition with other groups of Jesus followers.[67]

Mark and Q differ in how they conceptualize Jesus' identity as God's eschatological agent, conceptualizations that generate group identity in different ways. The previous chapter showed that the Double Tradition presented Jesus' exorcisms as evidence of the corporate victory of the kingdom of God over the kingdom of Satan, a victory in which those who followed Jesus could participate. Consistent with this participatory image of eschatological victory, the Commissioning in Q presents the disciples as co-workers with Jesus in the task of making God's eschatological blessings present through miracles, the task of instantiating the kingdom of God. These stories would inculcate an identity among early Jesus followers that their group was defined by its participation alongside Jesus in God's eschatological victory.

While the Double Tradition versions of the Beelzebul Controversy and the Commissioning present the healings and exorcisms as evidence of the incipient kingdom of God, of which Jesus is the preeminent figure, in the Markan versions of these pericopes, the healings and exorcisms show the divine authority of Jesus who single-handedly conquers Satan. Such an identity for Jesus leaves little opportunity for his followers' direct participation in the eschatological victory he brings. Indeed, in Mark's version, the disciples' mission only palely reflects that of Jesus, and the eschatological proclamation of the kingdom of God is missing from their mission. It might seem that this less participatory paradigm would not be as effective at generating group identity. However, in Mark's case, group identity is promoted not by an allegiance to the kingdom of God that is shared by Jesus and his followers, but by an allegiance to Jesus as God's special eschatological agent. The more Mark talks of Jesus in ways that blur the distinction between Jesus and God, the sharper the distinction becomes between those who follow Jesus and those who do not.

The investigation so far broadly supports a modified version of the Grand Inquisitor's thesis advanced in the first chapter: Q represents an early interpretation of Jesus' miracles which eschewed their use to authenticate Jesus' divine identity, while Mark demonstrates an early tradition that used miracles as just such tools. Yet to be examined is the pericope that inspired the Grand Inquisitor's discourse in the first place. It is finally time to take up the Temptation.

NOTES

1. For efforts to determine what belongs to Q, see Risto Uro, *Sheep Among the Wolves: A Study of the Mission Instructions in Q* (Helsinki: Suomaleinen Tiedeakatemia, 1987), 25, 73–226; Fledderman, *Q*, 403–37. For a helpful delineation of the overlaps among the four sets of mission instructions, see Robert E. Morosco, "Matthew's Formation of a Commissioning Type-Scene out of the Story of Jesus' Commissioning of the Twelve," *JBL* 103.4 (1984): 540.

2. Theodore Abel, *Why Hitler Came into Power* (New York: Prentice Hall, 1938); Hans Gerth, "The Nazi Party: Its Leadership and Composition," *American Journal of Sociology* 45 (1940): 517–41. For analysis and further examples of the penetration of Weber's idea of charisma into political and sociological scholarship, see Joshua Derman, "Max Weber and Charisma: A Transatlantic Affair," *New German Critique* 38.2 (2011): 51–88.

3. Stephan Feuchtwang, "Suggestions for a Redefinition of Charisma," *Nova Religio: The Journal of Alternative and Emergent Religions* 12.2 (2008): 90–105.

4. Max Weber, *Economy and Society: An Outline of Interpretive Sociology*, ed. Guenther Roth and Claus Wittich (Berkeley: University of California Press, 1978), 215.

5. Weber, *Economy and Society*, 216.

6. Weber, *Economy and Society,* 246–49.

7. Spencer C. Olin, Jr., "The Oneida Community and the Instability of Charismatic Authority," *The Journal of American History* 67.2 (1980): 293–96.

8. Catherine Wessinger, "Democracy vs. Hierarchy: The Evolution of Authority in the Theosophical Society," in Miller, *When Prophets Die,* 93–106.

9. Catherine Wessinger, "Charismatic Leaders in New Religions," in *The Cambridge Companion to New Religious Movements,* eds. Olav Hammer and Michael Rothstein (Cambridge: Cambridge University Press, 2012), 84–86.

10. Steven L. Shields, "The Latter Day Saint Movement: A Study in Survival," in Miller, *When Prophets Die,* 62–65.

11. Ibid., 71–73.

12. William D. Russell, "King James Strang: Joseph Smith's Successor?" in *Mormon Mavericks: Essays on Dissenters,* eds. John Sillito and Susan Staker (Salt Lake City: Signature Books, 2002), 131–57.

13. Gary R. Entz, "The Bickertonites: Schism and Reunion in a Restoration Church, 1880–1905," *Journal of Mormon History* 32, no. 3 (2006): 3.

14. Ian J. Elmer, "Setting the Record Straight at Galatia: Paul's *Narratio* (Gal 1:13–2:14) as Response to the Galatian Conflict," in *Religious Conflict from Early Christianity to the Rise of Islam,* eds. Neil Bronwen and Wendy Mayer (Berlin: Walter De Gruyter, 2012), 37.

15. John Howard Schutz, *Paul and the Anatomy of Apostolic Authority* (Lousville: Westminster John Knox, 2007), 264–78.

16. James A. Kelhoffer, "The Apostle Paul and Justin Martyr on the Miraculous: A Comparison of Appeals to Authority," *GRBS* 42.2 (2001): 163–75.

17. Philip F. Esler, *Galatians* (London: Routledge, 1998), 120.

18. Nachman Levine, "Twice as Much of your Spirit: Pattern, Parallel and Paranomasia in the Miracls of Elijah and Elisha," *JSOT* 85 (1999): 25–46.

19. Meier, *Marginal Jew,* 3.128–47; Collins, *Mark,* 297.

20. Collins, *Mark,* 302; Marcus, *Mark 1–8,* 388.

21. *TDNT* 2:562–63.

22. Klaus Scholtissek, *Die Vollmacht Jesu: Tradition- und redaktiongeschichtliche Analysen zu einem Leitmotiv markinischer Christologie* (Munster: Achendorf, 1992), 30–31, 47–48; James R. Edwards, "The Authority of Jesus in the Gospel of Mark," *Journal of the Evangelical Theological Society* 37.2 (1994): 218.

23. TDNT 2.562–63, δύναμις.

24. BDAG 207–8, δύναμις.

25. Scholtissek, *Vollmacht,* 285.

26. Aloysius M. Ambrozic, "New Teaching with Power (Mk 1:27)," in *Word and Spirit: Essays in Honor of David Michael Stanley, S.J. on his 60th Birthday,* ed. Joseph Plevnik (Willowdale, ON: Regis College Press, 1975), 122.

27. E.g., PGM IV.3019–20 features a conjuration through "Jesus, god of the Hebrews." For further examples of the invocation of a divine figure's name to exorcise or work miracles, see Collins, *Mark,* 446–47.

28. Marcus, *Mark 8–16,* 685.

29. Dale C. Allison Jr., *James: A Critical and Exegetical Commentary* (London: T&T Clark, 2013), 760.

30. Jeffrey John, "Anointing in the New Testament," in *The Oil of Gladness: Anointing in the Christian Tradition,* eds. Martin Dudley and Geoffrey Rowell (London: SPCK, 1993), 50; Allison, *James,* 760. Examples of oil's medicinal properties are to be found in Plato, *Menex.* 238A; Theophrastus, *Hist. Plant.* 9.11.1–2; Menander, *Georg.* 60; Philo, *Aet. 63, Somn.* 2.58; Josephus, *War* 1.657, *Ant..* 17.172. For magical and apotropaic uses, see *T. Sol* 18:33–34, *Eccl. Rab.* 1.8.4, PGM IV.3209–54; VII.211–12; VIII.200.

31. Allison, *James,* 759.

32. Bernd Kollman, *Jesus und die Christen als Wundertäter: Studien zu Magie, Medizin und Schamanismus in Antike und Christentum* (Göttingen: Vandenhoeck & Ruprecht, 1996), 345.

33. Helge Kjaer Nielsen, *Heilung und Verkündigung: Das Verständnis der Heilung und ihres Verhältnisses zur Verkündigung bei Jesus und in der altesten Kirche* (Leiden: Brill,

1987), 213; Sigurd Kaiser, *Krankenheilung: Untersuchungen zu Form, Sprache, traditionsges-chichtlichem Hintergrund und Aussage von Jak 5, 13–18* (Neukirchen-Vluyn: Neukirchener Verlag, 2006), 134; Allison, *James,* 758.

34. John, "Anointing," 54; Allison, *James,* 758.

35. Peter's mother-in-law 1:29–31; the man with leprosy 1:40–45; the paralytic 2:1–12; the man with the withered hand 3:1–6; Jairus's daughter 5:21–24, 35–43; the woman with the flow of blood 5:25–34; the deaf man 7:31–37; the blind man 8:22–26; Bartimaeus 10:46–52.

36. Reflected especially in the healing of the woman with a flow of blood (5:25–34). See Candida R. Moss, "The Man with the Flow of Power: Porous Bodies in Mark 5:25–34," *JBL* 129.3 (2010): 518.

37. Marcus, *Mark 1–8,* 473–74; Collins, *Mark,* 371.

38. E.g., Joel 4:13, Rev 14:14–15, *2 Bar.* 70.2, *4 Ezra* 4.26–29.

39. Davies and Allison, *Matthew,* 2.148–49.

40. For instance, Huneburg, *Jesus,* 164–65 argues that in the context of Q, ἤγγικεν indicates that the kingdom has already arrived. Davies and Allison, *Matthew,* 1.392 argue that ἤγγικεν indicates the extreme nearness, but not yet arrival, of the kingdom.

41. With Meier, *Marginal Jew,* 2.433.

42. Fledderman, *Q,* 434; Schulz, *Q,* 417; Huneburg, *Jesus,* 163.

43. Bovon, *Luke 1,* 282; Craig S. Keener, *The Gospel of Matthew: A Socio-Rhetorical Commentary* (Grand Rapids, MI: Eerdmans, 2009), 336; Hanna Stettler, "Die Bedeutung der Täuferanfrage in Matthäus 11,2–6 par Lk 7,18–23 für die Christologie," *Biblica* 89 (2008): 173–200; John J. Collins, "The Works of the Messiah," *DSD* 1.1 (1994): 98–112; Hermann L. Strack and Paul Billerbeck, *Kommentar zum Neuen Testament aus Talmud und Midrasch* (Munich: Beck, 1922), 1.593. David T.M. Frankfurter ,"The Origin of the Miracle-List Tradition and Its Medium of Circulation," *SBLSP* 29 (1990): 344–74. L. Novakovic, *Messiah, the Healer of the Sick* (Tübingen: Mohr Siebeck, 2003), 181; Graham Stanton, *Gospel Truth? New Light on Jesus and the Gospels* (Valley Forge, PA: Trinity Press Internations, 1995), 186–87; James D. Tabor and Michael O. Wise, "4Q521 'On Resurrection' and the Synoptic Gospel Tradition: A Preliminary Study," *JSP* 10 (1992): 149–62; Micheal O. Wise and James D. Tabor, "The Messiah at Qumran," *BAR* 18 (1992): 60–63; Benjamin Wold, "Agency and Raising the Dead in *4QPseudo-Ezekiel* and 4Q521 2 ii," *ZNW* 103 (2012): 1–19; Collins,"Works," 98–112.

44. Hans Kvalbein, "The Wonders of the End-Time: Metaphoric Language in 4Q521 and the Interpretation of Matthew 11.5 par.," *JSP* 18 (1998): 87–110. Joseph Fitzmyer, *The One Who is to Come* (Grand Rapids, MI: Eerdmans, 2007), 97; Rafael Rodriguez, "Re-framing End-Time Wonders: A Response to Hans Kvalbein," *JSP* 20 (2011): 237–38; F. Neirynck, "Q 6,20b–21; 7,22 and Isaiah 61" in Idem, *Evangelica III: 1992–2000. Collected Essays* (Leuven: Leuven University Press, 2001), 129–66; Huneburg, *Jesus,* 66–67.

45. Dunn, "Kingdom," 5.

46. Hüneburg, *Jesus,* 75.

47. For a summary of various proposals, see Hüneburg, *Jesus,* 62–63.

48. Exod 4:6 (Moses' hand); Num 12:1–15 (Miriam); 2 Kings 5:1–27 (Naaman); 2 Chr 26:19 (King Uzziah).

49. Huneburg, *Jesus,* 64.

50. Davies and Allison, *Matthew,* 2:246; Meier, *Marginal Jew,* 2:134; R. T. France, *The Gospel of Matthew* (Grand Rapids, MI: Eerdmans, 2007), 424.

51. C.M. Tuckett, *Q and the History of Early Christianity: Studies on Q* (Edinburgh: T&T Clark, 1996),127.

52. With Davies and Allison, *Matthew,* 2:245; Meier, *Marginal Jew,* 2:134–35; Hüneburg, *Jesus,* 79.

53. Kloppenborg, *Formation,* 117–20; Cotter, *Christ,* 107, David R. Catchpole, "The Centurion's Faith and Its Function in Q," in *Four Gospels 1992,* eds. F. Segbroeck, C. M. Tuckett, G. van Belle, and J. Verheyden (Louvain: Peeters, 1992), 1.519; Uwe Wegner, *Der Hauptmann von Kafarnaum* (Tübingen: Mohr, 1985), 381–83.

54. Catchpole, "Centurion's Faith," 535; Tuckett, *Q,* 217; John T. Carroll, *Luke: A Commentary* (Louisville: Westminster John Knox, 2012), 162.

55. Against Catchpole, "Centurion's Faith," 534–37. Bovon, *Luke 1,* 262, Huneburg, *Jesus,* 131–34. Also Daniel Marguerat *Le Jugement dans l'Evangile de Mattieu* 2nd ed. (Geneva: Labor et Fides, 1995), 246, and France, *Matthew,* 315.

56. With Tuckett, *Q,* 217; Schulz, *Q,* 243.

57. Wegner, *Hauptmann,* 344–61, 430.

58. 1 Kings 18:4; 19:10; 2 Chr 36:14-1; Neh 9:26; Jer 2:30. For a discussion of how this theme is present in the Q material, see Tuckett, *Q,* 168–70.

59. See Isa 5:8–24; 28:1–31:9; Jer 13:27; Amos 5:18–29; 6:1–7; Micah 2:1–5; Hab 2:6–19.

60. *TDOT* 14.497. See also Jer 3:22; 15:19; 36:3; Ezek 18:30–32.

61. Hüneburg, *Jesus,* 172.

62. *TDOT* 14.496. See also Hos 2:8–9; 5:15; 6:4; 7:14–16; 11:7; Isa 9:12.

63. *TDOT* 3.362.

64. Waldemar Janzen, *Mourning Cry and Woe Oracle* (Berlin: Walter de Gruyter, 1972), 81–90.

65. Luz, *Matthew 8–20,* 153; Marguerat, *Jugement,* 263; Ilija Cabraja, *Der Gedanke der Umkehr bei den Synoptikern: Eine exegetisch- religionsgeschichtliche Untersuchung* (Sankt Ottilein: EOS Verlag, 1985), 45–46.

66. Kloppenborg, *Excavating Q,* 393.

67. Molina and Neyrey, *Calling,* 135–36.

Chapter Six

The Testing of Jesus

The Grand Inquisitor describes two conflicting attitudes toward miracles. Jesus rejects miracles as instruments of coercive power, while the Church rejects Jesus' rejection of miracles. So far, this study has investigated the distinct ways that Mark and the Double Tradition talk about Jesus' miracles as part of God's promised defeat of evil. The previous chapters have shown that Jesus' miracles in Mark indicate his exalted status, efface the distinction between Jesus and God, and highlight the distinction between Jesus and his followers. Mark thus emphasizes Jesus' unique, God-like role in the eschatological script. Conversely, in the Double Tradition, Jesus' miracles indicate the incipient presence of eschatological blessing and emphasize the shared participation of Jesus and his followers in ushering in this kingdom of God. Further, the preceding chapters have looked at how framing Jesus' miracles in these ways generated group identity for Jesus' followers. However, the book has not yet shown that these two ways of talking about Jesus' miracles competed with each other to define Jesus' identity for his followers. Now we at last come to the Temptation, which the Grand Inquisitor saw as the confrontation between two views of miracles.

To understand the function of the Testing in Mark and Q, this chapter surveys stories narrating a hero's early testing from diverse cultures. In addition, the chapter also examines rites of passage to explore the function of initiatory testing. The chapter then turns to the Q version to see how Jesus' threefold Temptation fits into the pattern of stories and rites of initiation. The refusal to perform miracles fits awkwardly into this schema, and this refusal makes most sense as an effort to dispute the memory of Jesus as one who performed miracles to prove his divine identity. Turning to Mark, the chapter argues that Mark's laconic narrative of Jesus' encounter with Satan fits with the Second Gospel's use of miracles to show Jesus' divine status.

Typically this encounter between Jesus and Satan is called the "Temptation." Both Mark and the Double Tradition refer to Satan's action with the verb πειράζω, which denotes tempting, but which can also denote testing.[1] The meanings are related, but distinct. "Tempting" implies inducing someone to do something wrong, an inducement that the person should resist. The tempter tests the person's resolution in adhering to norms of behavior. "Testing" implies putting someone in a situation that gauges ability or some aspect of character. Thus, not all tests are temptations. One can undergo a test of strength or of courage, for example. When the Israelites in the wilderness cry out for water, Moses asks them, "Why do you test (תְּנַסּוּן/πειράζετε) the Lord?" (Exod 17:2). Moses here is not accusing the people of tempting God to do something God should not, but rather of demanding God prove God's power and solicitude. The encounter between Jesus and the devil in the Double Tradition clearly involves temptation, as the devil fails to induce Jesus to perform actions that the Torah forbids. Due to the Q version's fame, the pericope is commonly called the Temptation. However, in Mark, there is no indication that the devil tempts Jesus, and Mark uses πειράζω elsewhere to describe situations of testing rather than temptation. Thus, both Mark and Q depict the devil testing Jesus, but only Q presents this testing as temptation. This chapter will therefore refer to the devil's actions as the Testing of Jesus unless the topic is specifically the Temptations that the devil uses to test Jesus in the Double Tradition.

Mark has Jesus encounter the devil's testing immediately after the baptism: "And immediately the spirit cast him out into the wilderness, and he was in the wilderness forty days, being tested (πειραζόμενος) by Satan, and he was with the wild animals, and the angels were serving him" (Mark 1:12–13). Both Matthew and Luke give substantially longer descriptions of Jesus' post-baptismal encounter with Satan. They narrate similar events, but in a different order. To make the parallelism more apparent below, I have rearranged the order in Luke to follow that of Matthew (underlines represent material common to Matthew and Luke not shared by Mark):[2]

	And Jesus, filled with the holy spirit, returned from the Jordan and was led
Then Jesus was brought up into the wilderness by the spirit to be tempted (πειρασθῆναι) <u>by the devil.</u>	by the spirit into the wilderness. He was tempted (πειραζόμενος) <u>by the devil</u> forty days.
And after fasting forty days and forty nights, <u>he hungered</u> greatly.	And he did not eat anything in those days and when they ended <u>he hungered.</u>

And approaching, the tempter (ὁ πειράζων) said to him, "If you are God's son, say that these stones become bread."
But Jesus answering said, "It is written, 'Not by bread only shall a person live, but upon every word coming from the mouth of God.'"
Then the devil led him into the holy city and stood him on the pinnacle of the Temple and said to him,
"If you are the son of God, cast yourself down. For it is written, 'His angels he will command concerning you, and they will bear you on their hands lest you strike your foot on a stone.'"
Jesus said to him, "Again it is written,
'You shall not test (ἐκπειράσεις) the Lord your God.'"
Again the devil took him onto a very high mountain and showed him all the kingdoms of the world and their glory.
And he said to him, "All these I will give to you if you fall down and worship me."
Then Jesus said to him, "Depart, Satan.

For it is written, 'Worship the Lord your God and serve him only.'"
Then the devil left him, and, behold, the angles came and served him.
(Matt 4:1–11)

And the devil said to him,
"If you are God's son, say to this stone that it becomes bread."
And Jesus answered him, "It is written that not by bread only shall a person live."

And he led him into Jerusalem and stood on the pinnacle of the Temple and said to him,
"If you are the son of God, cast yourself down from here. For it is written, 'His angels he will command concerning you to guard you,' and, 'they will bear you on their hands lest you strike your foot on a stone.'" And, answering, Jesus said to him, "It is said,
'You shall not test (ἐκπειράσεις) the Lord your God.'"

And leading him up, he showed him all the kingdoms of the world at a moment in time.
And the devil said to him, "To you I will give all this authority and their glory, because it has been handed over to me and I give it to whomever I want. If then you worship before me, all this will be yours." And, answering, Jesus said to him, "It is written, 'Worship the Lord your God and serve him only.'" And having finished all his tempting, the devil went away from him until the right time.
(Luke 4:1–13)

The Double Tradition includes the threefold temptation of Jesus to turn stones into bread, to jump off the Temple, and to worship Satan. Matthew and Luke also set this testing in the wilderness after Jesus' baptism, a setting shared with Mark's briefer version. Scholars have debated whether this temporal and geographic location belongs to Q.[3] In the effort to remain neutral with respect to solutions to the Synoptic Problem, this study adopts a strict definition of the Double Tradition: the material common to Matthew and Luke but absent in Mark. Since Mark locates the testing in the wilderness and after Jesus' baptism, these elements do not belong to the Double Tradition, thus narrowly defined. What Mark and the Double Tradition do share is a story of Jesus being tested by the devil. This chapter will demonstrate how in the Double Tradition the Testing repudiates both the use of miracles as markers of Jesus' divine identity and the worship of Jesus that his divine identity would allow. The chapter will further demonstrate how Mark's silence on the nature of the testing fits with his use of miracles to illustrate Jesus' superhuman status. To accomplish these tasks, this chapter begins by looking at the function of narratives and rites of testing cross-culturally.

TESTING AND INITIATION

In both Mark and the Double Tradition, Jesus is tested by his adversary, the devil. A hero's early testing by an adversary recurs in literature across cultures. The appeal of such narratives also finds evidence in the widespread pattern of testing within rites of initiation. Exploring the similarities of Jesus' testing with the testing of other heroes illustrates the appeal of these kind of stories and explains why early followers of Jesus found the story of his testing worth telling. The appeal of testing is multifaceted, but clearly a pattern exists across cultures showing that testing endears heroes to their followers and groups to their members.

God famously tests (נסה/πειράζω) the faithfulness of Abraham by commanding him to sacrifice his son Isaac (Gen 22:1). In several Second Temple and rabbinic retellings, Satan or Mastema instigates this test, but it remains God who does the testing.[4] Abraham does face direct testing from an evil spirit in the *Apocalypse of Abraham,* an early Common Era expansion of the call of Abraham in Genesis 12. This *Apocalypse* opens with Abraham living in his father's house. God sends the angel Iaoel to give Abraham a revelation of the future, but first Iaoel leads Abraham to climb Mount Horeb and sacrifice to God. They walk together forty days and nights and Abraham does not eat or drink (12.1–2). When they climb the mountain, Abraham prepares to make the required sacrifice, but an unclean bird flies down onto the carcasses and tries to dissuade Abraham from his task by saying, "What are you doing, Abraham, on the holy heights, where no one eats or drinks, nor is there upon them food for men. But these all will be consumed by fire and they will burn you up. Leave the man who is with you and flee! For if you ascend to the height, they will destroy you" (*Ap. Abr.* 13.4–5). With the help of the angel, Abraham drives the bird away and completes his assigned sacrifice. Iaoel explains that this bird was actually the evil spirit Azazel who was tempting Abraham to abandon the sacrifice God commanded (13.6–14.14). Having successfully resisted this temptation, Abraham goes on to receive the vision that God has promised him.

Stories of confrontations between a hero and an evil spirit also appear in Zoroastrianism. Chapter 19 of the *Videvdad*, a part of the scriptures of Zoroastrianism, which was probably committed to writing in the third to fifth centuries of the Common Era, tells the story of Zarathustra's encounter with Angra Mainyu (the evil spirit, known also as Ahriman).[5] Zarathustra announces his intention to vanquish Angra Mainyu and his host of demons, so the evil spirit offers to make him a ruler of many nations if he will renounce the religion of Ahura Mazda (the Zoroastrian good principle).[6] Zarathustra refuses and promises to conquer evil by the word of Ahura Mazda.

In Buddhist literature the evil spirit Mara on several occasions tests the Buddha by trying to break his equanimity, incline him toward sensual desires, or frighten him from continuing on the path of Enlightenment.[7] Such temptations to desist from the path of Enlightenment occur at many points in the Buddha's life, but they are most frequently associated with Mara's trying to prevent major milestones, such as the Buddha's renunciation of his family, his attainment of Enlightenment, or his efforts to bring others to Enlightenment.[8] Several of these accounts have strong parallels to Jesus' testing. For example, one first-century BCE text has Mara approaching the pre-enlightened Buddha, lamenting how emaciated he has become during his meditations, and suggesting he return to society.[9] In another story, Mara tries to convince the pre-enlightened Buddha to become a king and establish universal peace rather than continue to strive for Enlightenment.[10]

The folklorist Vladimir Propp discovered a similar pattern of heroes undergoing testing in folktales, and his analysis established a paradigm for examining such folkloristic motifs as reflections of the cultures that produced them.[11] Propp famously provided a structural analysis of fairy tales, and one element of this structure is the hero undergoing testing. Early in the story, the hero leaves home and soon thereafter meets the testing character, often in a forest or other deserted place. The tester can be friendly or hostile, and the tasks proposed can include providing a service, performing feats of strength, or resisting a temptation.[12] Propp used this structure to study the origins and social settings of the folktales, which he believed to be the scripts of long-defunct Slavic rituals of puberty and death.[13]

Although most modern anthropologists and folklorists do not assume that folktales arise from rituals, the correspondences between stories and rituals can still provide useful insights.[14] Rather than adopting an etiologic approach that locates the origins of a story in a certain ritual, or vice versa, one can view rituals as folk practices, just as telling folktales is a folk practice. Much as different versions of a folktale illustrate its appeal and significance, so too can rituals offer fodder for better comparative understanding. Telling stories and performing rituals are both ways by which groups form their identities and shape a collective memory.[15] Therefore, analyzing rituals of testing helps clarify the wide appeal of stories of a hero's testing.

Many of the elements common to stories of the hero's testing, including Jesus' testing, appear also in rites of passage.[16] The separation from society and the endurance of some form of hardship feature prominently in many such rites. Before his investiture, the chief-elect of the Ndembu of central Africa is secluded in a hut a mile outside the village; there he must perform menial tasks, such as fetching firewood, and submit himself to verbal and physical abuse from other members of the tribe.[17] For North American Plains Indians, the Vision Quest has been a widespread feature of various rites of passage. These Vision Quests almost always involve the isolation of the subject from society as well as self-inflicted mortification, including fasting, as components of the seeker's attempt to obtain a vision from a spirit.[18] The spirits encountered in rites of initiation, however, are not always benign. A wide range of shamanic initiation practices from Asia, Australia, and the Americas involve physical isolation and deprivation that bring on attacks from hostile spirits; the aspiring shaman would endure these assaults to gain competence in manipulating the spirit world.[19] Rites of passage that involve enduring hardship also exist in modern society. Collegiate fraternity and sorority initiations often involve periods of isolation and endurance, as does military boot camp.[20]

The shamanic initiations can be viewed as one example of a larger category of rites of passage in which a symbolic death, manifested by isolation and ordeal, is followed by a symbolic resurrection or new birth, manifested by the participant's return to society.[21] This pattern of separation followed by reintegration was noted by Arnold Van Gennep who identified a threefold structure in rites of passage: 1) an act of separation whereby the participants remove themselves from normal society, followed by 2) a period of liminality wherein the participants exist on the margins of society and undergo a transformation from one state to another, and finally 3) an incorporation into society when the transformed individuals return to society with new roles, responsibilities, and relationships. The liminal period often involves hardships or tests that the participant must endure.[22] This liminal phase, with its attendant difficulties and ordeals, is crucial in the process of ritual transformation of participants from one social state to another.[23]

This widespread predilection for testing in initiation has caught the attention not just of anthropologists and students of religion, but also of psychologists. Some psychological research has examined how the perception of having passed an initiatory test generates positive feelings for the group; the more difficult the initial test is perceived to be, the more positive the feeling of group membership becomes. Aronson and Mills famously demonstrated the link between difficulty of initiatory testing and liking for a group by inviting their experimental subjects to join groups that discussed sex.[24] Aronson and Mills crafted three different initiation requirements to which the subjects were randomly assigned: a control condition, a mild initiation condition, and a severe initiation condition. In the control condition, subjects simply had to affirm that they were comfortable talking about sex; subjects in the other two conditions had to undergo an embarrassment test, ostensibly to prove that they could talk about sex openly. In the mild initiation condition, subjects read aloud five non-obscene words related to sex (e.g,. prostitute, virgin, petting). In the severe initiation condition, the subjects read obscene words (e.g., fuck, cock, screw) and vivid descriptions of sex from contemporary novels. In both the mild and severe initiation conditions, investigators told the subjects that they passed the test and could join the group. Subjects in all three conditions were then allowed to listen to the conversation of the group into which they had just been initiated, a conversation about sex in lower animals that was designed to be "one of the most worthless and uninteresting discussions imaginable."[25]

At the end of this dull conversation, subjects rated their liking for both the discussion and the group members. Subjects in the control and mild initiation conditions rated the discussion and the group similarly, but subjects in the severe initiation condition rated both the discussion and the group more highly than those in the other two conditions. The perception of having passed a strenuous admission test induced more positive feeling for the group and its activity.

Further experimental studies and fieldwork examining the difficulty of initiatory testing have shown it to be just one of many interrelated factors that affect strength of group affiliation; moreover, such studies reveal that initiation severity does not uniformly correlate with increased liking for a group.[26] Although the exact psychological mechanisms still remain a subject of debate, severe initiations often heighten the positive in-group feelings among members that have passed these tests. Such a psychological effect helps account for the persistence and ubiquity of testing, deprivation, and ordeals as fundamental parts of so many rites of passage across cultures and times.

Put another way, these severe initiations call attention to the desirability of group membership. Rituals create a sense of importance and sacredness by asserting difference: ritual actions create an environment that is marked off from the normal flow of ordinary life and signify that something extraordinary is occurring.[27] Severe initiations mark off the experience of joining a group from normal daily activity; they draw attention to the significance of joining the group, and they endow group membership with a special character. Telling stories functions similarly to performing such rituals. Listening to a story is, like participating in a ritual, a way of paying attention. The act of telling and listening to a story implies that what is told is worth hearing about, that it differs from run-of-the-mill events, and that it carries some significance making the telling and the hearing worth the effort.

Narratives of a hero's testing have a psychological appeal similar to the endurance of severe initiations. The difficulty of the hero's test heightens the sense that what the hero accomplishes is important, just as a strenuous initiation heightens the sense of group importance. The preparatory testing of the Russian folk hero sets the tone for the story and emphasizes that the hero will accomplish something important. In a hero's passing a test, the audience can also vicariously experience the satisfaction of completing a difficult task. For example, Abraham's encounter with Azazel emphasizes that the revelation he is about to receive is meaningful, for why else would the evil spirit try to dissuade him? The reader then can share in Abraham's triumph over Azazel and have access along with Abraham to the revelation that follows. The testing also shows that Abraham is someone who deserves to receive such a revelation since he obeys God's command even as Azazel tries to frighten him off.

Similarly, the Buddha's encounters with Mara and Zarathustra's meeting with Angra Mainyu demonstrate their commitment. Because they founded religious groups, their stories of testing have an even greater significance. If their missions were important enough to arouse the opposition of evil forces, then the movements they founded must be important indeed. Another analogy exists here between these stories and initiation rituals: difficult initiations for new members and the founding hero's overcoming hardships both emphasize the worth of the group. Thus, telling stories of the founder's testing increases in-group positivity, much like strenuous initiations.

The founder, in overcoming the test, becomes an exemplar for group members. Just as his followers face pressures to swerve from the Middle Way, so too did Buddha have to endure Mara's temptations. The Buddha faces the same struggles as do his followers, and his success shows that they too can succeed. Portrayal of such an exemplar performs an important task for group identity formation.[28] Groups promote a sense of their identity by emphasizing exemplars and showing the exemplars' similarity to other members of the group.[29] Individual Buddhists recognize themselves as part of a community of people who struggle to remain on the path to Enlightenment by resisting the temptations of fear and sensuality, a community exemplified by the Buddha in his struggle with Mara.

The story of Jesus' temptations would have had analogous appeal to early Jesus followers—Jesus' temptations make him an exemplar for his followers. Such appeal as an exemplar is manifested in patristic interpretations of the Temptation. For instance, John Chrysostom says of Jesus in the wilderness, "since for our teaching he both did and underwent all things, he endures to be led up there and to wrestle against the devil in order that each of those who are baptized, if after baptism should have to endure greater temptations, may not be troubled as if it were unexpected" (*Homilies on Matthew* 13.1). Similarly, Augustine sees Christ undergoing temptation by the devil "in order to be a mediator to overcome temptations, not only through assistance, but also through example" (*De Trinitate* 4.13). Although these examples come several centuries after the initial telling of the story, there is every reason to suppose that earlier followers of Jesus would have seen in his withstanding the devil's tempting an example for themselves as well.

The Double Tradition's Temptation narrative, with its rich description of the temptations Jesus faced in his testing by the devil, lends itself to this exemplary function as it shows just how Jesus faced these temptations. Indeed, in the other examples of the testing of a hero, we see that it is not some generic testing the hero faces, but a specific challenge that the hero overcomes: Abraham perseveres through the threats of Azazel; Zarathustra resists the lure of kingship; the Buddha faces a number of specific threats and inducements at the hands of Mara. Mark, however, presents only a summary of Jesus' testing by Satan. The Gospel records no details of the content, difficulty, or outcome of the test. The question then arises, why is Mark so vague about the Testing? This chapter will show that this vagueness fits with Mark's overall pattern of characterizing Jesus in ways that maximize the distinction between Jesus and his followers.

The Double Tradition Temptation also deviates in important ways from the cross-cultural pattern. The stories of Abraham, Zarathustra, and the Buddha show the hero facing a hostile spirit trying to dissuade him from carrying forward his mission, be it to receive God's revelation (Abraham), to assist in the victory of Ahura Mazda over Angra Mainyu (Zarathustra), or to gain Enlightenment (the Buddha). In the confrontation with the evil spirit, the hero proves his fidelity. According to this pattern, one would expect that the story of Jesus' testing would involve testing of Jesus' fidelity to God, and the Q version of the Temptation provides just such a test in the devil's inducement to worship him. However, the other two temptations that involve doing miracles do not fit so obviously into this type of temptation. It is not clear how performing miracles would betray Jesus' mission since miracles elsewhere in Q fit into this mission. In folktales, the testing often involved feats of strength, but in refusing to perform miracles, Jesus refuses to demonstrate his power. Moreover, a temptation to perform miracles was not likely to be a temptation to which many of Jesus' followers could relate, and so the centrality of miracles in these temptations lessens their exemplary effectiveness. Thus, this chapter will explore what function these temptations served and argue that their inclusion repudiates the use of miracles to authenticate Jesus' divine identity.

THE TESTING OF JESUS IN THE DOUBLE TRADITION

The Double Tradition rejects the use of miracles to prove Jesus' singular status in relation to God. Unless authors explicitly lay out a position which they dispute, to demonstrate that a text rejects a position involves a circumstantial argument that a polemical agenda of rejection makes the most sense of the textual data. In the case of the Double Tradition, strong circumstantial evidence exists that the composer(s) had the opportunity, motive, and means to reject miracles as indicators of Jesus' exalted status.

The opportunity to reject a viewpoint arises when authors are aware of a position that differs from their own. The last few chapters have demonstrated that Mark told stories of Jesus' miracles in ways that effaced the distinction between Jesus and God and that emphasized Jesus' special role in fulfilling God's eschatological promises. Mark gives evidence that some early Jesus followers interpreted Jesus' miracles to indicate Jesus' exalted status. The Double Tradition prefers instead to talk about miracles in ways that emphasize Jesus' participation along with his followers in the in-breaking kingdom of God. Thus, the Double Tradition promotes a view of Jesus' miracles that differs from that held by some other early Jesus followers. Direct evidence that the author(s) of the Double Tradition were aware of this differing view of Jesus' miracles does not exist, but Mark shows that this view held currency among early Jesus followers. Thus, those who told and retold the stories that make up the Double Tradition could have been aware of this other way of telling miracle stories and therefore had the opportunity to reject it.

The motive for an author to refute a viewpoint would be some problem that the author sees with that viewpoint. The review of Markan miracles has examined the appeal of using miracles to show Jesus' unique connection to God. However, using miracles in this way carries liabilities. The review of miracles and magic in chapter 2 showed that one way to impugn those who performed such deeds was to imply that they did so for their own self-aggrandizement. In the *Life of Apollonius,* the hero faces trial at the hands of the emperor Domitian under numerous charges, one of which is that he has used his miracles to set himself up to be worshiped and treated as a god (7.20–21). By depicting Jesus as performing miracles to demonstrate his divine identity, early Jesus followers opened Jesus to a similar accusation. For instance, Celsus claimed that Jesus, "having hired himself out in Egypt on account of his poverty, and having there acquired some powers (δυνάμεών) . . . returned to his own country, thinking himself great on account of these powers (δυνάμεσι), and by means of these proclaimed himself a god" (Origen, *Contra Celsum* 1.28). In the ancient world, using miraculous powers to convince others of one's divinity was disreputable. This disreputability would have motivated some followers to portray Jesus as rejecting such a use of miracles.

One means by which the Double Tradition effects this rejection is by having Jesus reject the devil's temptations to perform miracles. The rest of this section will examine Q's Temptation to show how this is the case. It will show that in many ways the three-fold Temptation presents Jesus as an exemplary hero enduring a testing in a way that affirms the values of the community that follows him, just as the testings of Zarathustra and the Buddha do. However, the inducements to perform miracles fit awkwardly with this exemplary function, and the best explanation for these temptations is as an attempt to repudiate using miracles as Jesus' divine credentials.

Turning Stones into Bread

The devil opens his dialogue with, "If you are God's son (εἰ υἱὸς εἶ τοῦ θεοῦ)" (Matt 4:3//Luke 4:3). What exactly the devil means by "God's son" the storyteller leaves vague. In the Tanakh and Septuagint, being a son or child of God indicates an especially close, but not necessarily unique, relationship to God.[30] Christians later came to use the idea of sonship to speak of Jesus' unique relationship with God. The Double Tradition, on the other hand, does not present the parent/child relationship with God as exclusive to Jesus. Jesus teaches his followers to pray to God as their father (Matt 6:9// Luke 11:2) and encourages them to rely on God as their father (Matt 7:11// Luke 11:13; Matt 6:32//Luke 12:30).[31] The anarthrous υἱός in the devil's statement fits this pattern of seeing divine sonship as not exclusive to Jesus. While the NRSV translates the devil's opening, "If you are the Son of God," one could just as well translate, "If you are *a* son of God."[32] By leaving out the definite article, the storyteller avoids having the devil imply that Jesus is uniquely God's son.

Although the devil does not imply a unique filial relationship between Jesus and God, he does first stipulate that Jesus possesses great power based on his relationship to God and next tempts him to deploy that power.[33] The storyteller gives no indication why Jesus should reject the invitation to turn stones into bread; the problem is less obviously the temptation than the one doing the tempting. On one level, the devil's instruction to produce bread from rocks simply gives Jesus an opportunity to parry with a quotation from Deuteronomy and thus to create a parallelism between Jesus and Israel.[34] In all three of the temptations, Jesus rejects the devil's inducements with quotations from Deuteronomy 6–8. In these chapters Moses speaks to the Israelites just before they cross the Jordan into the Promised Land. Moses reminds the Israelites that God provided them manna in the wilderness to teach them that "one does not live by bread alone, but by every word that comes from the mouth of the Lord" (Deut 8:3). The Israelites' demand that God provide them water at Massah should, according to Moses, teach them, "Do not put the Lord your God to the test" (Deut 6:16). Moses also instructs the Israelites not to stray from exclusive devotion to the Lord after they enter the Promised Land: "The Lord your God you shall fear; him you shall serve, and by his name alone you shall swear" (Deut 6:13). Jesus' responses to the devil prove that he is faithful to the instructions that Moses gave God's people, prove that he is an exemplar.

Jesus' affirmation that one does not live by bread alone not only illustrates his commitment to the teaching of Moses, but it also demonstrates how Jesus lives his own teaching as presented in Q. A major theme of Jesus' teaching in Q is relying on God for everyday needs rather than striving to acquire them. Jesus teaches his followers not to worry about acquiring food and clothing by offering them the example of the ravens and the lilies, for whom God provides (Matt 6:25–31//Luke 12:22–39). Instead, Jesus' followers are to rely on God's paternal solicitude and to strive for God's kingdom:

> For the Gentiles strive after all these things. For your Heavenly Father knows that you need all these things. But seek first the kingdom of God and His righteousness, and all these things will be added to you. (Matt 6:31–32)

> For the Gentiles of the world strive after all these things, but your Father knows that you need these things. Then seek His kingdom and these things will be added to you. (Luke 12:30–31).

When Jesus refuses the devil's first temptation with a quotation from Deuteronomy, he models a trust in the fatherly care of God that renders concern for material needs superfluous.

Jesus also teaches his followers to rely on God for their material needs, specifically for bread, when he teaches his followers how to pray:

> Our Father who is in heaven, let Your name be sanctified, let Your kingdom come. . . . Give us our daily bread today and forgive us our debts as even we have forgiven those who owe us, and do not lead us into testing. (Matt 6:9–13)

> Father, let Your name be sanctified, let Your kingdom come. Give us our daily bread each day, and forgive us our sins, for we ourselves forgive all who owe us, and do not lead us into testing. (Luke 11:2–4)

The prayer shares several keywords and ideas with the Temptation: a filial relationship with God and concern about bread (ἄρτος), testing (πειρασμός), and a kingdom (βασιλεία). With regard to the first temptation, the prayer offers a parallel outlook about reliance on God. In the prayer, Jesus teaches his followers to rely on God as a father for their bread. In the first temptation, Jesus shows that as God's son he will rely on God's providence rather than his own ability to procure his bread. By responding to the devil's inducement with the quotation of Deuteronomy 8:3, Jesus demonstrates the reliance on

God for bread that he instructs his followers to have in the rest of the Double Tradition.

However, Jesus' first quotation from Deuteronomy could have come as a response to many other possible temptations: the devil could have offered to give Jesus bread, much as he later offers to give Jesus the kingdoms of this world; the devil could have tempted Jesus to return to civilization much as Mara tempted the hungering Buddha; or, to make the connection with Israel even tighter, the devil could have suggested that Jesus pray for God to provide manna during his time of hunger. Instead, the devil suggests Jesus perform a miracle to feed himself, by which the storyteller indicates that there is something untoward in Jesus performing such a miracle. Since Jesus elsewhere performs miracles in the Double Tradition without the storyteller attaching opprobrium, the first temptation cannot be an outright rejection of miracle on Jesus' part.[35] Rather, the temptation implies that there is something wrong with performing a miracle in the way the devil suggests.

One possibility for the unacceptable element is using a miracle to gratify Jesus' material needs. However, the devil presents Jesus with another temptation about miracles beginning with the phrase, "If you are God's son," that has nothing to do with satisfying Jesus' physical needs. The unacceptable element is the use of a miracle to demonstrate Jesus' identity as God's son. For the Double Tradition, Jesus' miracles should not serve as proofs of his identity.

Leaping from the Temple

The second temptation (in Matthew's order) again centers on the miraculous, in this case a miraculous rescue from certain death. Again the devil links the miraculous to Jesus' identity as God's son, and again Jesus refuses to validate his identity with a miracle.

This vignette starts as the devil leads Jesus into Jerusalem and stands him on top of the Temple. For the temptation that follows, this detail is inconsequential—any sufficiently high place could have served as the setting for the devil to urge Jesus to jump. One unconvincing explanation for specifying the location is that by placing the encounter on the Temple, there is an audience of onlookers below, onlookers who would be amazed to see angels flying down to catch Jesus should he jump. Thus, the devil's tempts Jesus to provide a sign to convince the onlookers of his close relationship to God, paralleled by Jesus' refusal to provide a sign from heaven (Mt 12:38–42//Lk 11:29–32).[36] However, there is no mention of an audience in the Temptation, so the location must serve some other function.[37]

Listeners familiar with the basics of Jesus' story will recall, when they heard a story about Jesus risking death in Jerusalem, the danger Jesus faced in Jerusalem at the end of his life.[38] Although the Double Tradition does not include a narrative of Jesus' death in Jerusalem, it nevertheless does depict Jerusalem, and the Temple in particular, as a place of danger. Q's Jesus chastises his contemporaries as complicit with their ancestors in the shedding of righteous blood from Abel until Zechariah, whom Q describes as dying between the altar and the sanctuary (Matt 23:35//Luke 11:51), apparently referring to Zachariah the priest who condemned Judah's apostasy and who was killed within the Temple precincts during the reign of King Joash (2 Chr 24:17–22). In Zachariah's story, the Temple is a place of danger to those loyal to God. This idea of Jerusalem as a place of danger for the prophets surfaces again in the Double Tradition's account of Jesus' lament: "Jerusalem, Jerusalem, who kills the prophets and stones those sent to it" (Matt 23:37//Luke 13:34). According to Q's Jesus, the Jerusalemites' failure to turn from their murderous ways has consequences for the Temple at its center: "Behold, your house is abandoned" (Matt 23:38//Luke 13:35). In the Double Tradition, Jerusalem is the site of the people's abandonment of God, evidenced by their killing God's messengers; God in return abandons the Jerusalem Temple.[39]

In these passages the Double Tradition develops the irony that the Temple should be a place of refuge, but it is in fact a place of danger for prophets. This juxtaposition of actual danger and supposed safety also finds expression in the Double Tradition's note that the devil sets Jesus "upon the pinnacle of the Temple (ἐπὶ τὸ πτερύγιον τοῦ ἱεροῦ)" (Matt 4:5//Luke 4:9). Exactly where this site is in the Temple Complex is unclear since the phrase, "pinnacle of the Temple," is unknown in literature prior to the Gospels.[40] The word πτερύγιον, however, means not only pinnacle, but also wing, and the related form πτέρυξ appears in a number of Psalms describing God's protection:

In the shelter of your wings (πτερύγων) you cover me. (Ps 16:8 LXX)

The people's children will hope in the shelter of your wings (πτερύγων). They will drink from the abundance of your house (οἴκου). (Ps 35:8–9 LXX)

I will hope in the shadow of your wings (πτερύγων). (Ps 56:2 LXX)

I will dwell in your tabernacle (σκηνώματί) forever, I will be covered in the shelter of your wings (πτερύγων). (Ps 60:5 LXX)

In the shelter of your wings (πτερύγων) I will rejoice. (Ps 62:8 LXX)

You hope under God's wings (πτέρυγας). (Ps 90:4 LXX)

Just like the Temple, the wings of God should be a place of protection and security, but Jesus faces temptation and danger on the wing of God's Temple.[41] By locating this temptation "upon the pinnacle of the Temple," Q creates an environment charged with symbolism of putative divine protection and actual danger.

In this symbolically charged locale, the devil opens his second temptation with the same phrase used in the first: "If you are God's son (εἰ υἱὸς εἶ τοῦ θεοῦ)" (Matt 4:6//Luke 4:9). Again, the protasis implies that Jesus, based on his relationship to God, has immense power, and the apodosis again gives the devil's suggestion of how to use this power. In this instance, rather than tempting Jesus to use his power to satisfy his hunger, the devil suggests Jesus put his life at risk by jumping off the Temple. Having been rebuked by Scripture before, the devil now resorts to Scripture by quoting the LXX of Psalm 90 (91 in the MT) to explain how God will send angels to rescue Jesus.[42] The Psalm explains how one with a close relationship with God, who "hope[s] under God's wings" (90:4), can expect divine protection. Satan uses this promise to induce Jesus to test the degree of God's care.

Jesus stands ready again to respond from Deuteronomy and counter the devil's attack. His quoted passage is Moses' admonition to the Israelites not to test God the way they had at Massah. In Deuteronomy Moses refers to Massah, but the story is told in Exodus 17:1–7—the Israelites in the wilderness thirsted and demanded Moses give them something to drink, which Moses interprets as their testing God. God instructs Moses to strike a rock, from which water flows. In Deuteronomy, Massah becomes a byword for the Israelites' unwarranted testing of God. In the context of the Double Tradition, the quotation from Deuteronomy 6:16 repudiates the devil's suggestion that Jesus provoke God to provide the protection promised in LXX Psalm 90. The Temple temptation provides an entertaining battle of wits and scriptural citations, which allows Jesus once again to get the best of the devil.

By quoting Deuteronomy Jesus models obedience to God that does not test God's faithfulness, an obedience that Moses commands the Israelites to maintain when they enter the Promised Land. In the course of his Deuteronomic speech, Moses reminds the Israelites that God tested (ἐκπειράσῃ) them in the wilderness (8:2), but forbids them from testing (ἐκπειράσεις) God in return (6:16). It is God's prerogative to test the people, but the people should not test God. The Double Tradition inculcates just this attitude toward testing. The Temptation demonstrates that humans should not test God. The Lord's Prayer, with its petition "do not lead us into testing (πειρασμόν)" (Matt 6:13//Luke 11:4), reflects the idea that God has the right to test humans, but humans can petition God not to do so. In the Temple temptation, Jesus demonstrates the attitude toward testing God that Moses laid down in Deuteronomy.

The Temple temptation does not, however, provide any insight into why the devil's offer was tempting in the first place. In the case of turning stones into bread, the appeal directly responds to Jesus' hunger. Why Jesus should want to leap from the temple and invoke a divine rescue is less clear. As mentioned above, there is no notice of an audience to imply that the devil is tempting Jesus to impress observers. Nor does the text indicate that Jesus might wish to prove his power to the devil or to himself. Furthermore, the author could have chosen another temptation to which Jesus could have responded from Deuteronomy 6:16. Instead of taking Jesus to the pinnacle of the Temple and tempting him to jump, the devil could have suggested that Jesus ask God to provide water in the wilderness. Such a temptation would have complemented the bread temptation, and it would have made the connection between Jesus and the Israelites in the Exodus even tighter by recapitulating the scene at Massah. Instead, The Double Tradition poses the temptation as regarding a miraculous divine rescue.

The bread and Temple temptations have complementary lacunae in addressing questions of psychology. The appeal of the bread temptation is obvious, but why Jesus should resist it is not evident—just because one does not live by bread alone does not mean that getting bread is forbidden. Nor does the story indicate why turning stones to bread would be illegitimate, although the fact that Satan offers the temptation points to its illegitimacy. On the other hand, the Temple temptation does not clarify why jumping off the temple should appeal to Jesus, but it makes very clear why Jesus should feel compelled to resist—because doing so would violate a prohibition from Deuteronomy. Neither temptation presents Jesus wrestling with his desire to do something or with his commitment to norms that prohibit him from doing so. The two events do not present Jesus as a figure to whose inner anguish readers can relate in their own struggles with temptation. Instead, the temptations present Jesus as an exemplar in following God's commandments, commandments that are as valid for all of God's people as they are for Jesus.[43] Jesus models the principles by which the hearers of the stories should live—principles of reliance on God.[44]

However, as we have seen above, there were other ways aside from having him decline to perform two miracles which could have made Jesus an exemplary figure. Indeed, having the temptations center around miracles (rather than on obtaining food and water by more mundane, but illicit means), weakens the narrative's exemplary force for Jesus followers who lack miraculous power. Nor did the storyteller need to have Satan introduce both temptations with, "If you are God's son . . ." As noted above, the narrative does not detail the exact nature of the relationship between God and Jesus that the devil presupposes, but by introducing the two temptations with this phrase the devil anchors them in Jesus' close relationship with God. The devil tempts Jesus to draw on this close relationship and perform miracles. The storyteller thus connects miracles to Jesus' identity as God's son.[45] Jesus' refusal to perform miracles here cannot be read as a more general repudiation of miracles, for the Double Tradition elsewhere views Jesus' miracles positively.[46] What the refusal of miracles does demonstrate is that

Jesus rejects the use of miracles to prove his relationship to God. In the Temple temptation, the devil takes Jesus to a place where divine protection should be most in effect, but where those who have remained faithful to God have found danger. Jesus refuses to claim a special privilege of protection that has been denied to the prophets who have met their end in Jerusalem. The Father-Son relationship does not exempt Jesus from the strictures about putting God to the test.

Worshiping Satan

The temptation to bow down to Satan breaks the pattern established in the other two temptations. There is no, "If you are God's son," from the devil. Instead of urging Jesus to use his own power, the devil here offers to grant Jesus power. In a rather pessimistic statement on political power, the story-teller suggests that Satan possesses all the kingdoms of the world and can transfer possession to whom he chooses. The catch is that to access this power, Jesus must bow down to Satan. Unlike the previous two temptations, here the devil is clearly attempting to convince Jesus to do something illicit (worship someone other than God) with the offer of something desirable (power over all the kingdoms of the world). At this point, the episode reverts to the pattern of the other two: Jesus rebuffs the Devil's advance with an apposite quotation from Deuteronomy.

Jesus shares with Zarathustra and the Buddha a temptation to assume earthly political power. All three figures led influential movements but did not exercise political power. Such stories of temptation show that these leaders could have taken a short-cut to their ultimate positions of influence, but such a path would have required them to betray their fidelity to God, Ahura Mazda, or the pursuit of Enlightenment. By telling stories of their temptations to political power, their followers emphasized that these figures came by their influence because they committed themselves to the right cause and taught others to do the same. All three figures could have obtained political power, but they chose instead to adhere to their respective goals.

The Double Tradition juxtaposes the offer of kingdoms for Jesus to rule with Jesus' commitment to the dawning kingdom of God.[47] Jesus teaches his followers to pray that God's kingdom come (Matt 6:10//Luke 11:2) and to seek first God's kingdom (Matt 6:22//Luke 12:31). As the previous chapters have shown, Jesus' miracles indicate the partial presence of God's kingdom and presage the fullness of God's kingdom to come. In the Beelzebul Controversy, Q's Jesus claims that God's kingdom is in the process of overcoming Satan's kingdom (Matt 12:25–28//Luke 11:18–20). In Q's Temptation narrative, Jesus refuses to align himself with the kingdom of Satan and provides an implicit example of allegiance to the kingdom of God which he proclaims elsewhere in the Q material.

Despite this implicit contrast between allegiance to the kingdom of God and the kingdom of Satan, the focus of the temptation is on worship of God versus worship of Satan. The offer of kingdoms is merely the bribe Satan proffers to induce Jesus to worship him, and Jesus' response from Deuteronomy focuses on violating monolatry rather than on the offer of kingdoms. In the context of Deuteronomy, the injunction to worship God alone comes as the Israelites are about to enter the Promised Land and live among people who worship other gods. The possibility exists that they will abandon their exclusive worship of the God who brought them out of Egypt and assimilate to Canaanite practices. Moses enjoins the people to remember what the God of Israel has done for them in liberating them from Egypt so that they will worship God alone. Jesus again shows himself obedient to the Torah by refusing to worship anyone other than God.

Monolatry was a well-established feature of Second Temple Judaism, so it seems odd that the tellers of the Double Tradition version of the Temptation would have felt a need to inculcate exclusive devotion to God through Jesus' example. It could be that such authors envisioned a Gentile audience that would still feel the pull of the polytheistic worship practices that they abandoned in becoming Jesus-followers.[48] In that case, this temptation would impress upon the audience Jesus' adherence to the monolatry commanded by Deuteronomy. An alternative explanation for the felt need to demonstrate Jesus' commitment to monolatry comes from the devotional practices within some early groups of Jesus-followers. If the worship of Jesus arose within the Jewish matrix of the earliest followers of Jesus, then these early followers had to contend with the Jewish insistence on exclusive worship of God. One way to square worship of Jesus with monolatrous commitment was to assimilate Jesus to the God of Israel and include worship of him within exclusive devotion to Israel's God.[49] Another response was to repudiate the worship of Jesus altogether, and the third temptation implicitly provides such a repudiation. We have seen in Mark evidence for early Jesus-followers blurring the distinction between Jesus and God through miracles, and we have seen in the first two temptations an attempt by the Double Tradition to distance Jesus from such a use of miracles. Similarly, this last temptation demonstrates that Jesus bowed down only to the one valid object of worship, and that Jesus was not to be included within the divine identity such that Jesus became a valid object of worship himself. Telling this temptation story was a way for some early Jesus followers to distance Jesus from devotional practices among other Jesus-followers that the Double Tradition tradents found problematic.

Co-text: The Refusal of a Sign

Jesus' refusal to provide a sign (Matt 12:38–42//Mark 8:11/13//Luke 11:29–32) represents another Mark-Q overlap. We will examine the Markan version in its own right as a co-text for the Markan Testing narrative, but here we will look at it only to determine what elements belong to the Double Tradition:

> Then some of the scribes and Pharisees replied to him, saying, "Teacher, we wish to see a sign (σημεῖον) from you." And Jesus answered and said to them, "A <u>wicked</u> and adulterous generation seeks a sign (σημεῖον), <u>but a sign (σημεῖον) will not be given to it except the sign (σημεῖον) of Jonah</u> the prophet. For just as Jonah was in the belly of the sea-monster three days and three nights, so will the son of man be in the heart of the earth three days and three nights. <u>The men of Nineveh will rise in the judgment with this generation and they will condemn it, because they repented at the proclamation of Jonah, and look, something greater (πλεῖον) than Jonah is here. The Queen of the South will be raised in the judgment with this generation and condemn</u> it, <u>because she came from the ends of the earth to hear the wisdom of Solomon, and look, something greater (πλεῖον) than Solomon is here.</u>" (Matt 12:38–42)

> When the crowds increased, he began to say, "This generation is a <u>wicked</u> generation. It seeks a sign (σημεῖον), <u>but a sign (σημεῖον) will not be given to it except the sign (σημεῖον) of Jonah.</u> For just as Jonah became a sign (σημεῖον) to the Ninevites, thus too will the son of man be to this generation. <u>The Queen of the South will be raised in the judgment with</u> the men of <u>this generation and condemn</u> them, <u>because she came from the ends of the earth to hear the wisdom of Solomon, and look, something greater (πλεῖον) than Solomon is here. The men of Nineveh will rise in the judgment with this generation and they will condemn it, because they repented at the proclamation of Jonah, and look, something greater (πλεῖον) than Jonah is here.</u>" (Luke 11:29–32)

> And Pharisees came out and began to dispute with him, seeking from him a sign (σημεῖον) from heaven, testing (πειράζοντες) him. And groaning in his spirit he said, "Why does this generation seek a sign (σημεῖον)? Amen I tell you, if a sign (σημεῖον) should be given to this generation. . . ." And leaving them, he again embarked and came to the other side. (Mark 8:11–13)

In the Double Tradition, Jesus responds to a request for a sign by calling those who ask for it a wicked generation and saying that this generation will receive only the sign of Jonah. Jesus follows with the sayings about the men of Nineveh and the Queen of the South condemning this generation for not responding appropriately to that which is greater than Jonah and Solomon.

As in the Temptation, so too in this pericope Jesus refuses an inducement to action. The Double Tradition stipulates neither the nature of the requested sign nor what that sign would indicate. Although not synonymous with miracle, σημεῖον ("sign") has a range of meanings that includes a miracle or wonder.[50] In refusing to give the people a sign, Jesus refuses to provide some noteworthy action, including a miracle.[51] In Q, Jesus performs miracles when confronted by the need for healing or exorcism, but he does not perform a miracle to prove himself, either to Satan or to his contemporaries. The only sign the contemporaries will receive is the cryptic sign of Jonah.

Jesus does not explain what this sign is, but it does serve as a segue to his further condemnation of his contemporaries. Instead of seeking a sign, they should have recognized what was occurring in Jesus' ministry. Just as he does in the woes on the Chorazin and Bethsaida (Matt 11:21–22//Luke 10:13–14), Q's Jesus castigates his contemporaries for failing to recognize the importance of what is occurring in his ministry, a failure which makes them liable to eschatological judgment. The Queen of the South and the Ninevites will rise in judgment against those who failed to recognize "something greater" (πλεῖον) than Solomon and Jonah.

Jesus blames his contemporaries for their failure to recognize *something* greater, rather than *someone* greater. Although it is the actions of Jesus' ministry that his contemporaries should recognize, the significance of these actions does not lie in indicating that Jesus is greater than Solomon and Jonah. Rather, Jesus' ministry indicates something is happening, something with eschatological significance, and elsewhere the Double Tradition refers to this thing present in Jesus' actions as the kingdom of God. In the refusal to give a sign, Q's Jesus deflects attention from his own person and toward what God is doing through him. In the Temptation Narrative, this deflection is even more explicit: Jesus refuses miraculous actions that would verify his status as God's son, actions that would distance him from the rest of humanity. Instead, Jesus chooses to exemplify the obedience and allegiance humans owe God.

Testing and Miracles in Q

In the Double Tradition, Jesus teaches his followers that not one stroke of a letter of the Law will pass away before heaven and earth pass away too (Matt 5:18//Luke 16:17). In the Temptation, the Double Tradition shows that Jesus considers the Law binding on himself as he quotes the Torah against the devil. However, the devil could have come up with any number of inducements for which a refutation from Deuteronomy would have been just as appropriate. Temptations to perform or call for miracles were not necessary to show that Jesus relied on God for his material needs, refused to put God to the test, and sought God's kingdom. The Temptation Narrative sets Jesus as an example of the principles he teaches elsewhere in the Double Tradition, but by including miracles among the temptations, the storytellers do more than make Jesus an example: they also make Jesus a spokesperson for reject-ing miracles as proofs of a special identity he has with God.

For Q, Jesus may be God's son, but this sonship does not exempt Jesus from obedience to and reverence for God. Jesus' ability to perform miracles does not place him in a position of equality with God. In the rest of the Double Tradition material on miracles, we have seen that miracles indicate the presence of eschatological blessedness in Jesus' ministry. Because Jesus plays such a key role in making the kingdom of God present, he is important, but the miracles demonstrate Jesus' importance precisely as the one who is manifesting the kingdom of God. The Temptation Narrative rejects any im-plication that Jesus' miraculous powers indicate that he is a God-like figure or that anyone beside God should receive worship, Jesus included.

THE TESTING OF JESUS IN MARK

The three-fold Temptation of Jesus by Satan in the Double Tradition both establishes Jesus as an exemplar for his followers and repudiates the use of miracles as authenticating signs of Jesus' special relationship with God, so it is not surprising that Mark does not narrate these temptations. Mark tells stories of Jesus' miracles to emphasize Jesus' identity with God and to make Jesus distinct from his followers rather than a co-worker with them. It is impossible to know whether the absence of the Temptation narrative from Mark stemmed from Mark's ignorance of the tradition or from Mark's choice to exclude a story that would have undercut his depiction of Jesus elsewhere in the Gospel. Whatever the reason for this absence, it does not explain why Mark included Jesus' testing in the first place. The Gospel of John features no mention of Jesus being tempted by Satan, and Mark similarly could have ignored this encounter. There must have been a reason to include the brief mention that Jesus, after his baptism, "was in the wilderness forty days, being tested by Satan, and he was with the wild animals, and the angels were serving him" (Mark 1:13).

A hero's testing serves other functions besides establishing the hero as an exemplar. As seen earlier in this chapter, testing demonstrates the excellence of the hero and the importance of the hero's accomplishment. By briefly mentioning Jesus' encounter with Satan early in the narrative, Mark indicates that what Jesus does in his subsequent ministry is important without specify-ing what that importance is. By omitting any details about the nature of this satanic testing, Mark invites readers to interpret it in light of the only full discussion Jesus gives about his encounter with Satan: the Beelzebul Contro-versy (Mark 3:22–30). The lack of detail in the Markan Testing focuses attention on the bare fact that Jesus encountered Satan before Jesus started his ministry, and the later Beelzebul Controversy explicates the outcome and significance of this encounter.

To demonstrate that the Beelzebul Controversy is the interpretive key for Mark's brief statement of Jesus "being tested by Satan," this section turns to the other details in 1:13 concerning the Testing. The discussion will show that these details create a web of connections between Jesus' Testing and various events and figures from the Scriptures of Israel, but they do not specify what happened during the Testing. To look at what Mark implies about the encounter between Jesus and Satan, the section will next turn to the other appearances of Satan and testing in the Gospel to argue that Jesus' parable of the Binding of the Strong Man in the Beelzebul Controversy is best seen as illustrating what occurred when Jesus met Satan shortly after the baptism.

The Wilderness, Forty Days, Wild Animals, and Angels

Mark's lack of detail about how Satan tested Jesus has led many interpreters to look for clues in the other details in 1:13 to indicate what occurred in the Testing and what Mark saw as its significance. From the facts that Jesus was in the wilderness for forty days, with wild beasts, and served by angels, one can view Jesus as a new Adam or Israel, and then interpret the content and significance of Jesus' testing based on such typologies.[52] However, rather than creating a strong correspondence between Jesus and any particular biblical figure, Mark has in fact used the polysemy inherent in the details of 1:13 to link Jesus in many ways with figures from Israel's Scriptures without narrowly defining the content of the testing.

The wilderness (ἡ ἔρημος) in which Jesus' baptism and testing take place was a symbolically important locale in the traditions of Israel. The Pentateuch depicts the wilderness wanderings as a time of punishment for the disobedient Exodus generation (e.g., Num 14:32–33), but it is through the deprivations of the wilderness that the Israelites are disciplined and purified (e.g., Deut 8:5).[53] Testing also figures heavily in the wilderness traditions, as God tests the Israelites (Exod 16:4, 20:20, Deut 13:3), but the Israelites also test God (Exod 17:2–7, Num 14:22, Deut 6:16, 9:22). Mark's mention of a testing in the wilderness thus could bring to mind Jesus as a recapitulation of Israel, but it could also set up Jesus in the position of God, who was also tested in the wilderness. In addition to testing and hardship, the wilderness was also an abode of evil spirits (Lev 16:10, *1 Enoch* 10.4–5).

Testing, hardship, and evil spirits do not exhaust the biblical implications of the wilderness. The wilderness also allowed a special nearness to God. Many of the theophanies of Genesis and Exodus occur in the wilderness (Gen 16:7, Exod 3:1, Ex 16:10).[54] Similarly, Enoch receives some of his visions "in the wilderness" (*1 Enoch* 28.1, 29.1). Hosea speaks of the time in the wilderness as a honeymoon between Israel and God (2:14–15), and Eze-kiel describes the wilderness as the place where God will renew the covenant with the gathered people of Israel (20:33–38).[55] Qumran's Community Rule instructs the faithful to "separate from the session of perverse men to go to the wilderness, there to prepare the way of truth" (1QS 8.13). Similarly, in the *Martyrdom of Isaiah*, the prophet flees the corruption in the cities and goes to live in the wilderness (2.8–12). Elsewhere in Mark's Gospel the wilderness carries such positive valence. The wilderness is where John the Baptist appears with his baptism of repentance and his preparation of the way for Jesus (1:3–4), and it is where Jesus goes to pray (1:35) or to be alone with his disciples after their mission (6:31–32). By placing the testing in the wilderness, Mark allows the reader to see Jesus' activity as part of this broad matrix of wilderness traditions, but Mark does not fix a particular signifi-cance to the wilderness in this case.

Mark chooses a time period similarly rife with possible significations: forty days. Given the wilderness setting, one parallel for Jesus' forty days is Israel's forty-years wandering, with Jesus' wilderness experience recapitulat-ing Israel's.[56] Other parallels also exist. Moses spent forty days on Sinai receiving the Torah from God (Exod 24:18), and Elijah spent forty days fasting as he traveled to Horeb to receive his theophany (1 Kings 19:8).[57] Perhaps the most famous forty-day period is the flood that Noah endured. In the ark, Noah is also with wild beasts (Gen 8:1) and receives a sign in the form of a dove over water (Gen 8:8–12), elements present in the baptism of Jesus that immediately precedes the testing (Mark 1:9–10). Forty-day periods occur in less well-known cases as well: the spies sent by Moses spend forty days in the Promised Land (Num 13:25); during Antiochus's rule, an appari-tion of cavalry appeared in the air in Jerusalem for forty days (2 Macc 5:2); the people of Bethulia put God to the test by deciding that they would surrender to Holofernes if God did not deliver them from the siege before forty days had passed (Jdt 7:19–8:17).[58] Forty days also figures in extra-biblical traditions about Adam. In *Jubilees* 3.9, God places Adam in Eden forty days after his creation. In *The Life of Adam and Eve* 6.1, Adam spends forty days fasting in penance for his disobedience to God.[59] Just as the wilderness location does not specify a single meaning for the Testing but rather invites the reader to connect Jesus' story with various stories of Israel, so does the duration of forty days similarly offer a panoply of connections between Jesus and figures from Israel's history.

The forty days in the wilderness were a time not only for Jesus to be tested, but also for him to be with wild animals and served by angels. In the Septuagint, wild animals (θηρία) are most often presented as forces of de-struction and death.[60] Jesus' being with the wild animals could thus indicate his exposure to danger during his stay in the wilderness.[61] However, within the prophets there also existed visions of a future when humans and wild

animals would live in harmony (Isa 43:20; Ezek 31:6; Hos 2:18). Thus, Mark
leaves the passage open to the interpretation that Jesus lives in eschatological
harmony with the wild animals.[62]

The combination of angels and wild animals can suggest the situation
envisioned in Psalm 91, which is made explicit in the Q version:

> For he will command his angels concerning you to guard you in all your ways.
> On their hands they will bear you up, so that you will not dash your foot
> against a stone. You will tread on the lion and the adder, the young lion and the
> serpent you will trample under foot. (Ps 91:11–13)

Here the one under God's protection goes unharmed by hostile animals while
angels guard him. Mark's placement of Jesus with the wild animals and the
angels invites, but does not demand, a link between Jesus and the figure in
the Psalm.[63] For a reader (or author) familiar with the Double Tradition
version of the Testing, a contrast based on Psalm 91 suggests itself: in
Mark's Testing, Jesus enjoys the protection promised by the Psalm, whereas
in the Q version, Jesus refuses to invoke this same protection when the devil
quotes Psalm 91 on the pinnacle of the Temple. Whether Mark intended this
contrast or not, the presence of the angels suggests that in Mark's version
Jesus has the support of God, mediated through the angels, during his time in
the wilderness.

Rather than adding specificity about the content, result, or significance of
Jesus' testing, the other elements in Mark 1:13 connect the testing to a
multitude of events and figures from the history of Israel. This verse creates
an expansive network of allusions within which to situate the testing, but it
lacks sufficient detail to demand that any one single allusion is the overriding
interpretive key. To determine what specific ideas, if any, Mark has about
what happened in this encounter between Jesus and Satan, we must look to
the rest of his Gospel for clues.

Testing and Satan in the Markan Co-texts

Once familiar with the Double Tradition's Temptation, one struggles to
avoid seeing in Mark's mention of Jesus' Testing a demonic temptation to
violate God's commands. However, merely mentioning a testing by Satan
need not recollect the sort of Temptation narrated by Q. As noted in the
introduction to this chapter, πειράζω can indicate temptation, but its connotation is broader. In the LXX, the verb is very often used to describe actions
that test people's devotion to God, such as when God commands Abraham to
sacrifice Isaac (Gen 22:1), or when God allows other nations to afflict the
Israelites to determine if they would remain faithful (Judg 2:22). Nevertheless, this Septuagintal usage does not demand that Mark's readers take Jesus'
testing to be one of proving his faithfulness to God.[64] The Queen of Sheba

comes to test Solomon's wisdom, not Solomon's fidelity to God (1 Kgs 10:1; 2 Chr 9:1). The noun form, πειρασμός, also appears in the LXX to describe the plagues God sent on the Egyptians, which were not ways of proving the Egyptians' fidelity (Deut 4:34, 7:19). This example from Deuteronomy shows that this family of words also denoted a hostile action that had to be endured without reference to testing one's character or devotion to God.[65]

In the rest of Mark, the verb describes actions of Jesus' opponents with no mention of inducing Jesus to swerve from his devotion to God. In the Markan version of the Refusal of a Sign, Pharisees approach Jesus, "seeking from him a sign from heaven, testing (πειράζοντες) him" (Mark 8:11). Mark does not say what the Pharisees thought they were testing, but the most straight-forward reading is that they were testing Jesus' ability to perform a sign on demand. Jesus simply refuses to perform a sign, and he leaves without ex-plaining his refusal (8:12–13). One unsatisfactory way to interpret his refusal to give a sign is that Mark's Jesus views his ministry as self-authenticating and that therefore a miraculous sign would be superfluous or, indeed, contrary to the message of his ministry.[66] This interpretation is countered by the fact that Mark uses miracles extensively to demonstrate Jesus' identity. Indeed, Jesus heals the paralytic to prove his authority to the scribes who doubted him (Mk 2:10) and provides just the sort of authenticating sign that Jesus refuses to give to the Pharisees in 8:12. Moreover, the Transfiguration provides a striking sign from heaven to Peter, James, and John of Jesus' identity as Son of God (9:7). Mark 8:12–13 is more profitably interpreted as demonstrating that Jesus acts on his own initiative. If he had tried and failed to produce a sign, the Pharisees' opposition would be vindicated; if he suc-ceeded he would have shown that his opponents could manipulate him into acting as they demanded. Instead, Jesus chooses not to participate.

The Pharisees again test Jesus when they ask him about divorce: "Phari-sees came and, testing (πειράζοντες) him, asked if it is lawful for a man to divorce his wife" (10:2). Instead of answering the question, Jesus responds by asking another question: What did Moses command? When the Pharisees respond that Moses allowed divorce, Jesus begins his attack on his interlocu-tors by saying that Moses allowed divorce because of their hardness of heart. Jesus goes on to use the creation story from Genesis to show that divorce was not God's intention. The story does not detail what quality of Jesus the Pharisees thought they were testing, but the testing that they instigate ends with Jesus accusing them of being hard of heart.

Jesus similarly deflects the attack the third time the Pharisees test him. In Jerusalem, some Pharisees and some Herodians attempt "to trap him with a word," by asking him whether one should pay taxes to the emperor (12:13). Jesus, "knowing their hypocrisy, said to them, why do you test (πειράζετε) me?" (12:15). He then asks them whose bust appears on a denarius, and when they answer that Caesar's head appears on the coin, Jesus responds with the non-answer "Give to Caesar what is Caesar's and to God what is God's" (12:17). The Pharisees and Herodians come to trap him, but Jesus recognizes the trap and escapes it.

In these three instances of testing, the Pharisees present Jesus with challenging demands or questions, and the test concerns how Jesus responds. Mark does not indicate that these are tests of Jesus' loyalty to God, nor does Mark say what quality of Jesus these tests are supposed to illustrate. Rather, Mark focuses on Jesus' response to these tests, and in all three cases Jesus refuses to participate in the test as the opponents present it. The tests show Jesus' ability to avoid entrapment and to turn the Pharisees' hostile questions back on them. Mark is less interested in showing Jesus passing a test than he is in showing Jesus confounding those who try to test him.

These tests provide one set of cotexts for the Testing; the other useful set of cotexts are those about Jesus encountering Satan. The rest of Mark describes only two other encounters between Jesus and Satan. Following Peter's confession at Caesarea Philippi, Jesus tells his disciples that he will suffer, die, and rise again, at which Peter rebukes him. In response Jesus says to Peter, "Get behind me, Satan, because you do not think the things of God but the things of humans" (8:33). Mark most likely included this equation of Peter with Satan to provide a strong way for Mark's Jesus to rebuke the idea of avoiding the Passion. This brief rebuke hardly indicates Satan's agenda throughout the Gospel. Satan is very much absent from Mark's account of the Passion, and the one time when Mark presents Jesus as genuinely conflicted about whether or not to undergo his divinely appointed suffering, his prayer in Gethsemane (14:35–36), Satan does not figure as instigator. Therefore, no compelling reason exists to read into Jesus' Testing after the baptism an attempt to dissuade him from taking his path to the cross. [67]

The other description of an encounter between Jesus and Satan occurs in the Beelzebul Controversy, and this encounter provides the key to interpreting the Testing: the Testing is the occasion for Jesus' victory over Satan that he describes with the parable of the Strong Man. After Jesus refutes the scribes' accusation that he performs exorcisms through a pact with Satan, Jesus tells them in a parable what the exorcisms really demonstrate about his relationship with Satan: "No one is able to enter the house of a strong man to steal his property unless he first binds the strong man, and then he can plunder his house" (3:27). Jesus' exorcisms indicate that Jesus has conquered Satan. In Mark's telling, exorcisms are a feature of Jesus' public ministry from its inception (1:21–28), so the victory over Satan must have come before Jesus began his ministry. Mark thus implies that the encounter in the wilderness resulted in Jesus' conquest of the devil, a conquest that allowed him to perform his subsequent exorcisms. [68] In the tests that the Pharisees present, Jesus usually turns the test back on the testers and gains the upper hand. So also the Beelzebul Controversy shows that when Satan came to test Jesus, Jesus ensnared Satan.

The brevity of Mark's account of the testing speaks to Mark's purpose. Mark is not interested in telling how Jesus passes some particular test as a way to highlight a particular Christological virtue. Rather, Mark's interest lies in the fact that Jesus encountered and conquered Satan before he began his ministry. Because the Beelzebul Controversy makes clear that Jesus has bested Satan, the evangelist had no need to make the outcome of the testing explicit in chapter 1. The mention of the testing puts into the reader's mind that Jesus and Satan have encountered each other, and the lack of detail about the outcome creates suspense and invites the reader to infer what the outcome could be. The exorcisms show that Jesus has been victorious over Satan, and the Beelzebul Controversy makes the victory explicit.

CONCLUSION

The detailed telling of the Temptation in the Double Tradition shows Jesus repudiating the use of miracles to demonstrate his divine identity. By omitting details about the Testing, Mark allows the Beelzebul Controversy to describe the encounter between Jesus and Satan, so that the Testing in 1:13 becomes the genesis of Jesus' exorcistic miracles. Since the exorcisms and other miracles in Mark provide just the sort of demonstration of Jesus' divine identity that Q's Jesus rejects, it makes sense that Mark lacks an extended Temptation narrative similar to that of the Double Tradition. We cannot know whether Mark was familiar with the version of the story that the Double Tradition preserves, but if he were, it would have fit his agenda to omit it. That Mark's Gospel was preserved indicates that other early Jesus followers found its presentation of Jesus' life appealing and worth retelling and rerecording, and eventually some of these followers became aware of the Gospels of Matthew and Luke as well. That Mark continued to be copied and read speaks to the ongoing appeal of a depiction of Jesus using miracles to efface the distinction between himself and God, a depiction where such use of miracles is not a demonic temptation that Jesus must reject.

The inclusion of miracles within Q's Temptation narrative makes the most sense as a way of rejecting miracles as proofs of Jesus' divine identity. The absence of this narrative from Mark is consistent with a rejection of this rejection. Both Mark and the Double Tradition use the Testing to show the excellence of Jesus in overcoming a challenge from the devil early in his career, but it is a different type of excellence that each propounds. Q shows the exemplary excellence of Jesus as one faithful to God's commands who subjects himself to God; Mark shows Jesus as the one who conquers Satan and enacts the eschatological victory promised by God, as the evangelist leaves the implications of the Testing vague and invites the reader to view its significance through the lens of the Beelzebul Controversy. In Mark's way of depicting Jesus' excellence, miracles efface the distinction between Jesus and God, while such a function of miracles is anathema in Q's depicting Jesus' excellence. These two different ways of remembering Jesus and his miracles came into competition, and the Testing stories in Mark and the Double Tradition bear the marks of this competition.

NOTES

1. *BDAG* 640, πειράζω.

2. I have followed Matthew's order because 1) that is the order the Grand Inquisitor follows in interpreting the pericope and 2) Matthew groups the two temptations having to do with miracles consecutively, and structuring the discussion in this order streamlines the analysis of these two temptations.

3. For the argument that Q contains an account of Jesus' baptism leading into the temptation, see James M. Robinson, "The Sayings Gospel Q," in *Four Gospels 1992: Festschrift Frans Neirynck*, eds. F. Van Segbroeck, C. M. Tuckett, G. Van Belle, and J. Verheyden (Leuven: Leuven University Press, 1992), 1.382–85; for the argument against including the baptism in Q, see Harry T. Fleddermann, *Q: A Reconstruction and Commentary* (Leuven: Peeters, 2005), 233–35. For including the wilderness setting in Q, see James M. Robinson, Paul Hoffmann, and John S. Klopenborg, *The Critical Edition of Q: Synopsis Including the Gospels of Matthew and Luke, Mark and Thomas with English, German, and French Translations of Q and Thomas* (Minneapolis: Fortress, 2000), 22–23; for a reconstruction that omits the reference to the wilderness, see Fleddermann, *Q*, 235–38.

4. *Jub.* 17:15–18 and 4Q225 show Mastema as instigator; in *b. Sanh.* 89b it is Satan.

5. Mahnaz Moazami, "The Confrontation of Zarathustra with the Evil Spirit: Chapter 19 of the Pahlavi Videvdad," *East and West* 52.1 (2002): 151.

6. *Videvdad* 19:6.

7. Ananda W.P. Guruge, *The Buddha's Encounters with Mara* (Kandy, Sri Lanka: Buddhist Publication Society, 1997), 2–15; James W. Boyd, *Satan and Mara: Christian and Buddhist Symbols of Evil* (Leiden: Brill, 1975), 77–92.

8. Guruge, *Buddha's Encounters*, 14–15.

9. Ibid., 6.

10. Boyd, *Satan and Mara*, 144.

11. Vladimir Propp, *Morphology of the Folktale*, 2nd Ed., ed. Louis A. Wagner, trans. Laurence Scott (Austin: University of Texas Press, 1968); originally published in Russian as *Morfologiia skazki* (Leningrad: Academia, 1928). The pattern that Propp discerned in Russian folktales has been applied to tales from cultures around the world. For application to African stories, see Denise Paulme, "Le garcon traveti ou Joseph en Afrique," *L'Homme* 3.2 (1963): 5–21. For application to American Indian stories, see Alan Dundes, *The Morphology of North American Indian Folktales* (Helsinki: Suomalainen Tiedekatemia Academia Scientarum Fennica, 1964). For application to Africa, the Americas, Asia, and Europe, see Peter Gilet, *Vladimir Propp and the Universal Folktale: Recommissioning an Old Paradigm—Story as Initiation* (New York: Peter Lang, 1998), 59–120. The testing of the hero soon after his departure also features in Joseph Campbell's theory of the monomyth, *The Hero with a Thousand Faces* (New York: Pantheon Books, 1949), 97–108.

12. Propp, *Morphology*, 39–40.

13. Propp articulated this approach in his *Historical Roots of the Folktale*, published in Russian as *Istoricheskie korni volshebnoi skazki* (Leningrad: Izd-vo Leningradskogo gos. ordena Lenina universiteta, 1946). In this work Propp adopted the theoretical approach of mythritualism, which assumed that folklore and mythology derived from rituals. Gilet, *Propp*, 134; Jack Zipes, "Forward: Toward Understanding the Complete Vladimir Propp," in Vladimir

Propp, *The Russian Folktale by Vladimir Yakolevich Propp*, trans. Sibelan Forrester (Detroit: Wayne State University Press, 2012), ix–xi.

14. For a decisive critique of the myth-ritualist paradigm see Joseph Fontenrose, *The Ritual Theory of Myth*, University of California Folklore Studies 18 (Berkeley: University of California Press, 1966). For the positive contributions of the myth-ritualist paradigm, see Robert A. Segal, "The Myth-Ritualist Theory of Religion," *Journal for the Scientific Study of Religion* 19, no. 2 (1980): 173–85.

15. Paul Connerton, *How Societies Remember* (Cambridge: Cambridge University Press, 1989), 54, 70.

16. Gilet, *Propp*, 131–54, sees the entirety of Propp's morphological paradigm corresponding to the form of a rite of passage. Campbell, *Hero*, 382–86, similarly connects his monomyth with rites of passage. Mark McVann, "One of the Prophets: Matthew's Testing Narrative as a Rite of Passage," *BTB* 23, no. 1 (1993): 14–20, interprets Matthew's version of the Temptation as enacting a rite of passage.

17. Victor Turner, *The Ritual Process: Structure and Anti-Structure* (New York: de Gruyter, 1969), 100–102.

18. Kathleen Margaret Dugan, *The Vision Quest of the Plains Indians: Its Spiritual Significance* (Lewiston, NY: Edwin Mellen, 1985), 132–34, 143–44.

19. Mircea Eliade, *Shamanism: Archaic Techniques of Ecstasy*, trans. Willard R. Trask (New York: Pantheon, 1964), 33, 35–45, 45–50, 58–60.

20. Neil J. Smelser, *Odyssey Experience: Physical, Social, Psychological, and Spiritual Journeys* (Berkley: University of California Press, 2009), 182–90.

21. Mircea Eliade, *Rites and Symbols of Initiation: The Mysteries of Birth and Rebirth*, trans. Willard R. Trask (New York: Harper & Row, 1958), xii, 2–3, 21–40, 90–91.

22. Arnold Van Gennep, *The Rites of Passage* (Chicago: University of Chicago Press, 1960), 21, 65–115, 191.

23. Victor Turner, "Betwixt and Between: The Liminal Period in *Rites de Passage*," in *The Forest of Symbols: Aspects of Ndembu Ritual* (Ithaca, NY: Cornell University Press, 1967), 101.

24. Elliot Aronson and Judson Mills, "The Effect of Severity of Initiation on Liking for a Group," *Journal of Abnormal and Social Psychology* 59 (1959): 177–81.

25. Ibid., 179.

26. Harold B. Gerard and Grover C. Mathewson, "The Effects of Severity of Initiation on Liking for a Group: A Replication," *Journal of Experimental Social Psychology* 2 (1966): 278–87; Caroline Kamau, "What Does Being Initiated Severely Into a Group Do? The Role of Rewards," *International Journal of Psychology* 48, no. 3 (2013): 399–406; Ward D. Finer, Jacob E. Hautaluoma, and Larry J. Bloom, "The Effects of Severity and Pleasantness of Initiation on Attraction to a Group," *Journal of Social Psychology* 111 (1980): 301–2; Caroline F. Keating et al., "Going to College and Unpacking Hazing: A Functional Approach to Decrypting Initiation Practices Among Undergraduates," *Group Dynamics: Theory, Research, and Practice* 9, no. 2 (2005): 104–26; Hein F. M. Lodewijkx and Joseph E. M. M. Syroit, "Severity of Initiation Revisited: Does Severity of Initiation Increase Attractiveness in Real Groups?" *European Journal of Social Psychology* 27 (1997): 275–300.

27. Jonathan Z. Smith, *To Take Place: Toward Theory in Ritual* (Chicago: University of Chicago Press, 1987), 105–9.

28. For the important roles exemplars play in group identity formation, see Eliot R. Smith and Miachael Zarate, "Exemplar and Prototype in Social Categorization," *Social Cognition* 8, no. 3 (1990): 243–62.

29. Philip F. Esler and Ronald Piper, *Lazarus, Mary, and Martha: Social-Scientific Approaches to the Gospel of John* (Minneapolis: Fortress, 2006), 34–38.

30. C. Michael Robbins, *The Testing of Jesus in Q* (New York: Peter Lang, 2007), 97–98. The idea of a parent/child relationship with God could be applied to kings (2 Sam 7; 1 Chr 17:13; 22:10; 28:6; Ps 2:7; 89:26–27), the people of Israel (Exod 4:22–23; Deut 32:6–18; Jer 3:4,19; 31:9, 20; Hos 11:1; 2 Esdr 6:58; Wis 18:13; Sir 36:17), angels (Gen 6:2; Job 1:6; 2:1; 38:7; Dan 3:25) and righteous people (Wis 2:12–20; Sir 4:10).

31. C. M. Tuckett, "The Temptation Narrative in Q," in *The Four Gospels 1992: Festschrift Frans Neirynck,* ed. F. Van Segbroeck, C. M. Tuckett, G. Van Belle, and J. Verheyden (Leuven: Leuven University Press, 1992), 495–96. For God's solicitude as a father as a major theme in Q, see Ickhard Rau, "Unser Vater im Himmel: Eine These zur Metaphorik der Rede von Gott in der Logienquelle" *NT* 53, no. 3 (2011): 242.

32. Alfred M. Perry, "Translating the Greek Article," *JBL* 68, no. 4 (1949): 330.

33. Although Jeffrey B. Gibson, "A Turn on 'Turning Stones to Bread.' A New Understanding of the Devil's Intention in Q 4.3," *Biblical Research* 41 (1996): 38 argues that the devil is really tempting Jesus to ask God to turn the stones into bread, the apodosis does not indicate that Jesus is to petition God. Instead, Jesus is to order the stones to become bread, which implies that they will obey his word.

34. Robbins, *Testing,* 157–61; W. D. Davies and Dale C. Allison, Jr., *Matthew 1–7,* International Critical Commentary (Edinburgh: T&T Clark, 1988), 361.

35. Against Siegfried Schulz, *Q: Die Spruchquelle der Evangelisten* (Zürich; Theologischer Verlag, 1972), 177–90.

36. Tuckett, "Temptation," 500.

37. Davies and Allison, *Matthew 1–7,* 367.

38. Harry T. Fleddermann, "The Plot of Q," *ETL* 88, no. 1 (2012): 47–48, 56.

39. Kyu Sam Han, *Jerusalem and the Early Jesus Movement: The Q Community's Attitude Toward the Temple* (London: Sheffield Press, 2002), 177–90.

40. Davies and Allison, *Matthew 1–7,* 365.

41. Han, *Jerusalem,* 141.

42. William Richard Stegner, "The Use of Scripture in Two Narratives of Early Jewish Christianity (Matthew 4.1–11; Mark 9.2–8)," in *Early Christian Interpretation of the Scriptures of Israel: Investigations and Proposals,* ed. James A. Sanders and Craig A. Evans (Sheffield: Sheffield Academic Press, 1997), 100.

43. Tuckett, "Temptation," 488–89; Thomas Hieke "Schriftgelehrsamkeit in der Logienquelle: Die alttetstamentlichen Zitate in der Versuchungsgeschichte Q 4,1–13," in *From Quest to Q: Festschrift James M. Robinson,* ed. Jon Ma Asgeirsson, Kristin de Toyer, and Marvin W. Meyer (Leuven: Leuven University Press, 2000), 70.

44. Luigi Schiavo, "The Temptation of Jesus: The Eschatological Battle and the New Ethic of the First Followers of Jesus in Q," *JSNT* 25.2 (2002): 163; Tuckett, "Temptation," 506; John S. Kloppenborg, *The Formation of Q: Trajectories in Ancient Wisdom Collections* (Philadelphia: Fortress, 1987), 250–53; Rudolf Bultmann, *History of the Synoptic Tradition,* trans. John Marsh (New York: Scribner's, 1951), 256.

45. Martin Hüneburg, *Jesus als Wundertäter in der Logienquelle: Ein Beitrag zur Christologie von Q,* Arbeiten zur Bibel und ihrer Geschichte 4 (Leipzig: Evangelische Verlagsanstalt, 2001), 113.

46. Kloppenborg, *Formation,* 253–54; Jacques Schlosser, "Les tentations de Jésus et la cause de Dieu," *Revue des Sciences Religiuses* 76, no. 4 (2002): 420.

47. Tuckett, "Temptation," 504–5.

48. Fleddermann, *Q,* 262–63. For the argument that this temptation specifically arose in the context of early Christian disapproval of the Emperor Caligula, see Gerd Theissen, *The Gospels in Context: Social and Political History in the Synoptic Tradition,* trans. Linda M. Maloney (Minneapolis: Fortress, 1991), 206–21. N. H. Taylor, "The Temptation of Jesus on the Mountain: A Palestinian Christian Polemic Against Agrippa I," *JSNT* 83 (2001): 27–49, modifies Theissen's thesis slightly and sees Caligula's client Agrippa I as the target of the implied polemic.

49. Larry W. Hurtado, *Lord Jesus Christ: Devotion to Jesus in Earliest Christianity* (Grand Rapids, MI: Eerdmans, 2003), 50–53.

50. *BDAG* 747–48, σημεῖον.

51. Hüneburg, *Jesus,* 214–15; François Bovon, *Luke 2: A Commentary on the Gospel of Luke 9:51–19:27,* Hermeneia, trans Donald S. Deer, ed. Helmut Koester (Minneapolis: Fortress, 2013), 215. Other scholars see the request for a sign as equivalent to a request for a miracle, see Schulz, *Q,* 255; Ilija Cabraja, *Der Gedanke der Umkehr bei den Synoptikern: eine exegetisch- religionsgeschichtliche Untersuchung* (Sankt Ottilein: EOS Verlag, 1985), 110.

52. For the Adam typology, see Dale C. Allison, Jr., "Behind the Temptations of Jesus: Q 4:1–13 and Mark 1:12–13," in *Authenticating the Activities of Jesus,* ed. Bruce M. Metzger and Bart D. Ehrman (Boston: Brill, 1999), 196–98; Joel Marcus, *Mark 1–8: A New Translation with Introduction and Commentary,* Anchor Bible 27 (New York: Doubleday, 2000), 169–70. For the Israel typology, see John Paul Heil, "Jesus with the Wild Animals in Mark 1:13," *CBQ* 68, no. 1 (2006): 63–78.

53. Robert Barry Leal, *Wilderness in the Bible: Toward a Theology of Wilderness* (New York: Peter Lang, 2004), 223; Richard Dormandy, "Jesus' Temptations in Mark's Gospel: Mark 1:12–13," *ExpTim* 114, no. 6 (2003): 183.

54. Leal, *Wilderness,* 150.

55. Terry L. Burden, *The Kerygma of the Wilderness Traditions in the Hebrew Bible* (New York: Peter Lang, 1994), 179–80.

56. Jeffrey B. Gibson, "Jesus' Wilderness Temptation according to Mark," *JSNT* 53 (1994): 17–18.

57. Allison, "Behind," 202.

58. Jan W. Van Henten, "The First Testing of Jesus: A Rereading of Mark 1.12–13," *NTS* 45, no. 3 (1999): 360.

59. Allison, "Behind," 198 n.13.

60. Gen 27:20; Exod 23:29; Lev 26:6, 26:22; Deut 7:22, 28:26, 32:24; Josh 23:5; 1 Sam 17:46; 2 Macc 9:15; Ps 73:19, 78:2; Wis 12:9, 16:5; Hos 2:12, 13:8; Zeph 2:14, 3:1; Isa 5:29, 46:1; Jer 7:33, 12:9, 15:3, 16:4, 19:7, 41:20; Ezek 5:17, 14:15, 14:21, 29:5, 33:27, 34:5, 34:8, 34:29, 39:3; Dan 7:5–7

61. Heil, "Jesus," 65, 74; Dormandy, "Temptations," 184.

62. Martin Hasitschka, "Der Sohn Gottes—geliebt und geprüft: Zusammenhang von Taufe und Versuchung Jesu bei den Synoptikern," in *Forschungen zum Neuen Testament und seiner Umwelt: Festschrift für Albert Fuchs,* ed. Christoph Niemand (Frankfurt am Main: Peter Lang, 2002), 74.

63. Susan R. Garrett, *The Temptations of Jesus in Mark's Gospel* (Grand Rapids, MI: Eerdmans, 1998), 57; A. B. Caneday "Mark's Provocative Use of Scripture in Narration: 'He was with the Wild Animals and Angels Ministered to Him,'" *BBR* 9 (1999): 34; Gibson, "Temptation," 21–22.

64. *Contra* Gibson, "Temptation," 13.

65. LSJ 1354, πειρασμός.

66. Jeffrey B. Gibson, "Jesus' Refusal to Produce a Sign (Mk 8.11–13)," *JSNT* 48 (1990): 45–53; Jonathan Draper, "The Development of the Sign of the Son of Man in the Jesus Tradition," *NTS* 39 (1993): 1–21.

67. *Contra* Gibson, "Temptation," 33.

68. Ernst Best, *The Temptation and the Passion: The Markan Soteriology,* 2nd ed. (Cambridge: Cambridge University Press, 1965), 15.

Chapter Seven

Conclusion

Ivan Karamazov's Grand Inquisitor was onto something. This long investigation has shown that there were at least two different ways of conceptualizing the miracles of Jesus at the heart of the Synoptic tradition. Mark, like the Inquisitor's Church, emphasized the power of Jesus, whereas the Double Tradition made Jesus the messenger of the powerful kingdom of God. In showing how the Grand Inquisitor was right, this book has also examined the relationship between the three pairs in its title: Mark and Q, Christology and Social Identity, and Miracles and the Kingdom of God.

MARK AND Q

One of the novelties of this book is studying the Double Tradition without assuming a Synoptic Theory. However it came about, the Double Tradition exists and is available for scholars to examine. Bracketing the question its of origins does limit what we can claim the Double Tradition shows about early Jesus followers, but it does not eliminate the Double Tradition as a source of insight. Even if Q never existed, studying it is not necessarily vain.

Comparing Mark and the Double Tradition has shown the variegated ways Jesus' early followers remembered him. Just as the polyphony of the Kentucky Fried Rat story showed how twentieth-century Americans voiced their anxiety about social change, so does the variety present within Mark and Q show the striving of early Christians to articulate an identity for Jesus and for themselves. Chapters 4 and 5 demonstrated this variety and how Mark and the Double Tradition each articulates a sense of Jesus that differs in significant ways from the other.

The final chapter argued that the Double Tradition's famous Temptation narrative showed these two ways of thinking about Jesus to be in competition with each other. The evidence shows the tradents of Q being aware of and reacting to the way of talking about Jesus and his miracles that we find in Mark's Gospel, even if the creators of the Double Tradition were not familiar with the text itself. Were Mark aware of the story of the three-fold Temptation, then its absence in the Second Gospel speaks to the evangelist's rejection of the view of miracles it represents. Early Jesus followers contested the collective memory of Jesus, and Mark and the Double Tradition provide traces of this contest.

CHRISTOLOGY AND SOCIAL IDENTITY

The term "Christology" is a dangerous one in New Testament studies. It can be useful as a topical category by grouping together statements or stories that depict the importance of Jesus' identity and work. However, there is something insidious about the term that subtly induces a shift from grouping into systematizing, taking the statements and stories we have grouped and turning them into some sort of doctrinal system about Jesus' identity and work. Such systemization is the task of theology, and there is nothing wrong with this when done as theology explicitly. The problem comes when we assume such systemization was the prerequisite for making the statements in the first place, when we believe that we are discovering the theology that lies behind the text and therefore discovering the theological stances of the Biblical authors and the communities of which they were a part. As historians we have to entertain the possibility that these communities might not have had theological stances, in the sense of articulable systems of belief, at all. A history that assumes theology as the root of all religious expression runs the risk not only of misconstruing the nature of religion, but also of devolving into theology masquerading as history.

Recognizing the dangers of too blithely assuming a Christology that lies behind the texts, this study has engaged issues about early attitudes toward Jesus that are typically discussed under the rubric of early high Christology. This study both confirms and refutes the arguments for early high Christology. A maximalist argument states that high Christology was not only extremely early but ubiquitous in our sources, suggesting an origin in the early years of the Jesus-following movement before it diffused across the Eastern Mediterranean. Mark's presentation of Jesus is certainly consistent with what is usually identified as early high Christology. That the Double Traditions' Temptation implicitly refutes this construction of Jesus as divine stand-in and object of devotion speaks to sufficient prevalence to require refutation. Therefore, we can state that the two largest components of the Synoptic Tradition evince the ubiquity of *awareness* of high Christology, but they do not evince ubiquity of *holding* high Christology. In the Double Tradition, we have a rarely heard dissenting voice.

Such voices preserved in texts provide indirect evidence for the conversations occurring within the early Jesus movement. A statement about Jesus' identity or work gains traction by winning approval from other Christians so that they repeat it. Christians will find such a statement worth repeating to the extent that the image of Jesus created is one worth following, one that generates a positive sense of identity among his followers. One can therefore investigate not only what Christians of any era say about Jesus, but why they say that and not something else. A future direction for religious studies in general and early Christian history in particular is examining the success of certain beliefs in light of their potential to generate positive social identity. Answering why early Jesus followers depicted Jesus the way they did involves looking at the social function of affirmations about Jesus to see how they promote group identity in a way that makes them worth affirming. The Christological is simultaneously the sociological.

Why some followers would want to tell stories of Jesus in ways that effaced the distinction between him and God while others would tell the same stories in ways that emphasized Jesus' subservience to God's kingdom and his similarity to his followers probably owed much to their personal experiences. Although these preferences were likely highly personal and idiosyncratic, they are not inscrutable to us. How effective these different ways of remembering Jesus were in creating a positive and distinctive identity for Jesus followers likely influenced these preferences. The different ways of configuring the memory of Jesus, his miracles, and his proclamation of the kingdom of God each had benefits and liabilities in forming such an identity.

The configuration presented in the Double Tradition, in which Jesus and his miracles both point toward the kingdom of God, creates a sense of identity for Jesus followers by imagining them as his co-fighters in the confrontation between the kingdom of God and the kingdom of Satan. The configuration in Mark, in which the miracles and the kingdom of God point to Jesus, creates a sharper distinction between Jesus and the rest of humanity, which generates a more distinctive identity for the followers of the one who acts as God on earth. Mark and the Double Tradition can tell the same stories, but these different configurations allow them to shape both the memory of Jesus and the identity of his followers in distinct ways.

MIRACLES AND THE KINGDOM OF GOD

Both Mark and Q use "the kingdom of God," as an eschatological shorthand. The distinction between them is not that of eschatological vs. non-eschatological or of locative vs. diffuse. Rather, the difference lies in how Jesus, and by extension his followers, participate in the eschatological fulfillment that "the kingdom of God" indicates. Like the "kingdom of God," the "kingdom of Satan" was a novel term for a widespread idea—a demonic realm under the command of the evil spirit who was to be God's eschatological opponent. Q's use and Mark's avoidance of reference to Satan's kingdom again points to how differently Mark and Q envisioned Jesus' role in the final confrontation between good and evil.

The two views of Jesus' role correlate with two different conceptions about the role of Jesus' followers in the eschatological confrontation between good and evil. In Mark, the follower's role is limited to that of spectator and beneficiary of Jesus' victory over the devil. In Q, the followers become coworkers with Jesus and join in the battle between the kingdom of God and the kingdom of Satan. It is one of the great ironies of Christian history that this more participatory paradigm proved less popular and was less able to generate a sense of social identity than Mark's pattern.

Miracles allowed Mark and the Double Tradition to express the nature of the power of good with which Jesus and his followers aligned themselves. To the Grand Inquisitor, miracles signify power, the power to control and coerce human beings, a power that Jesus foolishly abjured in his Temptation. The link between power and miracle is by no means foreign to the Synoptic tradition. When Matthew, Mark, or Luke speak about a generic miracle, their word of choice is δύναμις, "power."[1] Jesus' miracles show that the normal rules of day-to-day life do not apply to him, that he is above the constraints that bind most people. As we have seen throughout this study, both Mark and the Double Tradition recount miracles to show the power at work in the ministry of Jesus. Both present Jesus' miracles as foretastes of the eschatological power that will become fully manifest in the near future—for Mark, when Jesus appears on the clouds in glory, and for the Double Tradition, when the kingdom of God comes in full. These accounts are not merely descriptions of power, but exercises of power as well. In telling the stories about Jesus' miracles, Mark and the Double Tradition exert their power to shape the collective memory of early Jesus followers. They are able to configure Jesus, his miracles, and his proclamation of the kingdom of God in ways amenable to their purposes and then encourage other early followers of Jesus to remember him in these ways.

The power evident in the miracle points toward something special about the one who bears this power. Miracles are signs, as the Gospel of John and the Hebrew Bible so often remind us.[2] The miracles of Jesus signify how he relates to the eschatological power, but Mark and the Double Tradition make this signification differently. Mark's miracles assign to Jesus divine activity and blur the distinctions between Jesus and God. Moreover, the miracles point to the distinctions between Jesus and his followers, and any similar power that the followers have comes by Jesus' delegation of it. The Double Tradition displays a much greater willingness to depict Jesus and his followers as sharing in a common mission to make manifest the kingdom of God; the Double Tradition also offers many fewer narrative elements conflating Jesus and God. Nevertheless, in these Double Tradition versions, along with their co-texts, Jesus retains primacy in the instantiation of the kingdom of God—Jesus is not merely one messenger among many.

These differing significations of Jesus' miracles imply different identities for Jesus. Mark's use of miracles involves talking about Jesus in ways that depict him as somehow divine, while Q's use of miracles involves talking about Jesus in ways that depict him as first among equals, among those other people who share his allegiance to the kingdom of God. While it goes beyond the evidence to impute to Mark and the Double Tradition full-fledged Christologies that their stories express, the elements in their stories nevertheless suggest differing ways of thinking about Jesus vis-à-vis God, and different configurations of the relationship among Jesus, his miracles, and the kingdom of God.

In the long-run, Mark's configuration won out. Christians focused on the victory and power of Jesus, and the miracles became indicators of Jesus' power and status as divine. By the time the Christological controversies started in earnest in the third and fourth centuries, the argument was not about *whether* Jesus was divine, but *in what sense* he was divine. The eschatological urgency of the early movement cooled, and the kingdom of God faded from importance in Christian proclamation. When eschatology was discussed, it was in terms of Jesus' second coming, just as in Mark. An alternative view lay hidden within the canon, a view that focused eschatological hope not so much on Jesus' coming again as judge, but on the alleviation of human suffering that the eschton would bring, a focus that makes Jesus' miracle working a foretaste of eschatological blessedness. That view lies ready for recovery in Christian theological and ethical thought about healing.

By the inclusion of all three Synoptic Gospels, the canon grants both the Markan and Double Tradition versions of these stories a place in a grander narrative. The miracles represent both the power of Jesus and the presence of the kingdom of God that he represents. At the same time, the canonical form presents an ambivalence about miracles: in the Temptations of Matthew and Luke, Jesus rejects miracles as a way to prove his divine identity, while Mark's Jesus is only too happy to use miracles in such a way. Ultimately, canonization did not resolve the competition between these two ways of remembering Jesus and his miracles, but instead enshrined this competition within the Christian tradition for thinkers such as Dostoyevsky to wrestle with for generations to come.

NOTES

1. Matt 7:22; 11:20–23; 13:54, 58; Mark 6:2, 5; 9:39; Luke 10:13; 19:37.

2. For authors referring to miracles as signs, see, for instance, Exod 4:8,30; 7:9; Num 14:11; Deut 4:34; 11:3; 2 Kgs 20:8; Neh 9:10; Ps 77:43; John 2:18; 3:2; 4:48,54.

References

Abel, Theodore. *Why Hitler Came into Power*. New York: Prentice Hall, 1938.

Allison, Dale C. Jr. "Behind the Temptation of Jesus: Q 4:1–13 and Mark 1:12–13." In *Authenticating the Activities of Jesus,* edited by Bruce M. Metzger and Bart D. Ehrman, 195–213. Boston: Brill, 1999.

———. *Constructing Jesus: Memory, Imagination, and History*. Grand Rapids, MI : Baker Academic, 2010.

———. *James: A Critical and Exegetical Commentary*. London: T&T Clark, 2013.

———. *The Jesus Tradition in Q*. Harrisburg, PA: Trinity Press International, 1997.

Alter, Robert. *The Art of Biblical Narrative*, rev. ed. New York: Basic Books, 2010.

Ambrozic, Aloysius M. *The Hidden Kingdom: A Redaction-Critical Study of the References to the Kingdom of God in Mark's Gospel*. Washington, DC: Catholic Biblical Association of America, 1972.

———. "New Teaching with Power (Mk 1:27)." In *Word and Spirit: Essays in Honor of David Michael Stanley, S.J. on his 60th Birthday,* edited by Joseph Plevnik, 113–50. Willowdale, Ontario: Regis College Press, 1975.

Anastasio, Thomas J., Kristen Ann Ehrenberger, Patrick Watson, and Wenyi Zhang. *Individual and Collective Memory Consolidation: Analogous Processes on Different Levels*. Cambridge, MA: MIT Press, 2012.

Andersen, Francis I. and David Noel Freedman. *Micah: A New Translation with Introduction and Commentary,* The Anchor Bible. New York: Doubleday, 2000.

Anderson, Graham. *Philostratus: Biography and Belles Lettres in the Third Century A.D.* London: Croom Helm, 1986.

Aronson, Elliot and Judson Mills. "The Effect of Severity of Initiation on Liking for a Group." *Journal of Abnormal and Social Psychology* 59 (1959): 177–81.

Assmann, Aleida. "Canon and Archive." In *Cultural Memory Studies: An International and Interdisciplinary Handbook,* edited by Astrid Eril, Ansgar Nünning, and Sara B. Young, 97–108. Berlin: Walter de Gruyter, 2008.

Assman, Jan. "Collective Memory and Cultural Identity," translated by John Czaplicka. *New German Critique* 65 (1995): 125–33.

———. "Communicative and Cultural Memory." In *Cultural Memory Studies: An International and Interdisciplinary Handbook,* edited by Astrid Eril, Ansgar Nünning, and Sara B. Young, 109–18. Berlin: Walter de Gruyter, 2008.

Aune, David E. "Form Criticism." In *The Blackwell Companion to the New Testament,* edited by David E. Aune, 140–55. Chichester, UK: Wiley-Blackwell, 2010.

Bamberger, Bernard J. *Fallen Angels: Soldiers of Satan's Realm*. Philadelphia: Jewish Publication Society, 2006.

Baranowski, Ann. "A Psychological Comparison of Ritual and Musical Meaning." *Method and Theory in the Study of Religion* 10, no. 1 (1998): 3–29.

Bauckham, Richard. *Jesus and the God of Israel: God Crucified and Other Studies on the New Testament's Christology of Divine Identity.* Grand Rapids, MI: Eerdmans, 2009.

Baughman, Ernest W. *Type and Motif-Index of the Folktales of England and North America.* The Hague: Mouton & Co., 1966.

Bazzana, Giovanni B. *Kingdom of Bureaucracy: The Political Theology of Village Scribes in the Sayings Gospel Q.* Leuven: Peeters, 2015.

Beardsley, Richard K. and Rosalie Hankey. "A History of the Vanishing Hitchhiker." *California Folklore Quarterly* 2.1 (1943): 13–25.

Beasley-Murray, George. *Jesus and the Kingdom of God.* Grand Rapids, MI: Eerdmans, 1986.

Beavis, Mary Ann. *Jesus and Utopia: Looking for the Kingdom of God in the Roman World.* Minneapolis: Fortress, 2006.

Bell, Catherine. *Ritual Theory, Ritual Practice.* Oxford: Oxford University Press, 2009.

Bennett, Gillian and Paul Smith. *Urban Legends: A Collection of International Tall Tales and Terrors.* Westport, CT: Greenwood Press, 2007.

Best, Ernst. *The Temptation and the Passion: The Markan Soteriology*, 2nd ed. Cambridge: Cambridge University Press, 1965.

Blain, Jenny and Robert J. Wallis. "Ritual Reflections, Practitioners Meanings: Disputing the Terminology of Neo-Shamanic 'Performance.'" *Journal of Ritual Studies* 20, no. 1 (2006): 21–36.

Blenkinsopp, Joseph. *Isaiah 1–39: A New Translation with Introduction and Commentary.* New York: Doubleday, 2000.

Boddy, Janice. "Spirit Possession Revisited: Beyond Instrumentality." *Annual Review of Anthropology* 23 (1994): 407–34

Boer, Roland, ed. *Bakhtin and Genre Theory in Biblical Studies.* Atlanta: Society of Biblical Literature, 2007.

Boobyer, G.H. *St Mark and the Transfiguration Story.* Edinburgh: T&T Clark, 1942.

Borg, Marcus. "Jesus and Eschatology: A Reassessment." In *Images of Jesus Today,* edited by James H. Charlesworth and Walter P. Weaver, 42–67. Valley Forge, PA: Trinity Press International, 1994.

Boring, M. Eugene. "The 'Minor Agreements' and Their Bearing on the Synoptic Problem." In *New Studies in the Synoptic Problem: Oxford Conference, April 2008: Essays in Honor of Christopher M. Tuckett,* edited by P. Foster, A. Gregory, J. S. Kloppenborg, and J. Verheyden, 227–51. Leuven: Peeters, 2011.

———. "The Synoptic Problem, 'Minor' Agreements and the Beelzebul Pericope." In *The Four Gospels 1992: Festschrift Frans Neirynck,* 3 Vols., edited by F. Van Segbroeck, C.M. Tuckett, G. Van Belle, and J. Verheyden, 1.587–619. Leuven: Leuven University Pres, 1992.

Boucher, Madeline. *The Mysterious Parable: A Literary Study,* Catholic Biblical Quarterly Monograph Series. Washington, DC: The Catholic Biblical Association, 1977.

Bovon, François. *Luke 1: A Commentary on the Gospel of Luke 1:1–9:50,* translated by Christine M. Thomas. Minneapolis: Fortress, 2002.

———. *Luke 2: A Commentary on the Gospel of Luke 9:51–19:27,* translated by Donald S. Deer. Minneapolis: Fortress, 2013.

Boyd, James W. *Satan and Mara: Christian and Buddhist Symbols of Evil.* Leiden: Brill, 1975.

Brewer, Marilynn B. "Ingroup Bias in the Minimal Intergroup Situation: A Cognitive-Motivational Analysis." *Psychological Bulletin* 86, no. 2 (1979): 307–24.

———. "The Social Psychology of Intergroup Relations: Social Categorization, Ingroup Bias, and Outgroup Prejudice." In *Social Psychology: Handbook of Basic Principles* 2nd ed., edited by Arie W. Kruglanski and Tory E. Higgens, 695–715. New York: Guilford Press, 2007.

Broadhead, Edwin Keith. *Teaching With Authority: Miracles and Christology in the Gospel of Mark,* Journal for the Study of the New Testament Supplement Series. Sheffield: JSOT Press, 1992.

Brown, Scott G. "Mark 11:1–12:12: A Triple Intercalation?" *Catholic Biblical Quarterly* 64, no. 1 (2002): 78–89.

Brunvald, Jan Harold. *The Vanishing Hitchhiker: American Urban Legends and Their Meaning.* New York: W.W. Norton, 1981.

Buchanan, George Wesley. *Jesus. The King and His Kingdom.* Macon, GA: Mercer University Press, 1984.

Bultmann, Rudolf. *History of the Synoptic Tradition,* translated by John Marsh. New York: Harper & Row, 1968.

Burden, Terry L. *The Kerygma of the Wilderness Traditions in the Hebrew Bible.* New York: Peter Lang, 1994.

Busby, Cylin. "'This Is a True Story': Roles of Women in Contemporary Legend." *Midwestern Folklore* 20, no. 1 (1994): 5–62.

Buss, Martin J. *The Changing Shape of Form Criticism: A Relational Approach.* Sheffield: Sheffield Phoenix, 2010.

Byrne, Joseph. *Encyclopedia of the Black Death.* Santa Barbara, CA: ABC-CLIO, 2012.

Cabraja, Ilija. *Der Gedanke der Umkehr bei den Synoptikern: Eine Exegetisch-religionsgeschichtliche Untersuchung.* Sankt Ottilein: EOS Verlag, 1985.

Cameron, J. A., J. M. Alverez, D. N. Ruble, and A. J. Fullgni. "Children's Lay Theories about Ingroups and Outgroups: Reconceptualizing Research on Prejudice." *Personality and Social Psychology Review* 5, no. 2 (2001): 118–28.

Campany, Robert Ford. "On the Very Idea of Religions (In the Modern West and in Early Medieval China)." *History of Religions* 42, no. 4 (2003): 287–319.

———. "Religious Repertoires and Contestation: A Case Study Based on Buddhist Miracle Tales." *History of Religions* 52, no. 2 (2012): 99–141.

Campbell, Joseph. *The Hero with a Thousand Faces.* New York: Pantheon Books, 1949.

Caneday, A.B. "Mark's Provocative Use of Scripture in Narration: 'He was with the Wild Animals and Angels Ministered to Him.'" *Bulletin for Biblical Research* 9 (1999): 19–36.

Carroll, John T. *Luke: A Commentary.* Louisville, KY: Westminster John Knox, 2012.

Catchpole, David R. "The Beginning of Q: A Proposal." *New Testament Studies* 38, no. 2 (1992): 205–21.

———. "The Centurion's Faith and Its Function in Q." In *Four Gospels 1992,* edited by F. Segbroeck, C. M. Tuckett, G. van Belle, and J. Verheyden, 1:517–40. Louvain: Peeters, 1992.

———. "The Mission Charge in Q." *Semeia* 55 (1991): 147–74.

Charlesworth, James H., ed. *The Old Testament Pseudepigrapha.* 2 Vols. Peabody, MA: Hendrickson, 1983.

Chester, Andrew. "High Christology: Whence, When, and Why?" *Early Christianity* 2, no. 1 (2011): 22–50.

Collins, Adela Yarbro. *Mark: A Commentary,* Hermeneia—A Critical and Historical Commentary on the Bible. Minneapolis: Fortress, 2007.

Collins, John J. "The Works of the Messiah." *Dead Sea Discoveries* 1, no. 1 (1994): 98–112.

Connerton, Paul. *How Societies Remember.* Cambridge: Cambridge University Press, 1989.

Cotter, Wendy J. *The Christ of the Miracle Stories: Portrait Through Encounter.* Grand Rapids, MI: Baker Academic, 2010.

———. *Miracles in Greco-Roman Antiquity: A Sourcebook for the Study of New Testament Miracle Stories.* London: Rutledge, 1999.

Crossan, John Dominic. *Jesus: A Revolutionary Biography.* San Francisco: Harper, 1994.

Czachesz, István. "Explaining Magic: Earliest Christianity as a Test Case." In *Past Minds: Studies in Cognitive Historiography,* edited by Luther H. Hartin and Jesper Sørensen, 141–66. London: Equinox, 2011.

Dahl, Nils. *Jesus in the Memory of the Early Church.* Minneapolis: Augsburg, 1976.

Dalman, Gustaf. *The Words of Jesus Considered in the Light of Post-biblical Jewish Writings and the Aramaic Language.* Edinburgh: T&T Clark, 1902.

Davies, W.D. and Dale C. Allison, Jr. *Matthew 1–7,* International Critical Commentary. Edinburgh: T&T Clark, 1988.

———. *Matthew 8–18,* International Critical Commentary. London: T&T Clark, 1991.

De Jonge, Marinus. "Mark 14:25 among Jesus' Words about the Kingdom of God." In *Sayings of Jesus Canonical and Non-Canonical: Essays in Honour of Tjitze Baarda*, edited by William L. Petersen, Johan S. Vos, and Henk J. DeJonge, 123–36. Leiden: Brill, 1997.

———. *God's Final Envoy: Early Christology and Jesus' Own View of His Mission*. Grand Rapids, MI: Eerdmans, 1998.

Demoen, Kristoffel and Danny Praet, eds. *Theios Sophistes: Essays on Flavius Philostratus' Vita Apollonii*. Leiden: Brill, 2008.

Derman, Joshua. "Max Weber and Charisma: A Transatlantic Affair." *New German Critique* 38, no. 2 (2011): 51–88.

Dibelius, Martin. *From Tradition to Gospel,* translated by Bertram Lee Woolf. Cambridge: James Clarke, 1971.

Dodd, C.H. *The Parables of the Kingdom*. New York: Scribner, 1961.

Donaldson, Terence L. *Judaism and the Gentiles: Jewish Patterns of Universalism*. Waco, TX: Baylor University Press, 2007.

Dormandy, Richard. "Jesus' Temptations in Mark's Gospel: Mark 1:12–13." *The Expository Times* 114, no. 6 (2003): 183–87.

Dostoyevsky, Fyodor. *The Brothers Karamazov: A Novel in Four Parts and an Epilogue*. Translated by David McDuff. London: Pengiun, 1993.

Draper, Jonathan. "The Development of the Sign of the Son of Man in the Jesus Tradition." *New Testament Studies* 39 (1993): 1–21.

Dugan, Kathleen Margaret. *The Vision Quest of the Plains Indians: Its Spiritual Significance*. Lewiston, NY: Edwin Mellen, 1985.

Dundes, Alan. *Holy Writ as Oral Lit: The Bible as Folklore*. Lanham, MD: Rowman & Littlefield, 1999.

———. *The Morphology of North American Indian Folktales*. Helsinki: Suomalainen Tiedeka-temia, Academia Sceintarum Fennica, 1964.

Dunn, James D. G. "Jesus and the Kingdom: How Would His Message Have Been Heard?" In *Neotestamentica et Philonica: Studies in Honor of Peder Borgen,* edited by David E. Aune, Torrey Seland, and Jarl Henning Ulrichsen, 3–36. Leiden: Brill, 2003.

Echterhoff, Gerald. "Language and Memory: Social and Cognitive Processes." In *Cultural Memory Studies: An International and Interdisciplinary Handbook,* edited by Astrid Eril, Ansgar Nünning, and Sara B. Young, 263–74. Berlin: Walter de Gruyter, 2008.

Edwards, James R. "The Authority of Jesus in the Gospel of Mark." *Journal of the Evangelical Theological Society* 37, no. 2 (1994): 217–33.

Eliade, Mircea. *Rites and Symbols of Initiation: The Mysteries of Birth and Rebirth,* translated by Willard R. Trask. New York: Harper & Row, 1958.

———. *Shamanism: Archaic Techniques of Ecstasy,* translated by Willard R. Trask. New York: Pantheon, 1964.

Elmer, Ian J. "Setting the Record Straight at Galatia: Paul's *Narratio* (Gal 1:13–2:14) as Response to the Galatian Conflict." In *Religious Conflict from Early Christianity to the Rise of Islam,* edited by Neil Bronwen and Wendy Mayer, 21–37. Berlin: Walter De Gruyter, 2012.

Eril, Astrid, Ansgar Nünning, and Sara B. Young, eds. *Cultural Memory Studies: An International and Interdisciplinary Handbook*. Berlin: Walter de Gruyter, 2008.

Esler, Philip F. *Galatians*. London: Routledge, 1998.

Esler, Philip F. and Ronald Piper. *Lazarus, Mary, and Martha: Social-Scientific Approaches to the Gospel of John*. Minneapolis: Fortress, 2006.

Eve, Eric. *The Healer from Nazareth: Jesus' Miracles in Historical Context*. London: SPCK, 2009.

Faraone, Christopher A. and Dirk Obbink, eds. *Magika Hiera: Ancient Greek Magic and Religion*. New York: Oxford University Press, 1997.

Fentress, James and Chris Wickham. *Social Memory*. Oxford: Blackwell, 1992.

Feuchtwang, Stephan. "Suggestions for a Redefinition of Charisma." *Nova Religio: The Journal of Alternative and Emergent Religions* 12, no. 2 (2008): 90–105.

Fine, Gary Alan. "The Kentucky Fried Rat: Legends and Modern Society." *Journal of the Folklore Institute* 17, no. 2/3 (1980): 222–43.

————. *Manufacturing Tales: Sex and Money in Contemporary Legends.* Knoxville: University of Tennessee Press, 1992.

Finer, Ward D., Jacob E. Hautaluoma, and Larry J. Bloom. "The Effects of Severity and Pleasantness of Initiation on Attraction to a Group." *Journal of Social Psychology* 111 (1980): 301–2.

Fitzmyer, Joseph. *The One Who is to Come.* Grand Rapids, MI: Eerdmans, 2007.

Fleddermann, Harry T. "The Discipleship Discourses (Mark 9:33–50)," *Catholic Biblical Quarterly* 43, no. 1 (1981): 57–75.

————. *Mark and Q: A Study of the Overlap Texts.* Leuven: Leuven University Press, 1995.

————. "The Plot of Q." *Ephemerides Theologicae Lovanienses* 88, no. 1 (2012): 43–69.

————. *Q: A Reconstruction and Commentary.* Leuven: Peeters, 2005.

Fontenrose, Joseph. *The Ritual Theory of Myth.* Berkeley: University of California Press, 1966.

Foster, P., A. Gregory, J. S. Kloppenborg, and J. Verheyden, eds. *New Studies in the Synoptic Problem: Oxford Conference, April 2008: Essays in Honor of Christopher M. Tuckett.* Leuven: Peeters, 2011.

Fowler, Robert M. *Let the Reader Understand: Reader-Response Criticism and the Gospel of Mark.* Philadelphia: Fortress, 1991.

France, R. T. *The Gospel of Mark: A Commentary on the Greek Text.* Grand Rapids, MI: Eerdmans, 2002.

————. *The Gospel of Matthew.* Grand Rapids, MI: Eerdmans, 2007.

Francis, James A. *Subversive Virtue: Asceticism and Authority in the Second-Century Pagan World.* University Park: Pennsylvania State University Press, 1995.

Frankfurter, David T. M. "The Origin of the Miracle-List Tradition and Its Medium of Circulation." *SBLSP* 29 (1990): 344–74.

Fredriksen, Paula. *From Jesus to Christ: The Origins of the New Testament Images of Jesus.* 2nd ed. New Haven: Yale University Press, 2000.

————. "The Question of Worship: Gods, Pagans, and the Redemption of Israel." In *Paul Within Judaism: Restoring the First-Century Context to the Apostle,* edited by Mark D. Nanos and Magnus Zetterholm, 175–202. Minneapolis: Fortress, 2015.

Freud, Sigmund. *Civilization and Its Discontents,* translated by James Strachey. New York: W.W. Norton, 1961.

————. *Group Psychology and the Analysis of the Ego,* translated by James Strachey. New York: W.W. Norton, 1959.

Friedrichsen, Timothy A. "'Minor' and 'Major' Matthew-Luke Agreements Against Mk 4,30–32." In *The Four Gospels 1992: Festschrift Frans Neirynck,* 3 Vols., edited by F. Van Segbroeck, C. M. Tuckett, G. Van Belle, and J. Verheyden, 1.541–61. Leuven: Leuven University Pres, 1992.

Fuchs, Ernst. *Studies in the Historical Jesus,* translated by Andrew Scobie. Naperville, IL: Allenson, 1964.

Garrett, Susan R. *The Demise of the Devil: Magic and the Demonic in Luke's Writings.* Minneapolis: Fortress, 1989.

————. *The Temptation of Jesus in Mark's Gospel.* Grand Rapids, MI: Eerdmans, 1998.

Gellner, Ernest. "Concepts and Society." In idem, *Selected Philosophical Themes.* Vol. 1. *Cause and Meaning in the Social Sciences,* 19–46. London: Routledge, 2003.

Gerard, Harold B. and Grover C. Mathewson. "The Effects of Severity of Initiation on Liking for a Group: A Replication." *Journal of Experimental Social Psychology* 2 (1966): 278–87.

Gerth, Hans. "The Nazi Party: Its Leadership and Composition." *American Journal of Sociology* 45 (1940): 517–41.

Gibson, Jeffrey B. "Jesus' Refusal to Produce a 'Sign' (Mk 8.11–13)." *Journal for the Study of the New Testament* 48 (1990): 37–66.

————. "Jesus' Wilderness Temptation According to Mark." *Journal for the Study of the New Testament* 53 (1994): 3–34.

————. "A Turn on 'Turning Stones to Bread.' A New Understanding of the Devil's Intention in Q 4.3." *Biblical Research* 41 (1996): 37–57.

Gilet, Peter. *Vladimir Propp and the Universal Folktale: Recommissioning an Old Paradigm— Story as Initiation.* New York: Peter Lang, 1998.

Goodacre, Mark S. *The Synoptic Problem: A Way Through the Maze.* London: Continuum, 2001.

———. *The Case Against Q: Studies in Markan Priority and the Synoptic Problem.* Harrisburg, PA: Trinity Press International, 2002.

Graf, Fritz. "Prayer in Magic and Religious Ritual." In *Magika Hiera: Ancient Greek Magic and Religion,* edited by Christopher A. Faraone and Dirk Obbink, 188–213. New York: Oxford University Press, 1997.

Grossardt, Peter. "How to Become a Poet? Homer and Apollonius Visit the Mound of Achilles." In *Theios Sophistes: Essays on Flavius Philostratus' Vita Apollonii,* edited by Kristoffel Demoen and Danny Praet, 75–94. Leiden: Brill, 2008.

Guijarro, Santiago. "The Politics of Exorcism: Jesus' Reaction to Negative Labels in the Beelzebul Controversy." *Biblical Theology Bulletin* 29, no. 3 (1999): 118–29.

Gundry, Robert H. *Mark: A Commentary on His Apology for the Cross.* Grand Rapids, MI: Eerdmans, 1993.

Guruge, Ananda W. P. *The Buddha's Encounters with Mara.* Kandy, Sri Lanka: Buddhist Publication Society, 1997.

Halbwachs, Maurice. *The Collective Memory,* translated by Francis J. Ditter, Jr. and Vida Yazdi Ditter. New York: Harper & Row, 1980.

Han, Kyu Sam. *Jerusalem and the Early Jesus Movement: The Q Community's Attitude Toward the Temple.* London: Sheffield Press, 2002.

Harkins, Angela Kim, Kelley Coblentz Bautch, and John C. Endres, eds. *The Watchers in Jewish and Christian Traditions.* Minneapolis: Fortress, 2014.

———. *The Fallen Angels Traditions: Second Temple Developments and Reception History.* Washington: Catholic Biblical Association, 2014.

Hasitschka, Martin. "Der Sohn Gottes—geliebt und geprüft: Zusammenhang von Taufe und Veruschung Jesu bei den Synoptikern." In *Forschungen zum Neuen Testament und seiner Umwelt: Festschrift für Albert Fuchs,* edited by Christoph Niemand, 71–80. Frankfurt am Main: Peter Lang, 2002.

Hays, Richard B. *Reading Backwards: Figural Christology and the Fourfold Gospel Witness.* Waco, TX: Baylor University Press, 2014.

Heil, John Paul. "Jesus with the Wild Animals in Mark 1:13." *The Catholic Biblical Quarterly* 68 (2006): 63–78

Hengel, Martin. *Studien zur Christologie: Kleine Schriften IV,* edited by Claus-Jürgen Thronton. Tübingen; Mohr Siebeck, 2006.

Hieke, Thomas. "Schriftgelehrsamkeit in der Logienquelle: Die Altetsamentlichen Zitate in der Versuchungsgeschichte Q 4,1–13." In *From Quest to Q: Festschrift James M. Robinson,* edited by Jon Ma Asgeirsson, Kristin de Toyer, and Marvin W. Meyer, 43–71. Leuven: Leuven University Press, 2000.

Hollenbach, Paul W. "Jesus, Demoniacs, and Public Authorities: A Socio-Historical Study." *Journal of the American Academy of Religion* 49, no. 3 (1981): 567–88.

Hooker, Morna D. "'Who Can This Be?' The Christology of Mark's Gospel." In *Contours of Christology in the New Testament,* edited by Richard N. Longenecker, 79–99. Grand Rapids, MI: Eerdmans, 2005.

Horsley, Richard A. *Hearing the Whole Story: The Politics of Plot in Mark's Gospel.* Louisville, KY: Westminster John Knox, 2001.

Humphries, Michael L. *Christian Origins and the Language of the Kingdom of God.* Carbondale: Southern Illinois University Press, 1999.

Hüneburg, Martin. *Jesus als Wundertäter in der Logienquelle: Ein Beitrag zur Christologie von Q.* Leipzig: Evangelische Verlagsanstalt, 2001.

Hunink, Vincent. *Apuleius of Madauros Pro Se De Magia (Apologia) Edited With a Commentary.* Amsterdam: J.C. Gieben, 1997.

Hurtado, Larry W. *Lord Jesus Christ: Devotion to Jesus in Earliest Christianity.* Grand Rapids, MI: Eerdmans, 2003.

———. *One God, One Lord: Early Christian Devotion and Ancient Jewish Monotheism.* Edinburgh: T&T Clark, 1998.

Janowitz, Naomi. *Magic in the Roman World: Pagans, Jews, and Christians.* London: Routledge, 2001.

Janzen, Waldemar. *Mourning Cry and Woe Oracle.* Berlin: Walter de Gruyter, 1972.

Japhet, Sara. *The Ideology of the Book of Chronicles and Its Place in Biblical Thought.* Frankfurt am Main: Lang, 1989.

Jetten, J., R. Spears, and T. Postmes. "Intergroup Distinctiveness and Differentiation: A Meta-Analyitic Integration." *Journal of Personality and Social Psychology* 86, no. 6 (2004): 862–79.

John, Jeffrey. "Anointing in the New Testament." In *The Oil of Gladness: Anointing in the Christian Tradition,* edited by Martin Dudley and Geoffrey Rowell, 46–76. London: SPCK, 1993.

Kaiser, Sigurd. *Krankenheilung: Untersuchungen zu Form, Sprache, tradistionsgeschichtlichem Hintergund und Aussage von Jak 5, 13–18.* Neukirchen-Vluyn: Neukirchener Verlag, 2006.

Kamau, Caroline. "What Does Being Initiated Severely Into a Group Do? The Role of Rewards." *International Journal of Psychology* 48, no. 3 (2013): 399–406.

Keating, Caroline F., Jason Pomerantz, Stacy D. Pommer, et al. "Going to College and Unpacking Hazing: A Functional Approach to Decrypting Initiation Practices Among Undergraduates." *Group Dynamics; Theory, Research, and Practice* 9, no. 2 (2005): 104–26.

Kee, Howard Clark. *Medicine, Miracle, and Magic in New Testament Times.* Cambridge: Cambridge University Press, 1986.

———. *Miracle in the Early Christian World: A Study in Sociohistorical Method.* New Haven, CT: Yale University Press, 1983.

———. "The Terminology of Mark's Exorcism Stories." *New Testament Studies* 14, no. 2 (1968): 232–46.

———. "The Transfiguration in Mark: Epiphany or Apocalyptic Vision?" In *Understanding the Sacred Text: Essays in honor of Morton S. Enslin on the Hebrew Bible and Christian Beginnings,* edited by J. Reumann, 135–52. Valley Forge, PA: Judson Press, 1972.

Keener, Craig S. *The Gospel of Matthew: A Socio-Rhetorical Commentary.* Grand Rapids, MI: Eerdmans, 2009.

———. *Miracles: The Credibility of the New Testament Accounts.* 2 Vols. Grand Rapids, MI: Baker Academic, 2011.

Kelber, Werner H. and Samuel Byrskog, eds. *Jesus in Memory: Traditions in Oral and Scribal Perspectives.* Waco, TX: Baylor University Press, 2009.

Kelhoffer, James A. "The Apostle Paul and Justin Martyr on the Miraculous: A Comparison of Appeals to Authority." *Greek, Roman and Byzantine Studies* 42, no. 2 (2001): 163–84.

Kirk, J.R. Daniel and Stephen L. Young. "'I Will Set His Hand to the Sea": Psalm 88:26 LXX and Christology in Mark." *Journal of Biblical Literature* 133, no. 2 (2014): 333–40.

Kloppenborg, John S. *The Formation of Q: Trajectories in Ancient Wisdom Collections.* Philadelphia: Fortress, 1987.

———. *Excavating Q: The History and Setting of the Sayings Gospel.* Minneapolis: Fortress, 2000.

Klutz, Todd. *The Exorcism Stories in Luke-Acts: A Sociostylistic Reading.* Cambridge: Cambridge University Press, 2004.

Knoppers, Gary N. *1 Chronicles 10–29: A New Translation with Introduction and Commentary,* The Anchor Bible. New York: Doubleday, 2004.

Knust, Jennifer Wright. "Roasting the Lamb: Sacrifice and Sacred Text in Justin's Dialogue with Trypho." In *Religion and Violence: The Biblical Heritage,* edited by David A. Bernat and Jonathan Klawans, 100–113. Sheffield: Sheffield Phoenix, 2007.

Koch, Klaus. "Ofenbaren wird sich das reich Gottes." *New Testament Studies* 25, no. 2 (1979): 158–65.

Kollman, Bernd. *Jesus und die Christen als Wundertäter: Studien zu Magie, Medizin und Schamanismus in Antike und Christentum.* Göttingen: Vandenhoeck & Ruprecht, 1996.

Koskenniemi, Erikki. "The Function of the Miracle Stories in Philostratus's *Vita Apollonii Tyanensis.*" In *Wonders Never Cease: The Purpose of Narrating Miracle Stories in the New*

Testament and its Religious Environment, edited by Michael Labahn and Bert Jan Lietaert Peerbolte, 70–86. London: T&T Clark, 2006.

Kozar, Joseph Vlcek. "Meeting the Perfect Stranger: The Literary Role and Social Location of the Encounter Between Jesus and the Strange Exorcist in Mark 9:38–41." *Proceedings of the Eastern Great Lakes and Midwestern Biblical Society* 24 (2004): 103–23.

Kuhn, Karl Allen. *The Kingdom According to Luke and Acts: A Social, Literary, and Theological Introduction.* Grand Rapids, MI: Baker, 2015.

Kümmel, W.G. *Promise and Fulfillment: The Eschatological Message of Jesus,* translated by Dorthea M. Barton. Naperville, IL: Allenson, 1957.

Kuntzmann, Raymond. "Le Trône de Dieu dans l'Oeuvre du Chroniste." In *Le Trône de Dieu,* edited by Marc Philonenko, 19–27. Tübingen: Mohr, 1993.

Kvalbein, Hans. "The Wonders of the End-Time: Metaphoric Language in 4Q521 and the Interpretation of Matthew 11.5 par." *Journal for the Study of the Pseudepigrapha* 9, no. 18 (1998): 87–110.

Lambrecht, Jan. "John the Baptist and Jesus in Mark 1:1–15: Markan Redaction of Q?" *New Testament Studies* 38, no. 3 (1992): 357–84.

———. "Three More Notes in Response to John P. Meier: Mark 1,7–8; 3,27 and 10,1–12." *Ephemerides Theologicae Louvainenses* 89, no. 4 (2013): 397–409.

Lange, Armin, Hermann Lichtenberger, and Diethard Römheld, eds. *Die Dämonen Demons: die Dämonologie der israelitisch-jüdischen und frühchristlichen Literatur im Kontext ihrer Umwelt.* Tübingen: Mohr Siebeck, 2003.

Lau, Markus. "Die Legio X Fretensis und der Besessene von Gerasa. Anmerkungen zur Zahlenangabe "ungefähr Zweitausend" (Mk 5,13)." *Biblica* 88, no. 3 (2013): 351–64.

Laufen, Rudolf. *Die Doppelüberlieferungen der Logienquelle und des Markusevangeliums.* Bonn: Peter Hanstein, 1980.

Leal, Robert Barry. *Wilderness in the Bible: Toward a Theology of Wilderness.* New York: Peter Lang, 2004.

Lee, Daniel B. "Ritual and Social Meaning and Meaninglessness of Religion." *Soziale Welt* 56, no.1 (2005): 5–16.

Leonhard, Nina. "Memory as a Means of Social Integration." In *Theorizing Social Memory: Concepts and Contexts,* edited by Gerd Sebald and Jutin Wagle, 109–21. London: Routledge, 2016.

Levine, Amy-Jill. "Matthew's Advice to a Divided Readership." In *the Gospel of Matthew in Current Study,* edited by David E. Aune, 22–41. Grand Rapids, MI: Eerdmans, 2001.

Levine, Nachman. "Twice as Much of your Spirit: Pattern, Parallel and Paronomasia in the Miracles of Elijah and Elisha." *Journal for the Study of the Old Testament* 24, no. 85 (1999): 25–46

Lewis, I. M. *Ecstatic Religion: A Study of Shamanism and Spirit Possession.* London: Routledge, 2003.

Lodewijkx, Hein F. M. and Joseph E. M. M. Syroit. "Severity of Initiation Revisited: Does Severity of Initiation Increase Attractiveness in Real Groups?" *European Journal of Social Psychology* 27 (1997): 275–300.

Longenecker, Richard N., ed. *Contours of Christology in the New Testament.* Grand Rapids, MI: Eerdmans, 2005.

Lorein, Geert Wouter. "מלכותא in the Targum of the Prophets." *Aramaic Studies* 3, no. 1 (2005): 15–42.

Luck, Georg. "Witches and Sorcerers in Classical Literature." In *Witchcraft and Magic in Europe: Ancient Greece and Rome,* edited by Bengt Ankarloo and Stuart Clark, 91–158. Philadelphia: University of Pennsylvania Press, 1999.

Luz, Ulrich. *Matthew 8–20: A Commentary.* Minneapolis: Fortress, 2001.

Mack, Burton L. "The Kingdom Sayings in Mark." *Foundations and Facets Forum* 3, no. 1 (1987): 3–47.

———. "Q and the Gospel of Mark: Revising Christian Origins." *Semeia* 55 (1991): 15–39.

MacMullen, Ramsay. *Enemies of the Roman Order: Treason, Unrest and Alienation in the Empire.* Cambridge, MA: Harvard University Press, 1966.

Malbon, Elizabeth Struthers. "Narrative Criticism: How Does the Story Mean?" In *Mark and Method*, edited by Janice Capel Anderson and Stephen D. Moore, 29–57. Minneapolis: Fortress, 2008.

———. *Mark's Jesus: Characterization as Narrative Christology.* Waco, TX: Baylor University Press, 2009.

Malina, Bruce J. And Jerome H. Neyrey. *Calling Jesus Names: The Social Value of Labels in Matthew.* Sonoma, CA: Polebridge Press, 1988.

Marcus, Joel. *Mark 1–8: A New Translation with Introduction and Commentary,* The Anchor Bible. New Haven: Yale University Press, 2000.

———. *Mark 8–16: A New Translation with Introduction and Commentary,* The Anchor Bible. New Haven: Yale University Press, 2009.

Marguerat, Daniel. *Le Jugement dans l'Evangile de Matthieu.* 2nd ed. Geneva: Labor et Fides, 1995.

Matera, Frank J. *New Testament Christology.* Louisville, KY: Westminster John Knox, 1999.

McCurley, F. R., Jr. "And After Six Days (Mark 9:2): A Semitic Literary Device." *Journal of Biblical Literature* 93 (1974): 67–81.

McNicol Allain J., David L. Dungan, and David B. Peabody, eds. *Beyond the Q Impasse— Luke's Use of Matthew: A Demonstration by the Research Team of the International Institute for Gospel Studies.* Valley Forge, PA: Trinity Press International, 1996.

McVann, Mark. "One of the Prophets: Matthew's Testing Narrative as a Rite of Passage." *Biblical Theology Bulletin* 23, no. 1 (1993): 14–20.

Meier, John P. *A Marginal Jew: Rethinking the Historical Jesus.* 4 vols. New York. Doubleday, 1991–2009.

Metts, H. Leroy. "The Kingdom of God: Background and Development of a Complex Discourse Concept." *Criswell Theological Review* 2, no. 1 (2004): 51–82.

Miles, Graeme. "Reforming the Eyes: Interpreters and Interpretation in the *Vita Apollonii.*" In *Theios Sophistes: Essays on Flavius Philostratus' Vita Apollonii,* edited by Kristoffel Demoen and Danny Praet, 129–60. Leiden: Brill, 2008.

Miller, Timothy, ed. *When Prophets Die: The Postcharismatic Fate of New Religious Movements.* Albany: State University of New York Press, 1991.

Misztal, Barbara A. *Theories of Social Remembering.* Philadelphia: Open Univeristy Press, 2003.

Moazami, Mahnaz. "The Confrontation of Zarathustra with the Evil Spirit: Chapter 19 of the *Pahlavi Videvdad.*" *East and West* 52, no. 1 (2002): 151–71.

Mollier, Christine. *Buddhism and Taoism Face to Face: Scripture, Ritual, and Iconographic Exchange in Medieval China.* Honolulu: University of Hawaii Press, 2009.

Morosco, Robert E. "Matthew's Formation of a Commissioning Type-Scene out of the Story of Jesus' Commissioning of the Twelve." *Journal of Biblical Literature* 103, no. 4 (1984): 539–56.

Moss, Candida R. "The Man with the Flow of Power: Porous Bodies in Mark 5:25–34." *Journal of Biblical Literature* 129, no. 3 (2010): 507–19.

———. "The Transfiguration: An Exercise in Markan Accommodation," *Biblical Interpretation* 12, no. 1 (2004): 69–89.

Moxnes, Halvor. *Putting Jesus in His Place: A Radical Vision of Household and Kingdom.* Louisville, KY: Westminster John Know, 2003.

Müller, H.P. "Die Verklärung Jesu: Ein motivgeschichtliche Studie." *Zeitschrift für die neutestamentliche Wissenschaft und die Kunde der älteren Kirche* 51 (1960): 56–64.

Myers, Ched. *Binding the Strong Man: A Political Reading of Mark's Story of Jesus.* Maryknoll, NY: Orbis, 1988.

Neirynck, F. "Assessment." In *Mark and Q: A Study of the Overlap Texts,* by Harry T. Fleddermann, 263–304. Leuven: Leuven University Press, 1995.

———. "Q 6,20b–21; 7,22 and Isaiah 61" in *Evangelica III: 1992–2000. Collected Essays.* 129–66. Leuven: Leuven University Press, 2001.

Neusner, Jacob. "The Kingdom of Heaven in Kindred Systems, Judaic and Christian." *Bulletin for Biblical Research* 15, no. 2 (2005): 279–305.

Nielsen, Helge Kjaer. *Heilung und Verkündigung: Das Verständnis der Heilung und ihres Verhältnisses zur Verkündigung bei Jesus und in der ältesten Kirche.* Leiden: Brill, 1987.

Novakovic, L. *Messiah, the Healer of the Sick* (WUNT 170). Tubingen: Mohr Siebeck, 2003.

Olin Jr., Spencer C. "The Oneida Community and the Instability of Charismatic Authority." *The Journal of American History* 67, no. 2 (1980): 285–300.

Olrik, Axel. "Epic Laws of Folk Narrative." In *The Study of Folklore,* edited by Alan Dundes, 129–41. Englewood Cliffs, NJ: Prentice-Hall, 1965.

O'Neill, John Cochrane. "The Unforgivable Sin,' *Journal for the Study of the New Testament* 19 (1983): 37–42.

Orlov, Andrei A. *Dark Mirrors: Azazel and Satanael in Early Jewish Demonology.* Albany: State University of New York Press, 2011.

Parker, D.C. *The Living Text of the Gospels.* Cambridge: Cambridge University Press, 1997.

Paulme, Denise "Le garcon traveti ou Joseph en Afrique." *L'Homme* 3, no. 2 (1963): 5–21.

Peabody, David B., Lamar Cope, and Allan J. McNicol, eds. *One Gospel from Two—Mark's Use of Matthew and Luke.* Valley Forge, PA: Trinity Press International, 2002.

Penner, Hans H. "Language, Ritual and Meaning." *Numen* 32, no. 1 (1985): 1–16.

Pero, Cheryl S. *Liberation from Empire: Demonic Possession and Exorcism in the Gospel of Mark.* New York: Peter Lang, 2013.

Perrin, Norman. *Jesus and the Language of the Kingdom: Symbol and Metaphor in New Testament Interpretation.* Philadelphia: Fortress, 1980.

Perry, Alfred M. "Translating the Greek Article." *Journal of Biblical Literature* 68, no. 4 (1949): 329–34.

Phillips, C.R. "*Nullum Crimen sine Lege:* Socioreligious Sanctions on Magic." In *Magika Hiera: Ancient Greek Magic and Religion,* edited by Chrisopher A. Faraone and Dirk Obbink, 260–76. New York: Oxford University Press, 1997.

Powell, Mark Allan. "Matthew's Beatitudes: Reversals and Rewards of the Kingdom." *Catholic Biblical Quarterly* 58 (1996): 460–79.

Propp, Vladimir. *Morphology of the Folktale.* 2nd ed. Revised and edited by Louis A. Wagner, translated by Laurence Scott. Austin: University of Texas Press, 1968.

———. *The Russian Folktale by Vladimir Yakovlevich Propp,* edited and translated by Sibelan Forrester. Detroit: Wayne State University Press, 2012.

Raabe, Paul R. *Obadiah: A New Translation with Introduction and Commentary,* The Anchor Bible. New York: Doubleday, 1996.

Rajak, Tess. "Talking at Trypho: Christian Apologetic as Anti-Judaism in Justin's *Dialogue with Trypho the Jew.*" In *Apologetics in the Roman Empire: Pagans, Jews, and Christians,* edited by Mark Edwards, Martin Goodman, and Simon Price, 59–80. Oxford: Oxford University Press, 1999.

Rau, Eckhard. "Unser Vater im Himmel: Eine These zur Metaphorik der Rede von Gott in der Logienquelle." *Novum Testament* 53, no. 3 (2011): 222–43.

Raynor, D. H. "Moeragenes and Philostratus: Two Views of Apollonius of Tyana." *The Classical Quarterly* 34, no. 1 (1984): 222–26.

Reimer, Andy M. *Miracle and Magic: A Study in the Act of the Apostles and the Life of Apollonius of Tyana.* London: Sheffield Academic Press, 2002.

Rhoads, David and Donald Michie, *Mark as Story: An Introduction to the Narrative of a Gospel.* Philadelphia: Fortress, 1983.

Rhoads, David. "Performance Criticism: An Emerging Methodology in Second Testament Studies—Part 1." *Biblical Theology Bulletin* 36, no. 3 (2006): 118.

Richards, K. H, ed. *Society of Biblical Literature 1984 Seminar Papers.* Missoula, MT: Scholars Press, 1984.

Rives, James B. "Magic in Roman Law: The Reconstruction of a Crime." *Classical Antiquity* 22, no. 3 (2003): 313–39.

Robbins, C. Michael. *The Testing of Jesus in Q.* New York: Peter Lang, 2007.

Robinson, James M. "The Sayings Gospel Q." In *The Four Gospels 1992: Festschrift Frans Neirynck,* 3 Vols., edited by F. Van Segbroeck, C.M. Tuckett, G. Van Belle, and J. Verheyden, 1.361–88. Leuven: Leuven University Pres, 1992.

Robinson, James M., Paul Hoffmann, and John S. Kloppenborg, eds. *The Critical Edition of Q: Synopsis Including the Gospels of Matthew and Luke, Mark and Thomas with English, German, and French Translations of Q and Thomas*. Minneapolis: Fortresss, 2000.

Rodriguez, Rafeal. "Re-framing End-Time Wonders: A Response to Hans Kvalbein." *Journal for the Study of the Pseudepigrapha* 20 (2011): 219–40.

Rowe, Robert D. *God's Kingdom and God's Son: The Background to Mark's Christology From Concepts of Kingship in the Psalms*. Leiden: Brill, 2002.

Russell, William D. "King James Strang: Joseph Smith's Successor?" In *Mormon Mavericks: Essays on Dissenters,* edited by John Sillito and Susan Staker, 131–57. Salt Lake City: Signature Books, 2002.

Schiavo, Luigi. "The Temptation of Jesus: The Eschatological Battle and the New Ethic of the First Followers of Jesus in Q." *Journal for the Study of the New Testament* 25, no. 2 (2002): 141–63.

Schlosser, Jacques. "Q et la christologie implicite." In *The Sayings Source Q and the Historical Jesus,* edited by Andreas Lindemann, 289–316. Leuven: Leuven University Press, 2001.

———. "Les Tentations de Jésus et la Cause de Dieu." *Revue des Sciences Religieuses* 76, no. 4 (2002): 403–25.

Scholtissek, Klaus. *Die Vollmacht Jesu: Tradition- und redaktionsgeschichtliche Analysen zu einem Leitmotiv markinischer Christologie*. Munster: Aschendorf, 1992.

Schüling, Joachim. *Studien zum Verhältnis von Logienquelle und Markusevangelium*. Würzburg: Echter, 1991.

Schulz, Siegfried. *Q: Die Spruchquelle der Evangelisten*. Zurich: Theologischer Verlag Zurich, 1972.

Schütz, John Howard. *Paul and the Anatomy of Apostolic Authority*. Louisville, KY: Westminster John Knox, 2007.

Scott, James M. *Paul and the Nations: The Old Testament and Jewish Background of Paul's Mission to the Nations with Special Reference to the Destination of Galatians*. Tübingen: Mohr Siebeck, 1995.

Sebald, Gerd and Jutin Wagle, eds. *Theorizing Social Memory: Concepts and Contexts*. London: Routledge, 2016.

Segal, Robert A. "The Myth-Ritualist Theory of Religion." *Journal for the Scientific Study of Religion* 19, no. 2 (1980): 173–85.

Shields, Steven L. "The Latter Day Saint Movement: A Study in Survival." In *When Prophets Die: The Postcharismatic Fate of New Religious Movements,* edited by Timothy Miller, 59–78. Albany: State University of New York Press, 1991.

Smelser, Neil J. *Odyssey Experience: Physical, Social, Psychological, and Spiritual Journeys*. Berkley: University of California Press, 2009.

Smith, Barry D. *Jesus' Twofold Teaching about the Kingdom of God*. Sheffield: Sheffield Phoenix, 2009.

Smith, Eliot R. and Micheal A Zarate. "Exemplar and Prototype in Social Categorization." *Social Cognition* 8, no. 3 (1990): 243–62.

Smith, Jonathan Z. "Adde Parvum Parvo Magnus Acervus Erit." *History of Religions* 11, no. 1 (1971): 67–90.

———. "Differential Equations: On Constructing the Other." In *Relating Religion: Essays in the Study of Religion,* 230–50. Chicago: University of Chicago Press, 2004.

———. *Drudgery Divine: On the Comparison of Early Christianities and the Religions of Late Antiquity*. Chicago: University of Chicago Press, 1990.

———. *To Take Place: Toward Theory in Ritual*. Chicago: University of Chicago Press, 1987.

———. "Trading Places." In *Relating Religion: Essays in the Study of Religion,* 215–29. Chicago: University of Chicago Press, 2004.

———. "What a Difference a Difference Makes." In *Relating Religion: Essays in the Study of Religion,* 251–302. Chicago: University of Chicago Press, 2004.

Smith, Morton. *Jesus the Magician*. New York: Harper & Row, 1978.

Snodgrass, Kyle. *Stories with Intent: A Comprehensive Guide to the Parables of Jesus*. Grand Rapids, MI: Eerdmans, 2008.

Spaulding, Mary B. *Commemorative Identities: Jewish Social Memory and the Johannine Feast of Booths.* London: T&T Clark, 2009.

Srubar, Ilja. "Lifeworld and Trauma: Selectivity of Social Memories." In *Theorizing Social Memory: Concepts and Contexts,* edited by Gerd Sebald and Jutin Wagle, 17–31. London: Routledge, 2016.

Staal, Frits. "The Meaninglessness of Ritual." *Numen* 26, no. 1 (1979): 2–22.

Stanton, Graham. *Gospel Truth? New Light on Jesus and the Gospels* Valley Forge, PA: Trinity Press International, 1995.

Stegner, William Richard. "The Use of Scripture in Two Narratives of Early Jewish Christianity (Matthew 4.1–11; Mark 9.2–8)," in *Early Christian Interpretation of the Scriptures of Israel: Investigations and Proposals,* ed. James A. Sanders and Craig A. Evans, 98–120. Sheffield: Sheffield Academic Press, 1997.

Steinbock, Bernd. *Social Memory in Athenian Public Discourse: Uses and Meanings of the Past.* Ann Arbor: University of Michigan Press, 2012.

Stephan, W. G. and C. W. Stephan. "An Integrated Threat Theory of Prejudice." In *Reducing Prejudice and Discrimination,* edited by S. Oskamp, 23–45. Mahwah, NJ: Erlbaum, 2000.

Stettler, Hanna. "Die Bedeutung der Täuferanfrage in Matthäus 11,2–6 par Lk 7,18–23 für die Christologie" *Biblica* 89 (2008): 173–200.

Strack, H. and P. Billerbeck. *Das Evangelium nach Matthäus erläutert aus Talmud und Midrash.* Munich: C. H. Beck, 1922.

Storkey, Alan. *Jesus and Politics: Confronting the Powers.* Grand Rapids, MI: Baker Academic, 2006.

Struch, Naomi and Shalom H. Schwartz. "Intergroup Aggression: Its Predictors and Distinctness from In-group Bias." *Journal of Personality and Social Psychology* 56 (1989): 364–73.

Swain, Simon. *Hellenism and Empire: Language, Classicism, and Power in the Greek World AD 50–250.* Oxford: Clarendon Press, 1996.

Sweeney, Marvin A. and Ehud Ben Zvi, eds. *The Changing Face of Form Criticism for the Twenty-First Century.* Grand Rapids, MI: Eerdmans, 2003.

Tabor, James D. and Michael O. Wise. "4Q521 'On Resurrection' and the Synoptic Gospel Tradition: A Preliminary Study." *Journal for the Study of the Pseudepigrapha* 10 (1992): 149–62.

Tait, Michael. *Jesus the Divine Bridegroom in Mark 2:18–22: Mark's Christology Upgraded.* Manchester: University of Manchester Press, 2008.

Tajfel, Henri. "Experiments in Intergroup Discrimination." *Scientific American* 223, no. 2 (1970): 96–102.

Taylor, N. H. "The Temptation of Jesus on the Mountain: A Palestinian Christian Polemic Against Agrippa I." *Journal for the Study of the New Testament* 83 (2001): 27–49.

Theissen, Gerd. *The Miracle Stories of the Early Christian Tradition,* translated by John Kenneth Riches. Edinburgh: T&T Clark, 1983.

———. *The Gospels in Context: Social and Political History in the Synoptic Tradition,* translated by Linda M. Maloney. Minneapolis: Fortress, 1991.

Treggiari, Susan. "Social Status and Social Legislation." In *The Cambridge Ancient History Volume 10: The Augustan Empire, 43 BC–AD 69,* 2nd ed., edited by Alan K. Bowman, Edward Champlin, and Andrew Lintott, 873–904. Cambridge: Cambridge University Press, 1996.

Tuckett, C. M. "The Current State of the Synoptic Problem." In *New Studies in the Synoptic Problem: Oxford Conference, April 2008: Essays in Honor of Christopher M. Tuckett,* edited by P. Foster, A. Gregory, J. S. Kloppenborg, and J. Verheyden, 9–50. Leuven: Peeters, 2011.

———. *Q and the History of Early Christianity: Studies on Q.* Edinburgh: T & T Clark, 1996.

———. "The Temptation Narrative in Q." In *The Four Gospels 1992: Festschrift Frans Neirynck,* 3 Vols., edited by F. Van Segbroeck, C.M. Tuckett, G. Van Belle, and J. Verheyden, 479–507. Leuven: Leuven University Press, 1992.

Turner, Victor. "Betwixt and Between: The Liminal Period in *Rites de Passage.*" In *The Forest of Symbols: Aspects of Ndembu Ritual.* Ithaca: Cornell University Press, 1967.

———. *The Ritual Process: Structure and Anti-Structure*. New York: Aldine de Gruyter, 1969.

Twelftree, Graham H. *Jesus the Exorcist: A Contribution to the Study of the Historical Jesus*. Tübingen: Mohr Siebeck, 1993.

———. *Jesus the Miracle Worker: A Historical and Theological Study*. Downers Grove, IL: InterVarsity, 1999.

Uro, Risto. *Sheep Among the Wolves: A Study on the Mission Instructions of Q*. Helsinki: Suomaleinen Tiedeakatemia, 1987.

Vaage, Leif E. "Q: The Ethos and Ethics of an Itinerant Intelligence." Ph.D. Disseratation, Claremont Graduate School, 1987.

Van Eck, Ernest. "Eschatology and Kingdom in Mark." In *Eschatology of the New Testament and Some Related Documents*, edited by Jan G. van der Watt, 64–90. Tübingen: Mohr Siebeck, 2011.

Van Gennep, Arnold. *The Rites of Passage*. Chicago: University of Chicago Press, 1960.

Van Henten, Jan Willem. "The First Testing of Jesus: A Rereading of Mark 1.12–13." *New Testament Studies* 45 (1999): 349–66.

Van Segbroeck, F., C. M. Tuckett, G. Van Belle, and J. Verheyden, eds. *The Four Gospels 1992: Festschrift Frans Neirynck*. 3 Vols. Leuven: Leuven University Press, 1992.

Van Uytfanghe, Marc. "La *Vie d'Apollonius de Tyane* et le discours hagiographique." In *Theios Sophistes: Essays on Flavius Philostratus' Vita Apollonii*, edited by Kristoffel Demoen and Danny Praet, 335–74. Leiden: Brill, 2008.

Watson, Duane F., ed. *Miracle Discourse in the New Testament*. Atlanta: Society of Biblical Literature, 2012.

Watson, Francis. *Gospel Writing: A Canonical Perspective*. Grand Rapids, MI: Eerdmans, 2013.

Weber, Max. *Economy and Society: An Outline of Interpretive Sociology*, edited by Guenther Roth and Claus Wittich. Berkeley: University of California Press, 1978.

Weeden, Theodore J. *Mark—Traditions in Conflict*. Philadelphia: Fortress, 1971.

Wegner, Uwe. *Der Hauptmann von Kafarnaum* (WUNT 2/14), Tübingen: Mohr, 1985.

Weiss, Johannes. *Jesus' Proclamation of the Kingdom of God*, translated by Richard Hyde Hiers and David Larrimore Holland. Chico, CA: Scholars Press, 1971.

Wenham, J.W. *Reading Matthew, Mark, and Luke: A Fresh Assault on the Synoptic Problem*. London: Hodder & Stoughton, 1991.

Wessinger, Catherine. "Charismatic Leaders in New Religions." In *The Cambridge Companion to New Religious Movements*, edited by Olav Hammer and Michael Rothstein, 80–96. Cambridge: Cambridge University Press, 2012.

———. "Democracy vs. Hierarchy: The Evolution of Authority in the Theosophical Society." In *When Prophets Die: The Postcharismatic Fate of New Religious Movements*, edited by Timothy Miller, 93–106. Albany: State University of New York Press, 1991.

Williams, James G. "Note on the Unforgivable Sin Logion." *New Testament Studies* 12, no. 1 (1965): 75–77.

Willis, Wendel, ed. *The Kingdom of God in 20th Century Interpretation*. Peabody, MA: Hendrickson, 1987.

Wise, Michael, Martin Abegg, and Edward Cook. *The Dead Sea Scrolls: A New Translation*. San Francisco: HarperSanFrancisco, 2006.

Wise, Michael O. and James D. Tabor "The Messiah at Qumran." *Biblical Archaeology Review* 18 (1992): 60–63, 65.

Witmer, Amanda. *Jesus, the Galilean Exorcist: His Exorcisms in Social and Political Context*. London: T&T Clark, 2012.

Wold, Benjamin. "Agency and Raising the Dead in *4QPseudo-Exekiel* and 4Q521 2 ii" *Zeitschrift für die neutestamentliche Wissenschaft und die Kunde der älteren Kirche* 103 (2012): 1–19.

Wray, T. J. and Gregory Mobley. *The Birth of Satan: Tracing the Devil's Biblical Roots*. Gordonsville, VA: Palgrave Macmillan, 2005.

Wright, Archie T. *The Origin of Evil Spirits: The Reception of Genesis 6.1–4 in Early Jewish Literature*. Tübingen: Mohr Siebeck, 2005.

References

Zipes, Jack. "Foreward: Toward Understanding the Complete Vladimir Propp." In *The Russian Folktale by Vladimir Yakovlevich Propp*, edited and translated by Sibelan Forrester, ix–xii. Detroit: Wayne State University Press, 2012.

Index

About the Author

Myrick C. Shinall Jr. is an assistant professor at Vanderbilt University Medical Center in the Center for Biomedical Ethics and Society; his research focuses on the intersection of illness, healing, and religion in both the contemporary setting and the formative period of Christian origins. He completed an M.D. and a Ph.D. in religion under the direction of Amy-Jill Levine.